The Sikhs

Their Religious Beliefs and Practices

The Library of Religious Beliefs and Practices

General Editor: John Hinnells

The University, Manchester

The Sikhs

Their Religious Beliefs and Practices

W. Owen Cole
and
Piara Singh Sambhi

ROUTLEDGE & KEGAN PAUL
London, Boston and Henley

First published in 1978
by Routledge & Kegan Paul Ltd
14 Leicester Square, London WC24 7PH
9 Park Street, Boston, Mass. 02108, USA and
Broadway House, Newtown Road,
Henley-on-Thames, Oxon RG9 1EN
Reprinted with corrections 1985
Set in 11 on 12pt Garamond by
Kelly and Wright, Bradford-on-Avon, Wiltshire
and printed in Great Britain by
Redwood Burn Ltd, Trowbridge
© W. Owen Cole and Piara Singh Sambhi 1978

British Library Cataloguing in Publication Data

Cole, William Owen

The Sikhs.—(Library of beliefs and practices).
1. Sikhism
I. Title II. Sambhi, Piara Singh III. Series
294.6   BL2018   78–40023

ISBN 0 7100 8842 6
ISBN 0 7100 8843 4 Pbk

To our parents

Contents

Contents

Contents

Illustrations

Illustrations

Preface

Until Sikhs from the Punjab and East Africa began to arrive in Britain in appreciable numbers in the late 1950s and early 1960s the Sikh religion seems to have been regarded as a minor faith scarcely worthy of serious attention. Consequently no introduction meeting the needs of students in Britain or America has yet been written. They have been compelled to use Professor W. H. McLeod's excellent *Guru Nanak and the Sikh Religion* for this purpose though it is in no sense a primer, being a specialised piece of research into a particular and important aspect of Sikh studies, namely the reliability of the sources which exist for studying the historical Nanak. In the course of achieving this object, especially in his chapter on the teachings of Guru Nanak, the author placed Guru Nanak in his religious context and provided a valuable corrective to the usual views of Sikhism which have been put forward by those few western scholars who have mentioned it in their writings (see p. 38).

The purpose of our book is to provide a multi-dimensional introduction to the Sikh faith, covering practices as well as beliefs. For the most part the approach will be descriptive and explanatory but attention will also be given to various ways in which Sikhism has been regarded by scholars. It is always difficult to decide how the vocabulary of a faith should be translated – amrit pahul is not baptism and the kara is not a bangle or a bracelet. We have decided to retain Sikh words as much as possible in the hope that readers will make the attempt to enter the world of Sikhism rather than try to bring it into their own. The authors wish to express their thanks to many people. Mr Cole has received kindness, friendship and help from every Sikh he has met both in Britain and in India. In many respects this book is an expression of his respect and gratitude. Among scholars they would like to acknowledge the help of Professor Harbans Singh of Patiala, Professor Parkash Singh of the Khalsa College, Amritsar, Dr S. S. Kohli of Chandigarh, Dr Trilochan Singh and Dr Gobind Singh Mansukhani.

Among non-Sikhs we have received kind help from Professor Hew McLeod of Otago, Professor Geoffrey Parrinder of London, Dr Ursula King of Leeds, Miss Travis, Librarian at India House, London and Terry Thomas of the Open University who made many detailed and helpful comments on the manuscript of this book. A very special mention must be made of John Hinnells, whose evening classes in Newcastle set Owen Cole on the path of religious studies some years ago and so prompted him to apply for a post in Leeds where he met Piara Singh Sambhi.

We are grateful to the editorial staff of Routledge & Kegan Paul for their help in the production of the book, and to Mrs Tricia Bulmer for reading and correcting the proofs. Finally, we owe a special and almost inexpressible debt to our families: to Pinki, Laddi, Eluned and Siân, our children, who often played together while we worked; to Avtar Kaur Sambhi who plied us both with food and to Gwynneth Cole who typed the manuscript. The patience, love and cheerfulness of our wives has always been an unlimited source of strength and encouragement and we are thankful for it.

Quotations from the Adi Granth are based on the version prepared by Manmohan Singh for the Shiromani Gurdwara Parbandhak Committee, with some revisions by the present authors.

For any blemishes and errors the authors must accept complete responsibility. However, whatever its defects they hope that this introduction will go some way towards stimulating the study of the Sikh religion in the west and placing it on a sound foundation.

W. Owen Cole
Piara Singh Sambhi

Primary sources for the study of Sikhism

In this brief essay we have attempted to list the main sources available in English which we have used in writing this book. We have divided them into sections to enable readers who wish to take their own studies of particular aspects of Sikhism further to do so.

The main primary source is the Adi Granth, a collection of devotional practical compositions (sabads) written by six of the Ten Gurus and by other Sikhs as well as Hindus and Muslims. The sacred scripture is available in two recent English versions under the title *Sri Guru Granth Sahib* as a result of the labours of Gopal Singh (Gurdas Kapur & Sons, Delhi, 1962), and Manmohan Singh (Shiromani Gurdwara Parbandhak Committee, Amritsar). The latter writer also compiled in a separate volume the hymns of Guru Nanak which was issued by the Language Department, Punjabi University, Patiala. Neither of these transla-tions is entirely satisfactory. Not only is the English rather stilted, but there are also many inaccuracies and the text is unintelligible when it keeps to the Punjabi or north Indian sant cultural idiom. A sound English translation, with commentary, is a task which a group of Sikh scholars might undertake, emulating the panels which have produced recent English translations of the Bible. UNESCO sponsored work which resulted in *Selections from the Sacred Writings of the Sikhs* (Allen & Unwin, 1960) and to this must be added *Hymns of Guru Nanak* translated by Khushwant Singh (Orient Longmans, Calcutta, 1972) which has a useful introduction to most of the hymns. A small anthology by G. S. Mansukhani, *Hymns from the Holy Granth* (Hemkunt Press, New Delhi, 1975), has become quite popular among Sikhs in Britain.

In the late nineteenth century Ernest Trumpp also translated the Sikh scriptures. This was only a partial version covering about a third of the volume; it was reprinted in 1970 with the title *The Adi Granth* (Munshiram Manoharlal, New Delhi). Only the introduction is recommended. If its polemical style and the insulting remarks can be set on one side it may be seen to contain insights of some value.

Most other major sources are not accessible in English. First there are the janam sakhis (literally birth evidences). These fall into four groups. The first is the Puratan or 'ancient' Janam Sakhi which was heavily used by Macauliffe (see p. 160), and Trumpp (op. cit., introduction). Included in this group are also the Hafizabad and Colebrooke Janam Sakhis and, with some reservation, the India Office Library manuscript known as Punjabi B40. The second tradition is known as the Miharban Janam Sakhi. Sodhi Miharban, its supposed author, was associated with a sect, the Minas ('dissembling scoundrels') who followed Prithia Chand, the eldest son of Guru Ram Das. Consequently this janam sakhi has tended to be distrusted by Sikh writers and ignored. The Bala Janam Sakhi on the other hand has often been very popular because of the legend that it was dictated by Ghai Bala, a close companion of the first Guru, in the presence of Guru Angad. It comes as something of a surprise to discover that the existence of a disciple and companion called Bala is somewhat doubtful as he occurs in no other janam sakhis and is not mentioned by Bhai Gurdas. The surviving manuscript has been influenced by a sect wishing to exalt Baba Hindal, a contemporary of Guru Arjan, and denigrates Guru Nanak. In 1823 Santokh Singh wrote an account of the life of Guru Nanak called Nanak Parkash. Its continued popularity has also strengthened the acceptance of the Bala tradition. The fourth collection is the Gyan-ratanavali or Bhai Mani Singh Janam Sakhi. In its present form it is certainly not the work of Guru Gobind Singh's great follower, Bhai Mani Singh, for it refers to him in the third person and linguistically it belongs to a period perhaps as late as the beginning of the nineteenth century. Nevertheless, it does provide some anecdotes which supplement the first Var (epic poem) of Bhai Gurdas.

The value of the janam sakhis as historical sources has been fully discussed in McLeod (1968 and 1976), Trilochan Singh (1969), Harbans Singh (1969), as well as in articles in the journals listed below. Their religious worth has yet to be explored. Clearly they are devotional biographies and can too easily be dismissed as hagiographic accounts, but the theological statements which they make and the insights they give into Sikh belief in the seventeenth century to which, for the most part they belong, have been ignored as scholars question or defend their historical reliability. *The B40 Janam-Sakhi*, Guru Nanak University, 1980, an annotated translation of one janam sakhi, now makes it possible for students to sample this genre of literature for themselves. Hopefully English versions of others will also become available before long.

The Vars of Bhai Gurdas have suffered a similar fate. Most of them are not available in English and they have scarcely been tapped as sources for understanding the beliefs of the Sikh religion in the days of the Fifth and Sixth Gurus. Bhai Gurdas was amanuensis to Guru Arjan, and nephew of Guru Amar Das. From 1579 when he was admitted to the Sikh community until his death in 1637 he was at the centre of affairs. Some passages from the Vars have been translated by W. H. McLeod in 'Sources on the Life and Teaching of Guru Nanak', *Punjab Past and Present*, vol. 3, 1969 (Punjabi University, Patiala). This particular volume has a number of other important translations besides reprinting writings by Malcolm and Wilson, Cunningham, Field and others who have had a considerable influence upon western evaluations of the Sikh religion. (See also the section on journals, p. 201, for a further discussion of *Punjab Past and Present*.)

The writings of Guru Gobind Singh were compiled some years after his death by Bhai Mani Singh and constitute what is now known as the Dasam Granth (Collection of the Tenth Guru) to distinguish it from the book of prime importance, the Adi Granth. No English version of the Dasam Granth is available, but much of its content may be read in Macauliffe (1909), or in C. H. Loehlin, *The Granth of Guru Gobind Singh and the Khalsa*

xvii

Brotherhood (Lucknow Publishing House, Lucknow, 1971). The following translations of particular works should also be noted: *Jap Sahib*, Trilochan Singh (Delhi, Gurdwara Parbandhak Committee, 1968) and *Thirty Three Swayyas*, Jodh Singh (Lahore Book Shop, Ludhiana, 1953).

This section would be incomplete without a mention of two important contributions by Christopher Shackle. *An Introduction to the Sacred Language of the Sikhs*, 1983, is a study course enabling the student to translate at least the simpler verses of the *Guru Granth Sahib* and some janam sakhis into English. *A Guru Nanak Glossary*, 1981, is a lexicon of words used by Guru Nanak in those of his compositions which are in the Guru Granth Sahib. Both are published by the School of Oriental and African Studies, University of London.

Glossary

adi	first, original.
ahimsa	reverence for life: non-violence.
Ahluwalia	Sikh section of Kalal, distiller caste.
akal	Timeless, a term used to describe God, sometimes used as a name of God.
akali	literally a worshipper of the Timeless God. Used of the Sikhs of Banda Singh Bahadur who, after 1708, worked for the overthrow of the Mughals. Custodians of the Akal Takht who did not recognise the authority of Maharaja Ranjit Singh. Since 1922 a movement dedicated to the recovery of Sikh shrines (successful Gurdwaras Act 1925) and regarding itself as the voice of Sikhism especially in political matters. Britain and other countries in which Sikhs have settled have an elected body, the Shiromani Akali Dal.
Akal Takht	literally the throne of the Timeless One. Originally the Amritsar palace of Guru Hargobind, its builder, now one of the four seats of Sikh spiritual authority, the others being at Anandpur Sahib, Patna Sahib and Nander. Its custodian (jathedar) is an employee of the Shiromani Gurdwara Parbandhak Committee. The main feature of the Akal Takht is a throne three times higher than the Mughal throne balcony in the Red Fort at Delhi, a symbol of Sikh sovereignty.

akhand path	a continuous reading of the Guru Granth Sahib taking forty-eight hours. Associated with occasions of great sorrow or joy and a means of observing Sikh festivals (gurpurbs).
amrit	nectar of immortality. Name given to sugar crystal (patasha) and water solution used at the initiation (pahul) ceremony.
anand	bliss, a quality or attribute of God and therefore of one who has realised moksha.
arati	worship using lighted lamps.
Ardas	an important Sikh prayer used at the conclusion of a service.
Arya Samaj	nineteenth-century Hindu reform movement.
assan	seat. Term used by Namdharis to describe the cushion of the current Sat Guru as distinguished from the gaddi of the absent Sat Guru Ram Singh.
atman	the soul or inner self (also jiva).
Baisakhi	first month of the year according to some Indian calendars. Spring harvest. One of the great Sikh festivals marked by an animal fair at Amritsar.
bani	speech, hymn confined to the composition of the Gurus and the other bhagats included in the Guru Granth Sahib.
baoli	man-made pool with brick sides and steps leading down to it.
Bedi	clan of Guru Nanak, belonging to the Kshatriya caste.
bhagat	a devotee or exponent of bhakti. Used as a general term for the Hindu and Muslim sants whose compositions are included in the Guru Granth Sahib.
bhai	brother, normally restricted to describe men of outstanding piety in the Sikh faith, e.g. Bhai Buddha, Bhai Gurdas.
bhakti	loving devotion to a personal God.
bija mantra	seed mantra, basic thought form.
chanini	fringed awning placed over Guru Granth Sahib.
charn pahul	foot initiation. The foot of the guru is placed in water which is then given to the initiate to drink and/or sprinkled on his face, eyes and hair. The Sikh method of initiation until it was replaced by amrit pahul.

Glossary

charn puja	foot worship: touching or kissing the feet: performed by anyone to his social or family superior (e.g. son to father) or as a sign of respect (e.g. to an elderly person), but especially by a disciple to his guru. The idea lies behind the custom of many Sikhs to touch the step of the gurdwara upon entering it.
chattri	umbrella, canopy over Guru Granth Sahib, symbol of honour.
chauri	yak hair or peacock feather fan waved over Guru Granth Sahib: symbol of authority.
chela	the disciple of a guru, used as a synonym for sishya.
dakshina	a voluntary fee given to a guru or to a priest for performing some rite or giving instruction.
darshan	view, vision; sight of a holy person or important person (e.g. King-Emperor George V) believed to bestow spiritual power or virtue.
das	slave, often suffix to name of a devotee, e.g. Tulsi Das, Ram Das.
Dasam Granth	collection of writings attributed to the Tenth Guru and made by Bhai Mani Singh twenty or thirty years after the Guru's death.
degg (degha)	cooking pot.
dharmsala	commonly in India the term means a hostel or inn. In the early Sikh period it was used to describe the place where Sikhs assembled for worship. Later it was superseded by the word gurdwara, but among Namdharis it is still used of a place of worship which has never been visited by one of their gurus.
diksha	initiation of a disciple by a guru, often including the giving of a mantra.
Diwali	a major Hindu festival falling at the beginning of the light part of the month Kartik (October–November). A time of Sikh assembly.
diwan	court, name given to a Sikh act of worship.
gadi (gaddi)	seat or throne of a guru.
giani (gyani)	a person well-read in the Sikh scriptures, a teacher.
gosht	a discourse.
granth	collection.

xxi

Glossary

granthi	one who looks after the Guru Granth Sahib (and should therefore be able to read it) and may also be custodian of the gurdwara.
grihastha	householder; second stage of Hindu life but the Sikh norm.
gurbani	Guru's teaching; the content of the Adi Granth.
gurdwara	literally the door of the guru, consequently a building in which the scriptures are housed. May refer to a room in a private house or to a place of public worship.
gurmukh	literally the guru's word. One who follows the Guru.
Gurmukhi	the script in which the Guru Granth Sahib is written.
gurpurb	anniversary of the birth or death of a Guru, usually observed by an akhand path.
guru	commonly explained by Sikhs as meaning gu = darkness, ru = light, so one who delivers a person from ignorance by giving him the message which liberates and the technique to realise it.
gurukripa	the grace of the Guru.
gurupades	the teaching of the Guru.
haumai	self, self-reliance, a word which sums up the nature of natural, unenlightened man.
hukam	order, command (used in Qur'an 18[26]).
janam sakhi	a traditional biography, literally birth evidences or life evidences.
janeu	sacred thread worn by high-caste Hindus.
jap	repetition – of the name of God or of a mantra.
Jat	a peasant caste dominant in the Punjab.
jiva	soul inner self (cf. atman).
jivan mukti	liberation whilst still in the flesh.
jullaha	weaver caste to which Kabir belonged, officially regarded as Muslim.
kach: kachcha	short trousers worn instead of the dhoti (loose-fitting lower garment), one of the Five K's.
Kaliyug: Kalyug	the fourth and last cosmic age, literally related to the losing throw at dice. Kali means 'strife, battle'; sometimes writers describe the Kalyug as the age of iron following the Greek tradition. The age is

	supposed to last for 432,000 years and is characterised by the deficiency of dharma. Instead of karma-marga and jnana-marga, bhakti-marga will be that most followed. The present age is the Kalyug.
kameeze	tunic covering the upper part of a woman's body.
kangha	comb, one of the Five K's.
kanpatha	literally split-eared: followers of Gorakhnath.
kara	the steel band worn on the right wrist, one of the Five K's.
karah parshad	parshad (the gift of God to his devotees) prepared in an iron bowl (karah). Made of flour, sugar and ghee in equal proportions. Shared at the end of Sikh gatherings to symbolise casteless equality and brotherhood.
kesh	uncut hair, one of the Five K's.
keshdari	literally one who wears the hair long or uncut. An initiated Sikh.
Khalsa	the Pure Ones. The brotherhood of initiated Sikhs.
khalsa diwan	the name given to the Singh Sabha of Amritsar founded in 1883.
khanda	the double-edged sword, one of the emblems of Sikhism.
khande ka amrit	Sikh form of initiation introduced by Guru Gobind Singh in 1699.
khuda	one of the names used by Muslims for God – the Holy, al-Quddus.
kirpan	sword, one of the Five K's.
kirtan	singing of songs in praise of God normally to the accompaniment of music.
Kuka	nickname given to Namdhari Sikhs.
langar	free kitchen instituted by Guru Nanak, perhaps influenced by Sufism.
Laws of Manu	code of life outlining brahminic tradition.
mahant	head of a religious institution or monastery; used of those who controlled gurdwaras.
maharaja	title given to an Indian ruler.
mala	rosary or woollen cord, sometimes called a seli.

Glossary

man (mun)	mind.
manji	small string bed (charpoy); used of twenty-two areas of jurisdiction established by Guru Amar Das.
manmukh	one who follows the guidance of his own mind rather than that of the Guru.
mantra	word or verse often believed to confer power and insight upon the one who possesses it; given by a guru when a disciple is initiated.
masand	authorised leaders of local assemblies of Sikhs.
maya	the natural word, created by God and therefore real but capable of distracting man from God-centred-ness. The five vices are part of maya.
mela	fair, festival.
mool	basic.
nam	name.
nam japo	repetition of God's name.
nam simran	meditation upon God's name.
Namdhari	upholder of the name. A Sikh movement following Guru Ram Singh whom it believes still to be living.
Nath	literally 'master'. A Yoga sect following Shaivite and Tantric Buddhist teachings. The traditional founder of the school was Shiva.
nihang	soldier-devotees, protectors of the gurdwaras.
Nirankari	worshipper of the Formless.
nirguna	unconditioned, without qualities.
nishan sahib	saffron or blue flag bearing the Sikh symbols of the wheel and two swords.
nitnam: nitneem	daily 'prayer book' containing important sabads.
pandit	teacher of traditional learning.
panj kakke	Five K's.
panj pyares	the beloved five: the original Khalsa members.
panth	literally path; used to describe the Sikh community.
patashas	sugar crystals used in preparing amrit.
patit	lapsed Sikh.
pauri	stanza (literally 'staircase') of a hymn ascending to a climax of praise.

pir	Muslim religious leader.
pothi	a book.
prasad	gift received by devotee at worship.
Purana	eighteen books containing the mythology of Hinduism, regarded as important guides to behaviour.
pyare	beloved.
qazi	a Muslim judge.
rag	musical form.
Ramgarhia	artisan or carpenter and smith caste, listed as Tarkhan by Hindus.
rishi	sage, usually a hermit.
sabad : sabd	word, hymn or song, cf. bani.
sadhana	spiritual discipline ordered by a guru.
saguna	with form or qualities, used of God.
sahaj	ultimate state of mystical union.
salwar: shalwar	loose, baggy trousers.
sampradaya	school, sect, tradition.
sangat	gathering, congregation.
sannyasin	someone initiated into an ascetic order.
sant	popularly a synonym for sadhu. In the context of Sikhism a member of the north Indian tradition to which Kabir and Nanak belonged.
Sat Guru	God. By Namdharis used of Baba Ram Singh or the living Guru.
sau sakhi	literally one hundred stories, a collection of traditions.
seli	rosary of woollen cord (see mala).
sewa (seva)	service on behalf of mankind or the Sikh community.
Shiromani Gurdwara Parbandhak Committee	committee responsible to the Indian government for Sikh affairs in the Punjab.
siddha	one of eighty-four perfected ones who gained immortality through yoga. Often confused with Nath in Sikh writings.
sishya	disciple.

Glossary

slok	couplet.
smarta	follower of smriti, the Sanskrit tradition (as opposed to vernacular teachings).
smriti	that which has been remembered (as opposed to sruti).
Sodhi	Kshatriya subcaste to which the last seven gurus belonged.
Sohilla (Arati Sohilla)	A group of hymns forming the Evening Prayer of the Sikhs.
sruti	that which has been heard, revealed scripture.
Sudra	fourth caste of Hindu society.
Sufi	a Muslim mystic.
takht	throne.
tirath	a place of pilgrimage.
trimurti	'triple form', the three aspects of divinity, creative, preserving and destructive; often personified in Brahma, Vishnu and Shiva.
udasi	(1) order of ascetics claiming Shri Chand, son of Guru Nanak, as their founder; (2) journey, preaching tour.
Var	ode, eulogy, ballad, epic.
varnashram dharma	code of conduct laid down in the shastras.
Waheguru	(Vaheguru) Wonderful Lord. According to one tradition formed from the initial letters V (Vishnu) A (Allah) H (Hari).
yoga	'union'. A technique leading to a state of liberation through the union of the human spirit with ultimate reality. One who practises yoga is called a yogi.

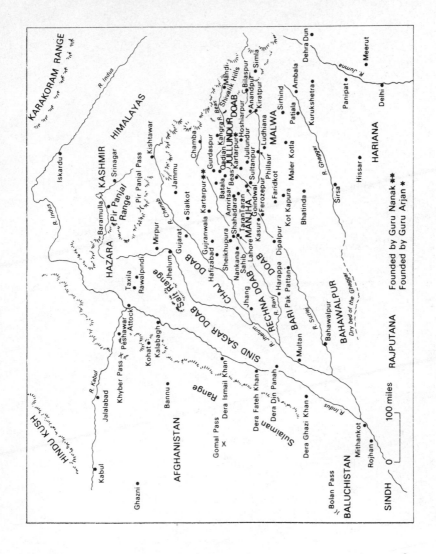

MAP 1 *The Punjab*

xxvii

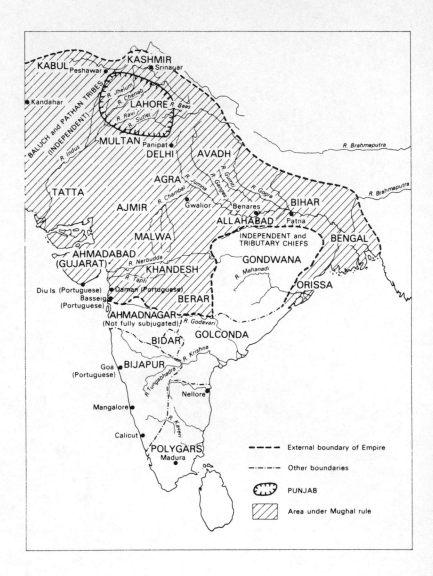

Map with the following labels:

KABUL, Peshawar, KASHMIR, Srinagar, Kandahar, BALUCH and PATHAN TRIBES (INDEPENDENT), R. Jhelum, R. Chenab, R. Ravi, LAHORE, R. Beas, R. Sutlej, MULTAN, Panipat, R. Indus, DELHI, AVADH, AGRA, R. Gumti, R. Jumna, R. Ganges, R. Gogra, TATTA, AJMIR, R. Chambal, Gwalior, Benares, BIHAR, R. Brahmaputra, ALLAHABAD, Patna, MALWA, INDEPENDENT and TRIBUTARY CHIEFS, BENGAL, AHMADABAD (GUJARAT), R. Nerbudda, KHANDESH, GONDWANA, R. Mahanadi, R. Tapti, Diu Is (Portuguese), Daman (Portuguese), BERAR, ORISSA, Basseig (Portuguese), AHMADNAGAR (Not fully subjugated), R. Godavari, BIDAR, GOLCONDA, Goa (Portuguese), BIJAPUR, R. Krishna, R. Tungabhadra, Nellore, Mangalore, Calicut, R. Kaveri, POLYGARS, Madura

Legend:
- - - - External boundary of Empire
-·-·- Other boundaries
PUNJAB
//// Area under Mughal rule

MAP 2   *The Mughal Empire at the death of Akbar (1605)*

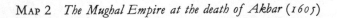

xxviii

CHAPTER ONE

The religious background of Guru Nanak

The homeland of the Sikh religion is the Punjab, the land of five rivers in north-western India. On a map of present-day India the Punjab will probably be shown as one of the states which comprises the republic but when the term is used in this book it refers to the much larger geographical region. To the north are the Himalayas which eventually, to the west, become the Hindu Kush and the mountains of Afghanistan. The Punjab consists of the foothills of these mountains and the extensive plain watered by the rivers Jhelum, Chenab, Ravi, Sutlej and Beas which in turn flow into the Indus. This area was once well forested, a countryside which the Mughal hunter could enjoy; now it is the richest agricultural region of the subcontinent.

The GT (Grand Trunk) road from the Khyber Pass to Calcutta passes through the Punjab as it winds its way from Rawalpindi to Delhi via Lahore and Amritsar, historically the two most important towns of the region, now divided, as the whole area is, by the arbitrarily drawn frontier between Pakistan and India. The archaeological sites of Mohenjodaro, Harappa and Taxila are reminders of ancient civilisations which flourished in the Punjab but whose existence, by the fifteenth century CE, had been forgotten only to be rediscovered during the nineteenth and twentieth. As all India's invaders have entered India from the north-west, with the exception of the Europeans, and as most

I

have used the Khyber Pass, the Punjab has become a land of ethnic and cultural variety.

Guru Nanak, first of the Sikh Gurus, was born at Talwandi in 1469. This village was situated fifty-five miles west of Lahore. It is now known by the name Nankana Sahib. The indigenous population of the Punjab was at this time predominantly Hindu. Many of them belonged to a warlike, landowning peasant class called Jats. One of the most important pilgrimage centres in north India, Hardwar, on the sacred river Ganges, lies close to the eastern edge of the region. This town figures in the story of Guru Nanak, who preached there. One of his successors, Guru Amar Das, successfully appealed to the Mughal Emperor against the tax which was imposed upon all pilgrims visiting Hardwar. Another pilgrimage centre in the Punjab was Kurukshetra where the famous battle described in the great epic, the Mahabharata, took place.

Both popular Hinduism and the Hindu philosophical systems are mentioned so frequently in the hymns of Guru Nanak that there can be no doubt of their importance. Sectarian Hinduism was no less prominent. North-east of Amritsar lie the Shivalik hills where devotion to the god Shiva was strong. Although there were many Shaivites, as the followers of Shiva are called, Vishnu seems to have been the most popular deity. His devotees, Vaishnavites, usually articulated their beliefs by telling myths and singing songs associated with Rama or Krishna. These were two of the human forms which Vishnu was believed to have taken when he incarnated himself in ancient India. Personal devotion to Krishna was often congregational. Both men and women gathered at his temples to chant hymns (kirtan). The customary general term for this devotion to a personal God is bhakti, an expression of Hinduism which had an important influence upon Sikhism. Its worship gives prominence to the congregational singing of hymns of their Gurus.

Sufism is the name given to Islamic mysticism. The enthusiasm of these mystics brought them into India before the end of the first millennium CE. Their humility and piety as well as their teachings about the immanence of God were congenial to the beliefs of many Indians. Devout men such as Sheikh Ismail Bokhari who went to Lahore in 1205, and Data Ganj Baksh, who died there sometime after 1088, or Sheikh Farid (died 1265) were often regarded as gurus by Hindus and won many converts to Islam. By the fifteenth century, according to at least one Muslim writer (Dr M. Mujeeb, in *Guru Nanak, His Life, Times and Teachings*, ed. Gurmukh Nihal Singh, 1969, ch. 7), Sufism had lost most of its dynamism and was ensnared by the manoeuvrings which accompanied Muslim political ascendancy. Terms which once referred to different religious traditions came to have political significance. Emperor Akbar visited the Chisti Sheikh Salim whose intercessions, he believed, resulted in the birth of his son, Prince Salim. Qadarite Sufis were not afraid that Akbar would be attracted to a form of Islam which encouraged repetition of the divine name and the singing of hymns in worship, they were concerned that he would come under the political influence of the order's leaders. On Akbar's death the struggle between the two major sects and orthodox Sunni Muslims who disapproved of Sufism intensified. Throughout the seventeenth century rivalry for dominance at the imperial court continued.

Hindu or Sikh histories of India in the seventeenth century often draw attention to Mughal persecution of their non-Islamic subjects. It must be recognised that very often the motive, from the imperial standpoint, was political, and that out-of-favour Muslims could find life as severe as Hindus or Sikhs. Aurangzeb, for example, ordered the closure of Hindu schools in 1669. He also began the demolition of temples. The jizya or capitation tax on all non-Muslims, which Akbar had abolished, was restored. However, Emperor Aurangzeb also re-established the department of moral censorship to impose Sunni orthodoxy upon his Muslim subjects.

Buddhism was extinct in India but not forgotten. Bhai Gurdas (1558–1637), the famous poet of the second generation of Sikhism, nephew of the Third Guru, quoted the following words as Guru Nanak's reply to a question put by Nath yogis: 'I have no refuge other than the Guru [God], the congregation of believers [sangat] and the sacred utterance [bani].' This is reminiscent of the famous Buddhist statement,

I go to the Buddha for refuge,
I go to the sangha [congregation] for refuge,
I go to the dharma [teaching] for refuge.

3

The Naths, who have been mentioned already, were a group of men and women who followed the teachings of Gorakhnath who probably lived in the twelfth century. It is said that he was born at Tilla near Jhellum in the Punjab. He taught that release from rebirth could be obtained through asceticism and yoga. The cult was essentially Shaivite but it had been influenced considerably by Buddhism. A Bengali tradition asserts that Gorakhnath was originally a Buddhist named Ramnavajra (Briggs, 1938, p. 151).

This abundance of religious expression was potentially influential. Even if much of the zeal and the perception of ideals for which they stood had given way to formalism and materialism, as Guru Nanak claimed, there were devout Hindus and Muslims in the Punjab of his day. For a young man like Nanak, searching for the truth, a variety of cults certainly claimed to possess it and were ready to instruct him in it.

Besides these groups a number of individuals must be mentioned, notably Lalla, Namdev and Kabir. Lalla or Lal Ded was a Kashmiri Shaivite who lived in the fourteenth century. In her verses she expresses a belief in a supreme being who can bring release 'nameless, without colour, lineage or form'. Liberation lies in the discovery that the One is within:

I Lalla, wearied myself in seeking for him and searching.
I laboured and I strove beyond my strength.
I began to look for him and lo I saw the bolts were
                                        on His door,
And even in me, as I was, did longing for him become fixed;
and there, where I was, I gazed upon him.

Outward forms of religion have no value for her, they are only likely to emphasise the duality which must be superseded if God is to be found:

He who hath deemed another and himself as the same,
He who hath deemed the day [of joy] and the night
                                        [of sorrow] to be alike,
He whose mind hath become free from duality,
He, and he alone, hath seen the Lord, the chiefest of gods.

Lalla does not name her guru. Even if she possessed a human preceptor, ultimately the guru is God who may be Shiva but is

4

also called 'gurunath', the preceptor of the gods. To her all the names of God are equal:

> Let him bear the name of Shiva or Kesava [Vishnu],
> or of the Jina [Mahavira], or of the lotus-born Lord,
> [the Buddha], – whatever name he bears –
> May he take from me, sick woman that I am, the disease
> of the world,
> Whether he be he, or he, or he, or he.

Of approximately the same period, but writing in medieval Hindi, was the Maharashtrian saint-poet Namdev. Although a Vaishnavite focusing devotion on the name 'Ram', he also never named his own human guru and emphasised the greatness of the 'satguru', God.

Kabir is probably the best known of the three. He named no human guru and the tradition linking him with Ramanand is probably to be discounted (Vaudeville, 1974, pp. 110–17). His guru was God, the Sat Guru. Only by knowing him could truth be perceived (Vaudeville, 1974, pp. 154–5):

> The grandeur of the Sat Guru is infinite, infinite
> in his bounty,
> He opened my eyes to the Infinite and showed me
> Infinity.
> I was just tagging along in the wake of the
> world and the Veda,
> Then the Sat Guru met me on the path and he put
> a lamp in my hand.
>
> A lamp full of oil he gave me whose
> wick will never run dry;
> All bartering is over,
> I will go to the market no more.

This group of devotees, among whom the Sufi Baba Farid (died 1265) should probably be included as well as other Hindus, Vaudeville (1974, p. 98) and McLeod (1968, p. 151) describe as the 'sant' tradition of northern India following the lead of P. D. Barthwal (*The Nirguna School of Hindi Poetry*, Benares, 1936) and P. Chaturvedi (*Uttari bharat me sant-parampara*, Prayag, 1951).

From Vaudeville's detailed summary of sant beliefs (1974, pp. 97–9), a number of characteristics might be mentioned to indicate those ideas which they shared. God was one, the all-pervading reality. Though the names 'Ram', 'Govind' or 'Hari', borrowed from Vaishnavism, are commonly used, God is also called 'Khuda'. The tendency to regard God as male in their poems should not be allowed to obscure the sant belief that God is essentially without form. Meditation was upon the Name (Nam) or Truth (Sat) which denotes his total being. Through such meditation the believer attained unity with God and all notions of duality disappeared as illusory. Consequently, all caste or sectarian distinctions were condemned and idol-worship opposed. Sants wrote their devotional poems in the vernacular, and taught men and women of any social status. None of them acknowledged a human guru though tradition has often provided them with one. God as self-communicating was their guru. It is in the context of this loose association of north-Indian sants that Guru Nanak is most satisfactorily understood.

CHAPTER TWO

The place of the Ten Gurus in the Sikh religion

Sikhism might be called the most materialistic of Indian religions in precisely the same way that William Temple once applied the epithet to Christianity, that is as a faith which takes the material world seriously as potentially useful for the good of mankind. It affirms the concept of a creator God (Sat Kartar, the True Creator) but does not believe that he ever became incarnate. Its ethics are based upon living as a householder (grihastha) and serving one's fellow men, and its rituals and festivals owe their origins to the men through whom the word of God was revealed. History is important to the Sikh in a way that it is not to the Hindu, Buddhist or Jain. He is conscious and proud of its influence, and aware that he is still an active participant in an historical process. Though Sikhism has no eschatology the individual believer is convinced of the work of God in past history and is proud of his own heritage. Also, because he has been reborn into a life where the Guru's teaching can be heard and obeyed, he has within his reach the opportunity of liberation. Any study of the Sikh religion must therefore include a survey of the lives of the Ten Gurus but in this book consideration will only be given to their importance within the context of that faith and not to an analysis of the documentary sources from which the biographical information is derived.

Sikhism had a beginning, if not in a moment then in a brief

period of time, in one man's lifetime. Something happened which fulfilled individual aspirations and met social and historical circumstances in such a way that something new and distinctive came into being and acquired permanence. This event was the life of Guru Nanak.

The First Guru has become a focus of devotion to a greater degree than any of his successors. Priority is naturally accompanied by a certain mystique and Guru Nanak is viewed by the Sikhs as the preacher of a new gospel, the founder of a new faith, the perfect example of piety and a person worthy of deep devotion, though this stops short of worship.

Guru Nanak (born 15 April 1469, died 22 September 1539)

Guru Nanak was born into a Kshatriya family of the Bedi subgroup and seems to have been brought up an orthodox Hindu in a district where there were both Hindus and Muslims in the population. His father was revenue superintendent for Rai Bular the Muslim owner of the village of Talwandi. Innumerable stories are told in the janam sakhis to show that Nanak was already destined for greatness. The pandit saw it in his horoscope, and the Muslim midwife, according to the same Bala Janam Sakhi, said that the new-born baby had laughed like a grown man. The pandit declared that the child would sit under a canopy:

'Both Hindus and Turks will reverence him; his name will become current on earth and in heaven. The ocean will give him the way, so will the earth and the skies. He will worship and acknowledge only the One Formless Lord and teach others to do so.'

At seven months, the Miharban Janam Sakhi states, he would already sit in the posture of a yogi. The same account also tells of his education in Sanskrit at the hands of the village pandit and in Persian and Arabic in the Talwandi Muslim school. He rejected the sacred thread ceremony at the age of ten and thwarted his father's ambition that his son should become an accountant. Though some narratives emphasise his rejection of all things worldly it is more probable that by the time Nanak came to the end of his teens he was an educated man already dissatisfied with the formal Hinduism which was his heritage. Descriptions of his

8

meetings with yogis, sadhus and sants may at very least point to a serious religious quest, supported as they are by a considerable number of references to the terminology, practices and beliefs of such groups in his compositions which are preserved in the Guru Granth Sahib.

Nanak's sister, Nanaki, had married Jai Ram, and gone to his town of Sultanpur where he was steward (modi) to Daulat Khan Lodi who later became governor of Lahore. The janam sakhis describe Nanak's attachment to his older sister. It is not unusual in the Indian tradition to see a younger brother going to the home of his older brother-in-law. Here he also found employment in the service of Daulat Khan. By now he was about sixteen years old. The Puratan Janam Sakhi attaches great importance to this period of the Guru's life. The considerable number of allusions to governmental structure in his hymns may reflect the knowledge which he gained at this time. Living in a much more Muslim context, as the employee of an Afghan administrator in a town on the main highway from Lahore to Delhi, it is attractive to see this as the period he met Muslim intellectuals and holy men but was again unable to find the answers he was seeking. When he was about nineteen he married and his two sons were born during the next few years. In every janam sakhi account he was already described as a spiritual preceptor rising before dawn to bathe in the river and after meditation lead his followers in singing kirtan before returning home for breakfast and work in the nawab's court. At the end of the day, after dinner, a congregation would gather at his home to sing kirtan far into the night. The janam sakhis, however, also describe an experience of enlightenment when he was thirty which preceded Nanak's emergence as a Guru.

One morning Nanak failed to return from his ablutions. His clothes were found on the river bank and the townspeople concluded that he had drowned. Daulat Khan had the river dragged but no body was discovered. After three days Nanak reappeared but remained silent. It was the next day before he spoke and then he made the enigmatic pronouncement: 'There is neither Hindu nor Mussulman so whose path shall I follow? I shall follow God's path. God is neither Hindu nor Mussulman and the path which I follow is God's.' Explaining what had happened to him he said that he was taken to the court of God and escorted into his presence. There a cup was filled with amrit (nectar) and was given to him with the command, 'This is the cup of the adoration of God's name. Drink it. I am with you. I bless you and raise you up. Whoever remembers you will enjoy my favour. Go, rejoice in my name and teach others to do so. I have bestowed the gift of my name upon you. Let this be your calling.' It is said that his first poetic utterance after this experience was the Mool Mantra in which the concept of the divinity which he had experienced is encapsulated. A passage in the Guru Granth Sahib is said to be another description of his experience.

> I was a minstrel out of work,
> The Lord gave me employment.
> The mighty One instructed me,
> 'Night and day, sing my praise.'
> The Lord summoned the minstrel
> To his High Court.
> On me he bestowed the robe of honouring
> him and singing his praise.
>
> On me he bestowed the Nectar in a cup,
> The nectar of his true and holy name.
> Those who at the bidding of the Guru
> Feast and take their fill
> of the Lord's holiness
> Attain peace and joy.
> Your minstrel spreads your glory
> By singing your word.
> Nanak, through adoring the truth
> We attain to the all-highest.

(AG 150)

This could well be the origin of the janam sakhi narratives. It bears witness to a deeply transforming experience, which resulted in a consciousness of being chosen to undertake a mission of revealing the message of God's name to the world.

The janam sakhi episodes of the earlier part of Nanak's life anticipate this calling. From this point onwards the accounts describe him as a Guru, popularly explained among Sikhs as one who dispels ignorance or darkness (gu) and proclaims enlightenment (ru). A series of journeys took him to the main centres of

Hinduism and Islam as well as to Sri Lanka and Tibet. He was often accompanied by Mardana, a Muslim disciple and musician. In some narratives Guru Nanak is seen as restoring a religion from the formalism which had overcome it to the truth which lay within it. Into this category come such anecdotes as that in which he joined the Qazi of Sultanpur and Daulat Khan Lodi in the mosque but stood alone while they performed prayer. When questioned why he, believing in the universality of God and prayer, had failed to join them at nimaz, he repeated that neither of them had offered prayer. The qazi's mind had been on his untethered foal which might fall down the well of his courtyard and the nawab had been thinking of his agent who was away at Kabul buying horses for him. Another incident of the same type describes Mardana's unwitting entry into the chauka, the sacred square marked out around the fire of a Vaishnavite pilgrim. When the Hindu reproved Mardana for polluting his food Guru Nanak replied:

> Perversity is like a drummer-woman,
> Heartlessness is like a butcher-woman,
> Slander is like a dirty scavenging woman,
> Wrath is like a heartless assassin.
> What is achieved by drawing sacred lines
>   on your kitchen floor
> When you are surrounded by these four vices?
>
> (AG 91)

The particular women mentioned in this verse were regarded as people who would automatically pollute on contact any high-caste Hindu. Guru Nanak says it is moral character not human birth which matters.

Of a slightly different kind are episodes in which immorality is reproved. Lalo was the poorest man of a village which the Guru visited. He was a carpenter and when the Guru invited himself to his house the Hindu steward of the local Muslim officer was indignant and tried to draw him away by inviting every sadhu and faqir in the district to a feast at his house. The Guru did not come and messengers were sent to fetch him. When he arrived he was asked why he preferred the poor food of a low-caste man. Sending for some of Lalo's coarse bread he squeezed it in his right hand. Drops of milk came from it. From Malik Bhago's in his left hand came drops of blood. Honest poverty was preferable to wealth gained by extortion and greed.

Some stories vindicate Nanak's claim to be sent by God. The Puratan Janam Sakhi describes the Guru's visit to Mecca. He lay down in the colonnade near the Ka'aba and went to sleep. At the time of evening prayer a qazi came to say prayers and seeing the Guru's feet stretched towards the Ka'aba reproved him. 'Do you call yourself a man of God, yet stretch your feet towards the house of God?' The Guru replied, 'Where the house of God is not turn my feet in that direction.' The qazi dragged his feet round but as he moved them the Ka'aba also moved. The qazi kissed the Guru's feet saying, 'Marvellous, marvellous! Today I have seen a true faqir of God.'

To point the folly of some religious practices is the chief reason for the inclusion of other episodes, as when at Hardwar he saw Brahmins throwing water eastwards towards the rising sun as pitra puja on behalf of their ancestors. He began to throw water in the opposite direction. 'If your water can reach your ancestors I am sure mine can reach my fields near Lahore which is barely a stone's throw from here,' he answered when they asked why he threw his water towards the west.

Many narratives are concerned with describing what true religion is. This motive lies behind such a story as the meeting of Sajjan and the Guru. Sajjan kept a mosque and a Hindu temple to meet the needs of travellers to whom he offered hospitality. At night he and his thags would kill and rob their guests. Far into the night the Guru sang hymns to the accompaniment of his companion Mardana and eventually the singing so affected Sajjan that he confessed his evil life and asked for forgiveness. This the Guru granted on condition that he gave up all his ill-acquired wealth. The robber obeyed, gave away everything in God's name and converted his home into a dharmsala (a Sikh place of worship). The true Sikh earned his living honestly and his home is a dharmsala whether it contains a copy of the Adi Granth or not.

From the janam sakhi episodes it is possible to argue that Guru Nanak was a reformer speaking and acting against the caste system and working to improve the status of women. Equally it can be asserted that he was a religious synthesiser attempting a blend of Hinduism and Islam in his own cult, or that he was a defender of pure religion against superstition, or that in saying 'there is no Hindu and no Mussulman' he was condemning their faiths as ultimately futile. A more satisfactory evaluation of Guru Nanak is probably to regard him as a mystic not in an other-worldly sense but as a person who, through his experience, perceived an ultimate unity in existence, so much so that he often spoke of 'the One without a second'. That he particularly wanted men to follow him is uncertain and even unlikely. It was the truth of his message not a community of followers which he seems most eager to establish. With regard to Hindus and Muslims he can be seen as encouraging them to perceive the truth which existed within themselves. It was the obscuring emphasis upon ritual which he deplored and condemned. Guru Nanak himself became the head of a community which gradually emerged as an independent religion with its own rituals and distinctive characteristics. The process began before his death.

When the Guru was about fifty years old, in about 1521, the journeys which occupy so much space in the janam sakhis came to a virtual end. He settled with his family at Kartarpur and a new phase in the development of Sikhism began. Previously the message had been of greater importance, now he turned his attention to the fruits of his preaching, the community which gathered around him.

> Baba Nanak then proceeded to Kartarpur and put aside all the garments of renunciation.
> He clad himself in ordinary clothes, ascended his gaddi and thus preached dharma to his people.
> He reversed the normal order, by before his death appointing [his disciple] Angad as Guru [and bowing before him].
> For his sons did not obey him becoming instead perfidious rebels and deserters.
> He gave utterance to words of divine wisdom, bringing light and driving away darkness.
> He imparts understanding through discourses and discussions, the unstruck music of devotional ecstasy resounded endlessly.
> Sodar and Arati were sung [in the evening] and in the early morning the Japji was recited.
> Those who followed him cast off the burden of the Atharva

Veda [and put their trust in the Guru's hymns]. (Bhai Gurdas, Var 1)

This is the earliest surviving description of the Kartarpur community. It is taken from the first Var of Bhai Gurdas (1558–1637), who was the nephew of Guru Amar Das and compiler of the Adi Granth under the direction of Guru Arjan. Rather tersely the passage gives an account of developments which were to have a lasting effect upon the followers of Guru Nanak and which would culminate in the devotees of a particular teaching and person becoming a distinctive community and a separate Indian religion. Soon after Babur's invasion of northern India, perhaps in 1521, Guru Nanak decided to end that stage of life in which he had been a wandering teacher. Though he did make a number of significant journeys in his remaining years he was for the most part resident in the village and received many visitors. The settlement grew upon land which had been donated by a rich devotee and although some traditions state that it had been established earlier in Nanak's lifetime, it is more likely that the village owed its origin to the Guru's decision to settle there at this time. Here he built his home, a place of worship, and erected a hostel and a dharmsala, which in Sikhism is the precursor of the gurdwara. During his travels he had adopted the garb of Sufis and sannyasins. Now he resumed the grihastha (householder) status even to the extent of dressing in a manner almost indistinguishable from other members of the community, though like other gurus he sat upon a specially reserved seat, a gaddi, to teach his followers. His teaching was not far removed from the sant tradition of north India. An important point which Bhai Gurdas makes, however, is that Guru Nanak on the one hand rejected the old traditions and the Atharva Veda and on the other encouraged the use of his own compositions, Japji, Sodar and Arati. The Atharva Veda consists largely, though not entirely, of magical spells and it was these aspects of popular Hindu thought and practice which the Guru discouraged. Worship of ancestors, the use of astrology, auspicious days, the acceptance of rituals related to the offices of brahmin priests, are all condemned in his hymns. Significantly Bhai Gurdas refers only to rejection. Nothing but the use of meditation and the Guru's hymns replaced Hindu rites. As yet the new community found the Guru and his teaching cohesive enough. It was only later that new rituals were needed to stand in the stead of the old.

At Kartarpur Guru Nanak was laying the foundation for the Sikhs to become a people of the Book. The philosophical teachings of the Vedas are not dismissed, though belief in the Vedic deities is often ridiculed. Bhai Gurdas speaks not of the rejection of the Rig Veda but of the Atharva Veda. Of greater significance is his mention of the use of the Guru's hymns. Guru Nanak was not only a Kshatriya usurping the right of the Brahmin to communicate divine knowledge; he was asserting that this knowledge was to be found in his utterances at least to the same degree as it was in the Vedas and by using his own hymns the way was being prepared for the bani, the utterances of Guru Nanak and his successors, to be revered, collected and ultimately regarded as scripture.

The Kartarpur community was exclusively Sikh. The village established itself around a person and was united in loyalty to him and to the message which he taught. The evidence of the Guru Granth Sahib testifies to the view that Guru Nanak and all his successors attempted to direct their followers to the gurbani, their teaching, and away from personal devotion to themselves, but in practice message and personality are always combined. Bhai Gurdas himself, though he emphasises the light-giving value of the Guru's utterances, in another of his Vars which will be mentioned in a later section almost exalts the Guru to a position of a divine incarnation (p. 100). The community was the beginning of the sangat.

The tradition of a community becoming a permanent body of believers is at least as ancient as Buddhism. The Buddhist sangha seems to have been envisaged as a vehicle for preserving and transmitting the Buddha's teachings from the outset. Gautama made no other provision for a successor. The Sikh sangat only gradually came to have these functions. Guru Nanak nominated and prepared one of his followers to take his place. Some years before Nanak's death, but during the Kartarpur period, a Trehan Kshatriya called Lehna (the name is also given as Lahina or Lahana), a devotee of Durga, became a follower of the Guru. He displayed the characteristics of humility and of obedience to the message (bani) to such a degree that Guru Nanak eventually chose him to be his successor in preference to his own sons. The elder, Shri Chand, was a pious man but the traditions describe him as an ascetic rather than a follower of his father's teachings, and full of self-importance. The other son, Lakshmi Chand, had no desire for the office of Guru or concern for the religious life. Therefore twenty days before his death, in September 1539, Guru Nanak summoned all his followers to assemble, delivered a stirring address in which he praised Lehna, and then initiated him as Guru by summoning him to him, placing five coins and a coconut before him and bowing at his feet. He gave Lehna a book of his own hymns (a pothi) and a seli, a woollen string symbolising renunciation worn by Sufis around their caps. He renamed him Angad and declared that the new Guru possessed his spirit and being. Angad is a pun on the word 'ang', limb, and means 'part of me'.

It is a matter of some dispute whether the ritual of appointing a successor was performed to this extent by Guru Nanak. However, this provides a convenient place to discuss the meaning of the various aspects which eventually comprised the installation ritual. The coconut is said to represent the created universe, the hairs on it being the vegetation. The coins are the five elements, air, earth, fire, water and ether. Being artefacts they also symbolise the skill of man. Thus to the new Guru was offered the world of nature and the world of man for his protection. The book of hymns indicated that Angad had now been entrusted with the divine message, the most important aspect of guruship in the Sikh context.

There can be no doubt about the meaning given later of the appointment of Guru Angad. Bhai Gurdas expresses it thus:

> Before he died he [Guru Nanak] installed Lehna and set the Guru's canopy over his head. Merging his light in Guru Angad's light the Sat Guru changed his form. None could comprehend this, he revealed a wonder of wonders, changing his body he made Guru Angad's body his own.   (Var 1, pauri 45)

The name and the body were different but both Gurus were enlightened by the same teaching and their message was one.

When Guru Nanak died on 22 September 1539 he left behind him not a fully developed Sikh religion but much more than an embryo.

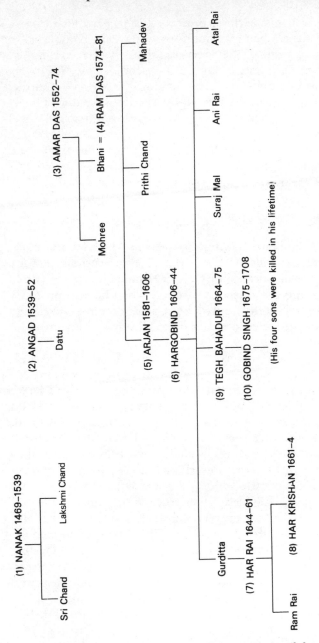

FIGURE 1 *Genealogical table of the Gurus with regnal dates*

17

First, there was his teaching preserved in 974 hymns many of which would already be in written form and others committed to memory and in regular use. Second, there was a community obedient to his discipline, living the householder life, regarding work as a form of divine service, singing the kirtan composed by Guru Nanak and meditating upon the divine name. Finally there was a second Nanak, Guru Angad, through whom God continued to speak (see Figure 1). From these emerged the sangat, the Guru Granth Sahib and the discipline of life and worship which are still, in the twentieth century, those things which give Sikhism its distinctiveness and cohesion.

Guru Angad (born 31 March 1504, Guru 1539–52)

It was humility and unhesitating discipleship which led to Lehna, a Kshatriya of the village of Khadur in the Amritsar district, being installed as his successor by Guru Nanak. He was converted to Sikhism during the Kartarpur period when he was probably in his twenties. Hitherto he had been a devotee of Durga and one janam sakhi account describes him as a pujari, someone who officiates at worship.

A number of anecdotes exist which show how he ultimately emerged as the most appropriate successor of Guru Nanak. One relates to a jug which had fallen into a muddy ditch. Shri Chand, Guru Nanak's elder son, refused to retrieve it because the filth would pollute him; the Guru's other son, Lakshmi Chand, considered the task too menial for the son of a Guru and refused. Lehna fetched the jug, washed it, and gave it to the Guru full of clean water. Another story describes a forest journey during which Guru Nanak made gold and silver coins appear on the path in front of his disciples. Their true loyalty quickly showed itself as they gathered all they could. Jewels also appeared and the Sikhs scrambled for these. Only two Sikhs continued to follow their Guru – one was Lehna, the other Bhai Buddha. He took them to a funeral pyre where he instructed them to eat the shrouded corpse. Bhai Buddha fled but Angad went forward and lifted the shroud. Underneath he found Guru Nanak!

As well as being a humble man Guru Angad was noted for his practice of meditation, austerities and abstinence (jap, tap and sanjam). During the last watch of the night he would rise from his bed, bathe and then meditate until daybreak. Kirtan was sung in his presence and then he would give darshan and spiritual comfort. Food was served daily in the langar and he participated in its distribution. In the afternoon he frequently played with the children of Khadur or watched wrestling matches. In the evening there would again be kirtan, after which he would give an address to his followers and any visitors. Generosity and wisdom were also famed characteristics of the Guru and Sikh children are still told of his love of children, which was such that on one occasion he kept the Mughal Emperor Humayun waiting for an audience whilst he played with the village children. Even during the life of Guru Nanak he seems never to have settled permanently at Kartarpur, and as Guru his gaddi was at Khadur. A reason for this may have been the presence of a Shri Chand faction at Kartarpur. Perhaps too much should not be made of this. During the period of the Ten Gurus succession never required settlement in the village of the predecessor or of an earlier Guru.

Only 62 or 63 hymns composed by the Second Guru are to be found in the Adi Granth. His importance is not that of a poet but of a consolidator. For thirteen years he held the community together and maintained its spread and growth. He is accredited with collecting all the hymns of Guru Nanak together for the first time, but if he did the pothi has not survived. Some traditions ascribe the invention of the Gurmukhi script of the Adi Granth to him but one hymn of Guru Nanak's composed in the form of an acrostic shows that an alphabet already existed. The renaming of the existing Tankre script and the instruction that it should be used in the collection of the Guru's hymns may well have been Angad's decision. Bhai Paira Mokha wrote down the hymns and Guru Angad scrutinised the resulting compilation. This not only prepared the way for a Sikh scripture, it marked the beginning of a vernacular Punjabi literature. There is also a tradition that Guru Angad encouraged Bala, a disciple of the First Guru, to compile a janam sakhi. The commissioning of a collection of hymns and 'life of Guru Nanak' would both be important in meeting the needs of an expanding community for many of whom, as time passed, Guru Nanak was not even a memory. They provided a focal point of piety and doctrine for those Sikhs who did not live near Khadur and, in the presence of sectarian rivalry, give a statement of orthodoxy. Unfortunately the so-called Bala Janam Sakhi is not attributable to this period and the very existence of a disciple named Bala, despite his fame in Sikh folklore, is a matter of doubt.

Guru Amar Das (born 5 May 1479, Guru 1552–74)

Guru Angad's two sons are dismissed in the traditions as irreligious. His daughter Amro was devout. She married and lived in her husband's village of Basarki in the district where Amritsar was later built. There her husband's uncle overheard her singing a sabad of Guru Nanak and after discussing her beliefs with her asked to be taken to Khadur to meet her father. This man was Amar Das who became a convert to the Sikh faith and a devoted follower of Guru Angad. Even when the Guru instructed him to live in the village of Goindwal some miles away he still returned to serve the Guru by bringing him water for his daily bath. This man, by then aged seventy-three, Guru Angad chose to be his successor despite the claims of Shri Chand the still-surviving son of the First Guru. It is a sign of the character of Guru Amar Das that he was able to hold the community together in the early years of his leadership and leave behind him a growing and well-organised faith when he died.

One of his significant acts was the construction of a baoli at Goindwal. This was a well or water-tank with eighty-four steps leading down to it. He built it so that it should be a tirath (place of pilgrimage) for Sikhs and the number of steps corresponds to the eighty-four lakhs of rebirths which there are in the Hindu cycle of existence. The first generation of believers may spurn rituals and find enough to give them cohesion in their own shared personal experience of enlightenment, in the devotion to a cause or in the personal qualities of a leader. Guru Amar Das himself had never met the First Guru and by the time he died probably only Bhai Buddha survived of those who could remember Guru Nanak. The Third Guru perceived the need to adapt to the changing consistency of the panth.

Just as Guru Angad had provided scattered congregations with copies of the sabads of his predecessor so the Third Guru divided the communities into twenty-two manjis under the direction of heads called sangatias. The number corresponds to the provinces of Akbar's Empire but the Sikh division was confined to the geographical Punjab and adjacent areas. The word manji is used of a charpoy or bedstead and refers to the seat of the provincial Sikh leader, distinguishing it from the gaddi which the Guru alone occupied. The Guru also appointed some women to undertake preaching work. They were called peerahs from the Punjabi word for chair.

Guru Amar Das also maintained the tradition of Guru Nanak's social and political action. There is a statement in the janam sakhis that Guru Nanak was imprisoned by the Emperor Babur and upon his release obtained the freedom of many other captives. It is recorded of the Third Guru that he succeeded in persuading the Mughal government to repeal the tax it imposed on pilgrims going to Hardwar. Also on one occasion when Akbar's army had been campaigning in the Lahore district for about a year and food had consequently become scarce and costly, it is said that the Guru obtained a remission of taxes for the year. The Mughal Emperor Akbar figures prominently in the lives of the Third, Fourth and Fifth Gurus. His broad interest in religion is attested. Jesuits at his court daily hoped for his conversion to Christianity and the Muslim scholars and religious leaders daily feared it. The Emperor hoped, by a policy of generous rather than grudging tolerance or oppression, to unite the Hindus and Muslims of his Empire; it is not surprising to discover him showing an interest in the new religion which was emerging in the Punjab, nor to find him behaving respectfully towards the Gurus. One charming story tells of Akbar visiting Guru Amar Das at the village of Goindwal on the Beas. Instead of being ushered into the Guru's presence or being met by the Sikh leader he was asked to sit on the ground with other visitors and share a meal. It was pointed out that a rule of the Guru was 'Pehle pangat piche sangat', first eat together then meet together. This is the tradition of the langar or free kitchen and Akbar accepted it. Akbar hoped to unite Hindus and Muslims by a policy of generous tolerance and acceptance. Today the tradition of langar, found wherever there is a gurdwara, is linked primarily with hospitality. The langar in the presence of the Guru at Kartarpur or Goindwal or wherever he happened to be had an additional, greater significance. The Guru Ka Langar was a means of emphasising the unity and equality of mankind. Sikhs have not succeeded in abolishing caste distinctions even within their community. The Gurus demanded through this common meal that all who came to them, Hindu or Muslim, Brahmin or Untouchable, Emperor or beggar, should lay aside their distinctions and become one in seeking the Guru's presence. The langar in Sikhism goes back to Guru Nanak, but the Third Guru emphasised it as a device for expressing the theoretical notion of equality in a practical way.

Guru Amar Das also initiated the tradition of commanding Sikhs to appear in his presence at the Hindu spring and autumn festivals of Baisakhi and Diwali. Although the historical incidents which Sikhs associate with these occasions still lay in the future, they now became times when the Guru's followers were required to decide which faith they belonged to. Sikhs could not enjoy the celebrations which took place in their Hindu villages and be disciples (sishyas) of the Guru.

Guru Ram Das (born 24 September 1534, Guru 1574–81)

Before Guru Amar Das died he nominated his son-in-law, Jetha, to be his successor. The new Guru took the title Ram Das, slave of God. He is mainly remembered as the founder of the city of Amritsar where his son later built the Harmandir or Darbar Sahib, a place of worship and pilgrimage which stood on the site now occupied by the Golden Temple. There are two traditions concerning the establishment of the town. Both mention the Emperor Akbar and indicate the respectful relationship which existed between him and the Fourth Guru. According to one source the land was given by the Emperor to the Guru's wife. He had wished to make an offering to the Guru but, in keeping with a tradition begun by Nanak, Guru Ram Das refused any gift for himself. Another explanation is that Guru Ram Das erected a hut by a pool which had been a favourite resort of Guru Nanak. Soon after 1577 he was granted the site and additional land nearby when the Emperor agreed to the purchase. A village, Guru Ka Chak, the Guru's village, grew up. Eventually its name became Ramdaspur and a little later Amritsar, the pool of nectar.

The foundation of Amritsar marked another distinct development in Sikhism. The town was well sited near the Delhi–Kabul trade route so its prosperity grew quickly. During the guruship of Ram Das it became a focal point for Sikhs on the festival days of Baisakhi and Diwali. The Darbar Sahib built by Guru Arjan turned Amritsar into a pilgrimage centre. It has been regarded as the holy city of the Sikhs ever since even though Guru Gobind Singh never visited it and at times, in the eighteenth century, Sikhs were forbidden entry on pain of death.

Guru Ram Das continued the work of welding the Sikhs into a self-conscious, coherent community outside Hinduism by initiating certain social reforms. He forbade the practice of burning widows on their husbands' funeral pyres and the veiling of women. Widows were permitted to remarry. Guru Ram Das also composed a wedding hymn which now constitutes the major part of the Sikh marriage service. Although this form of marriage was not legally recognised until 1909 some attempt to achieve cultural distinction can be discerned in these actions of the Fourth Guru.

By the time Guru Ram Das died (1581) the state of Sikhism might be summarised thus. Numerically the panth was not large, probably being counted in tens of thousands rather than hundreds of thousands. However, it was growing steadily and beginning to attract the Jat peasantry, especially after Guru Amar Das had emerged as their champion. Almost all its members were Hindu. Geographically, its strength still lay in the Punjab where it was always to remain. A sense of distinctiveness and self-awareness was developing, fostered by adherence to a living Guru, the exclusive use of vernacular hymns in congregational worship and the use of Hindu festival occasions for the assembly of Sikhs. The Mughal Empire was to be a major influence upon the development of Sikhism in the seventeenth and eighteenth centuries. However, during its first one hundred years the faith moved in a direction which was the natural consequence of the insights, and possibly the intentions of its founder Guru Nanak.

Guru Arjan (born 15 April 1563, Guru 1581–1606)

The whole of his period as Guru was influenced by the opposition of his elder brother Prithi Chand which continued during the reign of the Sixth Guru, Hargobind. The Handaliya Janam Sakhi, though ostensibly written about Guru Nanak, reflects this schism and rivalry to some extent. Towards the end of Guru

Arjan's lifetime Prithi Chand, with Mughal courtiers and officials, combined successfully to turn the Emperor's mind against the Sikhs and it was this which, to a large extent, was responsible for the Guru's death. However, for most of Akbar's long reign the story is one of mutual respect and confidence in a time of peace and harmony. In political terms the influence of Mian Mir the Qadirite Sufi was in the ascendant. The consequence was religious liberty. In matters of culture Emperor Akbar did not attempt to make India an Islamic country. One of his wives was a Rajput princess and Hindu princes served as administrators. Akbar was himself suspect in the eyes of many Muslims for his religious beliefs. Though his practices were those of a devout Muslim he was ready to listen to the teaching of other faiths. In such a climate the Sikh panth could flourish and even hope to rival and replace Hinduism and Islam as the major religion of the Mughal Empire.

Guru Arjan seems to have been groomed for the succession by his father. He was the first Guru to have been born a Sikh. It is even recorded that Guru Amar Das had perceived the qualities of guruship in his grandson and had predicted his eventual succession. One story is of interest not so much because it describes jealousy but because of its relevance to the concept of Guru as one who utters the divine word, the sabd. Guru Ram Das wished Prithi Chand to represent him at a wedding in Lahore. The son refused and Arjan took his place. He remained there some months awaiting permission to return. His messages were intercepted by his brother but one at last reached the Guru. In it Arjan compared himself to a chatrick, a pied cuckoo, which traditionally is in constant search for water. He said that his thirst was not quenched and there was no peace without a sight of the Guru. In his request he wrote three stanzas, on his return his father asked him to complete the poem and he did so with this line: 'It is my good fortune to have met the holy Guru. The immortal Lord I have found in my own home' (AG 97). The words, though uttered by someone who was not yet Guru, seem to have been regarded as an utterance of the sabd and may even have been seen as evidence that this was the divinely designated successor. It is interesting that the word 'father' does not occur in the poem. The human relationship had been replaced by that of Guru and chela.

Guru Arjan's reign saw the full flowering of Sikhism perhaps to an even greater degree than when, some years later, Guru Hargobind was to enjoy the favour of Jehangir, because as yet there had been no setback to temper optimism. The Guru embarked upon missionary journeys to the Manjha region between the rivers Sutlej and Ravi especially, and the Jat influx into the Sikh panth seems to have begun at this time. Ever since Guru Amar Das championed the cause of pilgrims going to Hardwar the panth seems to have attracted peasant members, but the Jats were small landowners, not landless peasant employees. With the Rajputs they were to constitute a major part of the opposition to Mughal rule in the revolts of the eighteenth century. McLeod (1976) sees them as the primary influence in the evolution of the Sikhs from being a religious panth to becoming the militant Khalsa. Sikh tradition would emphasise the initiative of the Gurus in converting many Jats and leading them in the fight against Mughal tyranny.

The panth was taxed on a regular basis, the Daswandh or tax of 10 per cent being collected by the sangatias first appointed by the Third Guru and now called masands. The revenue was used to construct large reservoirs, to counter the perennial threat of water shortage, and buildings. The most famous building of Guru Arjan's reign was the Harmandir at Amritsar. The artificial lake was enlarged and work on the building began in 1589. The foundation stone was laid by the Sufi Mian Mir and construction work was supervised by Bhai Buddha. The building was designed to have a doorway in each side, unlike the Hindu temples which had only one entrance. In this way it was shown to be open to all four castes. Also the Harmandir was constructed on a lower platform than the surrounding area so that to enter it the worshipper must step downwards and recognise that God is attained by bending low in submission and humility. Guru Arjan wrote, 'The four castes of Kshatriyas, Brahmins, Sudras and Vaisyas are equal partners in divine instruction' (AG 747).

While Guru Arjan was engaged in missionary work and visiting Sikhs in other parts of the Punjab, Prithi Chand compiled a collection of hymns, including compositions of his own, and seems to have attempted to put these forward as the authentic scriptures of the Sikhs. This prompted Guru Arjan to produce an authoritative collection. Mohan the son of Guru Amar Das possessed his father's compilation of the hymns of the first three Gurus. To these Guru Arjan could add those of his father and his own. Near the side of the Amritsar tank, on a site now marked by the Gurdwara Ramsar, Bhai Gurdas wrote the collection under the instruction of the Guru. In August 1604 the task was complete and the volume, known as the Adi Granth, was installed in the Harmandir. Its first granthi, or reader, was Bhai Buddha. There is a tradition that during the work the Emperor Akbar was informed that the new compilation contained teachings which were hostile to Islam. A copy was brought to him, he learned that it contained the compositions of Hindus and Muslims as well as those of the Gurus, and to express his satisfaction he made a gift of gold to the Book and of clothing to Bhai Buddha and Bhai Gurdas who had brought it and to the Guru. Guru Arjan's own claim for the Book was, 'In this verse you will find three things – truth, peace and contemplation: in this too the nectar that is the Name of the Master and which is the uplifter of all mankind' (AG 1429).

Amritsar was only one of four towns built by Guru Arjan. The others were Taran Taran (raft over the world ocean), eleven miles south of Amritsar where a large dharmsala and leprosarium were built; another was Kartarpur (city of the Creator) in the Jullundur Doab, and Shri Hargobindpur on the river Beas, named after his son.

In 1605 Sikh fortunes were at their height. The forty-two-year-old Guru enjoyed the Emperor's confidence. His panth was increasing and within it he was an important temporal as well as spiritual figure using the title Sacha Padshah, a Persian form used by the Mughal and meaning the True Emperor. Sikhs were to be found in Central and Western Asia trading especially in horses. The sangat in his hymns is almost as important as the Guru. In it the Lord becomes manifest, in their company the world-ocean can be crossed and moksha found. Under Guru Arjan a theocracy seemed to be emerging. Everything was set fair for the achievement of a great destiny. In 1595, after many years of anxiety, a son was born and the succession ensured. Though at that time Guru Arjan was only thirty-two this was a late age to become a father in Indian culture, especially when Prithi Chand still hoped to become leader of the panth. This dynastic as well as spiritual concern may be seen in the Guru's hymn composed on the birth of his son whom he named Hargo-bind (World Lord). Perhaps this hymn signifies his vision of Sikhism as the faith to unite India spiritually under enlightened and tolerant Mughal rule.

The true Sat Guru has sent the child.
The long-lived child has been born by destiny.
When he came and acquired an abode in the womb his mother's heart became very glad.
The son, the saint of the world-lord (Gobind) is born. The primal writ has become manifest amongst all.
In the tenth month by the Lord's command the baby has been born. Sorrow has left and great joy has become manifest.
The Sikhs sing the gurbani in their joy.   (AG 396)

To Sikhs the Sukhmani or hymn of peace, sung at funerals, is probably Guru Arjan's best known composition. In books written for non-Sikhs the following hymn is invariably included:

I do not keep the Hindu fast or the Muslim Ramadan. I serve him alone who is my refuge. I serve the One Master who is also Allah. I will not worship with the Hindu, nor like the Muslim go to Mecca, I shall serve him and no other. I will not pray to idols nor say the Muslim prayer. I shall put my heart at the feet of the One Supreme Being, for we are neither Hindus nor Muslims.   (AG 1136)

It is easy to see it as a negative renunciation of the paths of Hinduism or Islam but is more than this, it is a statement of the distinctiveness of Sikhism and a proclamation that it is a third and only true path. It is tempting to see the hymn as being written during the last dark days when, with the death of Akbar, the party of Sheikh Ahmad Sarhindi gained the ascendancy and the almost favoured position of non-Muslim holy men was replaced by an attempt to make India Islamic. However, it is equal in its rejection of Hinduism as well as Islam and instead of a consequence of a period of persecution it should be seen as the culmination of a period beginning with Guru Amar Das, and perhaps traceable to Guru Nanak at Kartarpur during which the ritual and social fabric of a new religion was being woven. Up to this point at least it can be argued that the religion owed little to the Mughal Empire; it was a monument to the personal

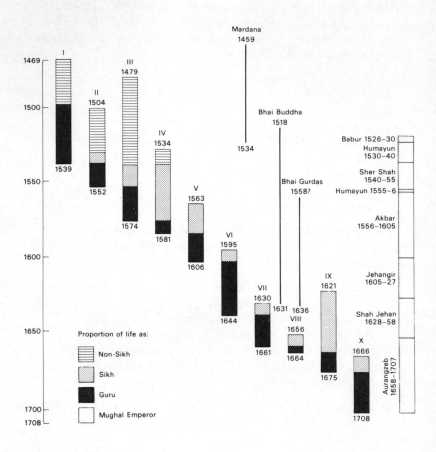

FIGURE 2 *The Sikh Gurus in their Mughal context*

The graph indicates the amount of overlap between the lives of the
Gurus. It was not until the accession of Arjan that the Sikhs had
a leader who was a birthright Sikh who had experienced no other
way of life. Guru Nanak was about thirty years old when he began
to teach; Angad was his disciple for seven years before being made
Guru. Amar Das became Guru after eleven years and Ram Das
was taken to the Guru's village at the age of about eight years,
after being orphaned.

qualities and teachings of the First Guru and the ability of his successors to weld a group of devotees into a vital society. After this period interaction between the Sikhs and the Mughal Empire was much closer (see Figure 2).

Religion is divisive as well as cohesive even to the point of provoking conflicting scholarly opinion. As Protestant and Catholic scholars differ in their views of the sixteenth-century Reformation in Europe so Muslims and Sikhs disagree over the reasons for the death of Guru Arjan and even its details. To the Mughals he was a dissident, suspected of supporting the succession of Khusrau who attempted to usurp the throne on the death of his grandfather but was defeated by his father Jehangir. To the Sikhs he is their proto-martyr. His death in the river Ravi was an execution carried out, as often is the case with Indian holy men, in such a way that no blood was shed. His body was never recovered from the water but a gurdwara was built in Lahore by Guru Hargobind at the place where his father entered the river.

Guru Hargobind (born 14 June 1595, Guru 1606–44)

Guru Hargobind obeyed the last injunction of his father, 'let him sit fully armed on his throne and maintain an army to the best of his ability'. He declared, 'My seli shall be the sword-belt and on my turban I shall wear the aigrette, the symbol of royalty.' Some traditions state that at his installation he asked to be invested with a sword and that when Bhai Buddha placed it on the wrong side of his belt he commanded it to be left and another put on the correct side. The story itself is unlikely; far from not knowing how to fasten a sword the centenarian disciple had been his fencing master. However, the story provides a convenient origin for the main religious contribution of Guru Hargobind, the idea of piri and miri, the two-sword theory of Sikhism. Piri is derived from the same root as the word 'pir', used in Sufism to denote religious teacher. It is of Persian origin and in the Guru Granth Sahib it is used as the Muslim equivalent of the word guru. Miri is derived from another word which entered India with Islam. The title Amir meaning commander of the faithful was certainly used by the Caliph Umar.

The use of piri and miri by the Sixth Guru is regarded as

bringing a new emphasis to a concept which is as old as Sikhism. Guru Nanak had confronted Babur with his unjust imprisonment of Indian princes, and though he is usually depicted as a pacifist he certainly sanctioned resistance to evil.

Both the Third and Fifth Gurus engaged in politics to the extent of siding with the over-burdened or unjustly treated tax payer against the Mughal rulers. Guru Arjan clearly had some of the trappings of a temporal prince. The concept of piri and miri persisted in Sikhism in a manifest form until the death of the Tenth Guru and was revived to some extent by Maharaja Ranjit Singh in the nineteenth century. Sikhs today speak less of piri and miri and more of tegh and deg, sword and cooking pot, by which is meant the protection of the oppressed and the feeding of the hungry. These terms, popularised by the Ninth and Tenth Gurus, epitomise the householder concept of Sikhism in terms of social responsibility. Strictly speaking the use of arms is an extension of the giving of alms! It is a way of protecting the defenceless and, though Sikhs have a military reputation, warfare should be a last resort only to be undertaken in the cause of justice. The Ninth Guru, Tegh Bahadur, youngest son of Guru Hargobind, gave his life for such a cause.

Outwardly Guru Hargobind seems to have been concerned more with miri than with piri, so much so that it is said that Goswami Ram Das, guru of the famous Indian nationalist Sivaji, put the following question to him: 'I hear that you are the successor of Guru Nanak. Guru Nanak had renounced the world while you wear the sword, keep horses and an army and people call you Sacha Padshah. What kind of a sadhu are you?' The Guru replied, 'Saintliness is within. Sovereignty is external.' ('Batan faqiri, zahir amiri.') There is little wonder that his contemporary Bhai Gurdas felt moved to mention such criticisms in one of his Vars. He voices the popular accusations thus:

> Formerly the Gurus used to sit in the dharmsala,
> The present Guru does not stay in any one place.
> Emperors called at the residence of former Gurus,
> The present Guru was imprisoned by an Emperor.
> Formerly the disciples could not find room in the
>   ever-crowded congregations,
> The present Guru leads a roving life fearing no one.

Former Gurus gave consolation sitting on a manji,
The present Guru keeps dogs and hunts.
The former Gurus would compose hymns, listen to
them and would sing;
The present Guru does not compose, listen or sing.
His companions are not Sikhs,
He has wicked and bad people as his guides.

(Var 26)

Bidi Chand, one of his famous companions, was certainly a
reformed bandit and in the Guru's later years, during the struggle
against Shah Jehan, he was a leader of men of very mixed motives.
His own were summed up in the concept of miri and piri, for in
his own mind his warfare was not that of a political rebel but that
of an opponent of Shah Jehan's destruction of Hindu and Sikh
places of worship and his policy of forcibly dissolving the
marriages of Hindus to Muslim women. In his later years Guru
Hargobind established a refuge at Kiratpur in the Shivalik hills
in the territory of Raja Tarachand who had renounced his
allegiance to Shah Jehan. Earlier, until the death of Jehangir and
except for a brief period of imprisonment, the Guru had been
Jehangir's friend and hunting companion and must have given
the impression of being a prince rather than a sadhu. Nevertheless,
from his own closeness to the Guru Bhai Gurdas could speak of
the devotion of his followers, which extended beyond Sikhs and
his consciousness of responsibility. Bhai Gurdas continues:

Yet the truth cannot be concealed,
The Sikhs are enamoured of his lotus feet like bees.
He supports an intolerable burden
But he does not complain of it.

(Var 26, pauri 24)

Besides developing the concept of miri and piri the Sixth Guru's
contributions to Sikhism were threefold. He restored the dharmsalas associated with the earlier Gurus where he found they had
fallen into neglect; he provided a pennant for his troops which
became the flag of Sikhism known as the nishan sahib; and his
troops used the kettledrum, which explains the surprising injunction in the Rehat Maryada or regulations governing the Sikh
faith that there should be a kettledrum in each gurdwara (see
Appendix 1).

The place of the Ten Gurus in the Sikh religion

Guru Har Rai (born 30 January 1630, Guru 1644–61)

Guru Hargobind's last years were saddened by the deaths of all his sons except Tegh Bahadur, the youngest, a man who had fought bravely at the skirmish of Kartarpur in 1638 but whose withdrawn nature did not commend him as a candidate for the position of Guru. Har Rai, the younger son of Guru Hargobind's eldest son, was therefore chosen. That he was only fourteen might cause some surprise, but Akbar became Emperor at thirteen. The Indian way of life accelerates maturity with respect to responsibility and outlook, and the Guru like any other ruler would have his advisers, though nothing is known about any council which assisted any of the Gurus. In Sikh tradition he is mainly remembered for three things. First, though he continued to hunt in the manner of his grandfather, he trapped animals and kept them in his gardens in preference to killing them. Second, he grew herbs and was interested in medicine so that it is reported that when Prince Dara the son of Shah Jehan was ill the remedy was supplied from plants grown by the Guru. These two episodes suggest a reversion to the type of guruship which existed before the reign of Guru Arjan.

Though tender-hearted is an epithet often used of the Seventh Guru, his resolution is shown by the third anecdote. With the imminent death of Shah Jehan, war broke out between his sons. Guru Har Rai supported Dara with an army of 2,000 men but the prince was indecisive and victory went to his brother Aurangzeb. The Guru was summoned to the Mughal court but he sent Ram Rai, his son, instead. At the court he was asked to explain a verse of Guru Nanak's found in the Granth Sahib, 'The dust of a Muslim is kneaded by a potter into clay and he converts it into pots and bricks which cry out as they burn' (AG 466). The original context is a discussion of cremation and inhumation in which the Guru expresses the view that the choice is unimportant. The Muslim remains may find themselves part of the potter's clay, so, in a sense, the one who practises burial may be accidentally cremated in the kiln!

Ram Rai answered that a scribal error had been responsible for the use of the word 'Musulman', it should have been 'beiman', faithless. Guru Har Rai's comment on hearing of his son's failure to stand by the words of Guru Nanak and the text of the

Granth Sahib were: 'The Guruship is like a tiger's milk which can only be contained in a golden cup. Only he who is ready to devote his life thereto is worthy of it. Let Ram Rai not look on my face again.' Harsh words to speak about the failure of a fourteen-year-old, but the episode conveys the importance which the scripture now possessed in the Sikh community.

Guru Har Krishan (born 7 July 1656, Guru 1661–4)

Ram Rai remained at the Mughal court and was used as a rival to the Gurus, both Har Rai and especially his five-year-old son who succeeded him. The little boy was taken to Delhi to live in the city residence of Raja Jai Singh so that the Emperor could decide on a suitable leader for the Sikhs. There, on a site now occupied by the gurdwara Bangla Sahib, he contracted small pox and died, but not before he had nominated a successor, 'Baba Bakale', his great-uncle who lived in Bakala.

Guru Tegh Bahadur (born 1 April 1621, Guru 1664–75)

The man who became Ninth Guru was one who had twice been passed over in earlier years. Although his courage in battles against Mughal forces had earned him the name Tegh Bahadur, 'brave sword', to replace his birth name Tyag Mal, he was clearly not the person to continue Guru Hargobind's political development of guruship. Guru Har Rai's reason for nominating a five-year-old boy in preference to his uncle is less easy to discern until one remembers the tradition that twenty-two members of the Sodhi family appeared at Bakala each claiming to be the person designated by Guru Har Krishan. Presumably to choose a son was a way of averting the dynastic problems which would arise from nominating some other relative, and the establishment of guruship in the Sodhi family was so firm by now that no choice which went outside it could be contemplated.

Once installed Guru Tegh Bahadur proved to be the man to meet the demands of the time. He possessed inner qualities which alone were capable of countering a period of harassment. Something of his approach to life may be seen from his self-given nickname Degh Bahadur, brave cooking pot, which he preferred to brave sword. It was as feeder of the hungry that he wished to be known. However, there were few occasions when he could live peacefully as he wished. Within the sangat there was faction. Not only was Ram Rai being used by the Mughals as a rival, perhaps willingly by now, but his other kinsmen still maintained their opposition. When he visited Amritsar the massands slammed the doors of the Harmandir in his face. Dhirmal, his nephew, plotted his assassination but the bullet only grazed his shoulder. The marksman was pardoned. As the Guru said, 'It is a great act to exercise forgiveness. To forgive is to give alms. It is equal to bathing at all places of pilgrimage. Forgiveness ensures man's liberation. There is no virtue equal to forgiveness.'

As the reign of Aurangzeb proceeded (effective ruler 1658–1707, though Shah Jehan lived to 1666) the process of Islamisation developed. In 1669 he ordered the closing of Hindu schools and the demolition of temples. Sometimes, as in Agra, this work was carried out and mosques were erected on the sites. Elsewhere practice only slowly followed command as opposition grew. Forcible conversions to Islam, the reimposition of pilgrim taxes and, four years after the Ninth Guru's death, the introduction of the jizya, a tax imposed on non-Muslims, provoked civil war. Sikhs and Hindus alike suffered, the rivals for the Guru's position vanished with the hard times leaving Guru Tegh Bahadur to rally the community. This he did by travelling about north-west India until he was summoned to Aurangzeb's court. Imprisonment followed. After four of his companions had been executed in his presence he like them refused to become a Muslim; instead he accepted death. His martyrdom is seen not only as the act of a man dying resolutely for his own faith but on behalf of Hinduism and religious liberty as a principle. The view is well summed up in some verses composed by his son Gobind Rai whom he had nominated as his successor.

> To preserve their right to wear their caste marks and their
>   sacred threads,
> Did he, in the dark age, perform the supreme sacrifice.
> To help the saintly he went to the utmost limit,
> He gave his head but never cried in pain.
>
> He suffered martyrdom for the sake of his faith.
> He lost his head but did not reveal his secret.

He disclaimed to perform miracles or jugglers' tricks
For such fill men of God with shame.
He burst the bonds of mortal clay
And went to the abode of God.
No one hath ever performed an act as noble as his.

(Vichitar Natak)

Guru Gobind Singh (born 22 December 1666, Guru 1675–1708)

The last Guru was a person who, in Sikh eyes, combined the qualities of his most illustrious predecessors. He is the perfect example of manhood, highly educated, skilled in horsemanship and the use of arms, chivalrous and generous in character. Whereas in his father's lifetime passive resistance alone was possible, before Guru Gobind Rai was very old armed revolts were breaking out in much of Aurangzeb's Empire. From an historical point of view it is difficult to assess his period. In terms of what actually happened the end was tragedy and chaos. For the Sikh, the significance of his Guruship is of greatest importance. As the last and greatest Guru after Nanak, the subsequent development of Sikhism is telescoped in his reign and his achievements. For example, the decision of Ahmad Shah Abdali of Afghanistan who invaded India nine times between 1747 and 1769 to present his campaigns as a jihad (holy war) reflected itself in historical writing, and the earlier struggles of the Tenth Guru were seen as the defence of Sikhism or Hinduism against the Muslim assault of Aurangzeb. It is easy to forget that a possible meeting between the Guru and Aurangzeb was being arranged when the Emperor died and that the Guru's forces were campaigning with those of the new ruler Bahadur Shah at the time of the Guru's assassination in 1708.

The two major religious acts of the Guru's reign have also been telescoped by tradition. This should not be allowed to diminish their religious importance within the community. Rather it served to underline their importance. On Baisakhi 1699 the Guru ordered his Sikhs to assemble before him as was customary at this festival, but he issued his command with a greater urgency than usual. He reminded them of the perilous time in which they were living and spoke of a plan to replace their weakness by strength and unity. It would demand supreme loyalty to the

Guru. He then asked for men to come forward who would give their heads to him. He made the request in a spectacular manner with drawn sword. No one responded for some time, save with a hushed and fearful silence. At last one Sikh came forward and was led into the Guru's tent. The Guru reappeared alone, with a bloodstained sword. Four more men followed, though in the time it took the volunteers to come forward many other Sikhs departed from Anandpur. After the last of the panj pyares (beloved five), as they are now called, had entered the tent the Guru emerged with them. Some Sikhs say that he had raised them to life, others that the blood was that of a goat, but all agree on their fearless devotion to the Guru and his ideals. The five were given nectar (amrit) made from water and sugar crystals (patashas) prepared in an iron bowl and stirred with a two-edged sword, and then the Guru himself received the same initiation followed by many thousands from all castes and Untouchables. Finally the Guru proclaimed a Code of Discipline. Tobacco, the eating of meat from animals slaughtered according to the Muslim ritual (hallal), and sexual intercourse with Muslim women were to be avoided. The members of the new brotherhood, which was called the Khalsa (Pure Ones), were to have no dealings with those who followed rival leaders or their successors and were also instructed to wear five symbols – uncut hair, a comb, a steel wrist guard, a sword, and short breeches. Initiated men took the name 'Singh' (lion) and henceforth the Tenth Guru was known as Gobind Singh. Two other important features belong to the tradition. First, women were admitted to the Khalsa, taking the name 'Kaur' (princess). Second, of the panj pyares one came from the Kshatriya caste and another from the Jat and the rest from the Sudra group, symbolising the ideals of caste and sex equality. A consequence of the Guru's action certainly seems to have been to place the strength of eighteenth- and nineteenth-century Sikhism in the third, fourth and fifth orders of Indian society, though some of its leaders still came from the Kshatriya varna.

Sometimes pictures of the first amrit ceremony show two dead hawks on their backs on the ground while two doves, their killers, sit proudly on the bowl of nectar. By drinking from it the doves had gained the strength of hawks. Self-respect and cohesion through loyalty to the Guru was the purpose of the formation of the Khalsa but before his death the Guru took another step. On 7 October 1708, knowing that he would not recover from a knife wound he had sustained, the Guru is reputed to have taken five coins and a coconut which he placed before a copy of the Granth Sahib, thus installing it as Guru. He had once said,

> 'Where there are five there am I,
> When the five meet, they are the holiest of the holy.'

Now the new concept of Guru became not only that of the message contained in the Book but that of the Guru Panth, the spirit of the Guru present wherever members of the Khalsa deliberated and made decisions in the presence of the Guru Granth Sahib.

Guru Gobind Singh's mission was above all religious. He saw himself as a restorer of dharma in the finest Indian tradition, by which he meant true religion, and played with the language of avatar to the point that some scholars have concluded that he saw himself as one. In fact he accepted the role but reinterpreted the concept of stressing his own humanity. None the less he was a man of destiny in his own eyes:

> The divine Guru sent me for righteousness' sake
> On this account I have come into the world to
> Extend the faith everywhere and to
> Seize and destroy the evil and the sinful.
> Understand this, ye holy men, in your souls.
> I assumed birth for the purpose
> Of spreading the faith, saving the saints
> And extirpating all tyrants.

His identity with the Khalsa was to the point of asserting that

> There is no difference between the Guru and the sangat.
> The sangat and the True Guru are one and the same.

His respect for the Khalsa is nowhere better seen than in one of his poems:

> All the battles I have won against tyranny
> I have fought with the devoted backing of the people;
> Through them only have I been able to bestow gifts,
> Through their help I have escaped from harm;

The love and generosity of these Sikhs
Have enriched my heart and home.
Through their grace I have attained all learning;
Through their help in battle I have slain all my enemies.
I was born to serve them, through them I reached eminence.
What would I have been without their kind and ready help?
There are millions of insignificant people like me.
True service is the service of these people.
I am not inclined to serve others of higher caste:
Charity will bear fruit in this and the next world,
If given to such worthy people as these;
All other sacrifices and charities are profitless.
From toe to toe, whatever I call my own,
All I possess and carry, I dedicate to these people.

The Guru frequently used epic poetry as a means of rallying his followers. His court, even more than that of Guru Arjan, was a centre of bardic activity, but when he revised the Granth Sahib to include the hymns of his father he inserted none of his own, with the possible exception of one verse. His own poetry, he told those who wanted him to include it in the Granth Sahib, was mere play. It was left for a follower Bhai Mani Singh to collect it together early in the eighteenth century in the Dasam Granth or Book of the Tenth Guru.

Guru Nanak in the eyes of western scholars

In the present chapter the Sikh view of the contribution of the Ten Gurus has been expressed. Only Guru Nanak has attracted the serious attention of western writers, who have usually combined a study of his work with an appraisal of Sikhism.

Earlier in this book (p. 6), it was asserted that Guru Nanak is most satisfactorily understood if he is placed within the sant tradition. This interpretation of his location in the Indian religious firmament has not always been accepted. Some scholars have described Sikhism as syncretistic (Noss, 1963; Parrinder, 1961; De Bary, 1958). Sen (1970), Renou (1953), Smart (1972) and Sharpe (Hinnells and Sharpe, 1972) did not necessarily reject the sant tradition but explicitly described Guru Nanak as a disciple of Kabir. An earlier exponent of this view was J. N. Farquhar in his *Primer of Hinduism* (1912), a book which has had a considerable influence upon western studies of the religions of India. Guru Nanak's purpose has often been explained in words reminiscent of those of John Malcolm, who wrote his *Sketch of the Sikhs* in 1812:

Born in a province on the extreme verge of India, at the very point where the religion of Muhammed and the idolatrous worship of Hindus appeared to touch, at the moment when both tribes cherished the most violent rancour of animosity towards each other, his great aim was to blend those jarring elements in peaceful union, and he only endeavoured to effect this purpose through the means of mild persuasion. His wish was to recall both Muhammedans and Hindus to an exclusive attention to that sublimest of all principles, which inculcates devotion to God, and peace towards man. He had to combat the furious bigotry of the one and the deep-rooted super-stition of the other; but he attempted to overcome all obstacles by the force of reason and humanity (quoted *Punjab Past and Present* vol. 3, 1969, p. 113).

Hew McLeod (McLeod, 1968, and to a lesser extent Basham, 1975, ch. 20) examines the eclectic, eirenic view in some detail and concludes that in the life and teaching of Guru Nanak, 'The intention to reconcile was certainly there, but not by the path of syncretism. Conventional Hindu belief and Islam were not regarded as fundamentally right but as fundamentally wrong' (1968, p. 161).

The picture of Guru Nanak as a bridge-builder between the two militant antagonists of Islam and Brahminical Hinduism receives some support from a reading of the Sikh biographies of the Guru known as janam sakhis. It is also an interpretation which Sikhs in our present ecumenical age are often happy to present. Sometimes the view is accompanied by a misleading quotation of the words 'There is neither Hindu nor Mussulman'. However, the Guru went on to add, 'so whose path shall I follow? I shall follow God's path. God is neither Hindu nor Mussulman and the path which I shall follow is God's.' The early janam sakhis belong to the time of the Fifth and Sixth Gurus when there was some hope that Sikhism might prove to be the unifying faith of the Mughal Empire. An inclination to show the Guru's universal appeal may be discerned in some of the episodes, but behind this interpretation many if not most of the individual narratives portray the superiority of Sikhism at the expense of the other faiths with which the Guru came in contact. From his hymns contained in the Adi Granth come such quotations as

> The vedas and the semitic texts (lit. Kitab) know not the Lord's mystery.   (AG 1021)

> In Vedas and Puranas I see not another.   (AG 1022)

> The Muslims praise the shariat. They read and reflect upon it. Lord's servants are they who fall into captivity trying to perceive him. The Hindus praise the praiseworthy one whose vision and beauty are incomparable, but they bathe at pilgrimage places, make flower offerings and place the perfume of sandal wood before idols.   (AG 465)

Text upon text may be put forward in discussing Guru Nanak's attitude to the religions of his day. The following three, each to do with ritual, suggest to the present writers that he did not regard them as 'fundamentally wrong' but as potentially distracting. They were likely to become ends in themselves rather than the means whereby ultimate truth might be realised. In the passages cited the emphasis is not on salvation through the sacred texts but only by commitment.

> If they happen to know the nature of God, they will realise that all rites and beliefs are futile.   (AG 470)

> Rituals and ceremonies are chains of the mind.   (AG 635)

> Cursed be the ritual that makes us forget the Loved One. (AG 590)

When the Guru said,

> Let compassion be your mosque, faith your prayer carpet and righteousness your Qur'an.
> Let modesty be your circumcision and uprightness your fasting.
> Thus you will become a true Muslim.
>
> (AG 140)

we contend he was not denouncing Islam as futile but was seeking to recall it to the truth of its revelation in the classical prophetic manner. In doing so he was, like similar figures before and since, expressing something of his own personal dissatisfaction, holding faiths and practices up to the scrutiny of his own insights.

Kabir stood in a similar position to Guru Nanak with regard to the religious systems of his day. As his elder, probably dying in 1518, it has been usual to postulate a relationship between the two sant-poets in which Kabir is described as Nanak's guru, especially as many of Kabir's hymns are included in the Sikh scriptures. In two of the janam sakhis, meetings between the Guru and Kabir are described. In one (Meharban) Kabir bows before the Guru and describes him as jagat-guru or enlightener of the world. The Handaliya account is associated with a break-away sect which left the Sikhs during the time of the Third Guru; its statement that Guru Nanak was the disciple of Kabir may be regarded as part of the attempt to deprecate the importance of Sikhism's founder figure. The Handaliya account was accepted by Westcott (*Kabir and Kabir Panth*, 1907) and through this medium the tradition gained ground in Europe. A kinship of thought between Guru Nanak and Kabir cannot be denied and some if not all of the hymns of Kabir in the Adi Granth would seem to have been collected by Guru Nanak. However, it is likely that he also gathered hymns of Namdev and Baba Farid and that the link with Kabir lies in the common sant tradition and not in a direct personal connection. A detailed comparison of the teachings of Kabir and Guru Nanak would reveal no similarities which could not have arisen from the common sant tradition as well as a few differences. Most notably the Guru does not share Kabir's preference for the name 'Ram'.

Guru Nanak was a strict monotheist and this seems to be the main doctrinal reason for claiming that he was influenced by Islam. However, as with Kabir there is remarkably little Sufi influence in his writings and apart from the terms which he could have picked up from his daily life in a Muslim environment it would be as easy to argue that his model was Buddhism as Islam. As has been pointed out above, monotheism was as much part of the sant tradition as it is fundamental to Islam and there is no need to look beyond the sants. Though Sufism may have been responsible for their insistence on the oneness of God their denial of duality must be seen as belonging to the Indian rather than Arabian tradition. It was Islam in the political form of the Mughal Empire more than the Sufis which influenced Sikhism, and this in outward form rather than doctrine. In this respect the militant Sikh brotherhood, the Khalsa, instituted in 1699 is only a step in a process lasting ninety years, during which the Sikhs had been transforming themselves from a purely religious fellowship (or panth) to an independent, largely Punjabi, Indian freedom movement. This process seemed to have reached its culmination when Maharaja Ranjit Singh ruled over an independent Punjab, but this was not a Sikh state, and despite the ruler's personal religious beliefs, it should be regarded as a state in which religion could be expressed freely but was not accompanied by privilege. At what point militant Sikhism came to have the aim of winning independence from the Mughals it is difficult to say. It first expressed itself in Banda Singh's warcry of 1710, 'Raj Karega Khalsa', 'The Khalsa will rule!' When Aurangzeb died Guru Gobind Singh was on his way to the court at Agra for an audience, he was received by his successor Bahadur Shah, presented with a jewelled scarf and other gifts and remained at the court for four months. His army marched with the Emperor's though it does not seem to have taken part in any campaigns.

In 1968 McLeod's study of Guru Nanak was published. It was this which placed Guru Nanak within the sant tradition of north India. However, much of the book is concerned with the quest of the historical Guru Nanak. The janam sakhis were subjected to rigorous scrutiny as historical sources and McLeod concluded that for the most part they did not form a reliable basis upon which to construct a biography. Sikhs have often reacted by defending the janam sakhi traditions (especially Trilochan Singh, 1969). Students who cannot read Punjabi must stand frustrated on the sidelines until either they have mastered the language or the janam sakhis have been rendered into satisfactory English translations.

Contemporary Indian scholars often see Guru Nanak as a reformer anticipating the work of Mahatma Gandhi. See the volumes of essays published to celebrate the quincentenary of Guru Nanak's birth listed on p. 199 and annual anniversary tributes in the *Spokesman* or *Sikh Review*.

CHAPTER THREE

The Sikh scriptures

One of the most fascinating aspects of Sikhism is the process which began with a human Guru, continued during a period of duality in which there were human Gurus and a collection of sacred writings, and ended with the present situation in which full authority is enjoyed by the scripture.

The development can be appreciated visually by looking at one of the many pictures of Guru Nanak with his companions Bala and Mardana. He is to be seen sitting on a cushion or low stool, a halo round his head and above him a tree shading him with its branches. Bala usually stands at his side with a peacock feather fan in his hand or a chauri of yak hairs embedded in a wooden or silver holder. The tree is intentionally reminiscent of the chattri (umbrella or parasol) which Lakshman holds over Rama in similar Hindu devotional pictures or which is to be found above the dome of a Buddhist temple. Compare such a portrait of Guru Nanak with enthroned scriptures in any Sikh temple and the similarity will immediately be seen, in fact their position is not similar but identical. In every respect the scripture is what the Gurus were. The Ten Gurus were not worshipped, neither is the Book even though the worshipper will bow or prostrate fully before it on entering the gurdwara. However, some gurdwaras will install it in the morning and put it to bed at night in much the same way as Rama and Krishna are cared for in Hindu temples.

It is not unusual to come across denunciation of such practices in Sikh periodicals.

Both the Gurus and the Book deserve the respect which they are accorded because of the bani which they express, the word of divine truth. Therefore it was possible for Guru Arjan, the fifth in the human line, to bow before the collection which he had compiled and installed in the newly-built Darbar Sahib in 1604, for he was acknowledging the higher authority of the bani to that personal importance and significance which he possessed as Guru. This is discussed further in the section on the nature and role of the Guru (p. 100).

The emphasis upon the bani is so complete that the position of the human Guru in Sikhism might seem, to the casual observer, to be one in which complete reverence has given way to complete indifference. A Sikh should not bow to a picture of a Guru as a Hindu would offer puja to a picture of Rama. Pictures of the Gurus should not be displayed near the scripture. In the 1930s paintings of the Gurus were discouraged in gurdwaras but in more recent times this stricture seems to have been ignored. The proper Sikh attitude was once summed up in a single pithy comment, 'The picture of the Guru is the gurbani' (Bhai Gurdas, Var 24, pauri 11).

The bani did not begin with Guru Nanak and in a sense it has not ended with the compilation of a scripture for Sikhs believe that where the congregation of believers gathers to hear the bani, God himself is present interpreting it to the needs of their situation. From it both the individual and the community can obtain consolation, joy and encouragement. It is therefore the focal point of all important events. The naming of a child is at its direction, a wedding performed by walking round it four times is regarded as valid in Sikh tradition regardless of civil requirements, and it is often read when a family moves into a new house or a firm into new business premises. Chapter 6 describes the Book's importance in domestic life.

Two names are usually given to the Sikh scriptures, the Adi Granth and the Guru Granth Sahib. The first title is earlier. The second, often preceded by the honorific Shri (Lord), frequently used of Krishna, only occurs after 1708 when the Tenth Guru installed the scripture as his successor. 'Granth' simply means collection, anthology or book and the word 'Adi' means 'first'.

It is customary to explain the title Adi Granth as distinguishing the scriptures from the collection of the Tenth Guru's writings known as the Dasam Granth. However, 'adi' often means first in sense of importance and not only time and the name should be seen as referring to the unique scriptural status which the anthology possesses. Perhaps the point can be reinforced by noting that Guru Nanak is 'pehle Guru' (First Guru), the Adi Guru is God.

The origin of the Guru Granth Sahib lies in the hymns of Guru Nanak. Mardana features in many janam sakhi accounts as the Guru's companion and the one who accompanied the Guru by playing a stringed instrument called a rebeck. When the Guru sensed the imminence of an inspired utterance he would warn Mardana to be ready with his music. Once when his companion was looking after a horse the Guru broke the silence of meditation and exclaimed, 'Mardana, touch the chords, the Word is descending.' 'But master,' his friend replied, 'my hands are occupied in holding the reins of this grazing horse. If I let go it may run away.' 'Let the horse go,' insisted Guru Nanak. Such a consciousness of inspiration must have led to the memorising or writing down of the Guru's compositions during his lifetime. Tradition is uncertain here. Sometimes Guru Angad is named as the first person to assemble the Guru's hymns but it seems more likely that when he was invested as Guru the most important object which he received was a bani pothi, an anthology of at least some of the Guru's hymns.

Two other narratives indicate the existence of some kind of collection during the Guru's lifetime. The Puratan Janam Sakhi states that a disciple Mansukh spent three years at Kartarpur with the Guru preparing a pothi under his supervision. More intriguing is the statement of Bhai Gurdas that when Guru Nanak visited Mecca 'he carried a staff in his hand, a book under his arm, a water pot and a prayer carpet for the call to prayer' (Var 1, pauri 32). Perhaps this book contained the bani of Farid, Namdev and Kabir and other pre-Nanak sants whose hymns are found in the Adi Granth. It is impossible to be sure and conclusions have often been reached which are based on theories of the Guru's dependence upon Kabir. It has already been pointed out that the common sant tradition may account for the many similarities which exist between the teachings of Kabir and those of Guru

Nanak. There is no trustworthy evidence that the two men ever met but it would be surprising if the Guru had never heard of such a famous person whose beliefs were in such agreement with his own. If he did know of him he could be expected to collect his writings and those of other teachers of similar views. Nothing could be more natural.

The Mohan Pothi compiled on the instructions of Guru Amar Das is the first anthology to have survived and whose contents are, therefore, known in detail. The two-volume pothi of 600 and 448 pages respectively includes works by Guru Nanak then Guru Angad and Guru Amar Das himself, followed by hymns of Kabir, Namdev, Trilochan, Sein, Ravidas and finally Jaidev. Here is clear evidence that non-Sikh material (called the bhagat bani by Sikhs) had a place in Sikh writings before the time of Guru Arjan. The initiative to include it may have come from Guru Amar Das but this is unlikely when the reasons for compiling the pothi are examined. A significant absentee is Baba Farid. It is tempting to speculate that his compositions were included by Guru Arjan as part of his attempt to commend Sikhism as the faith which could cement the Mughal Empire during the favourable reign of Akbar the Great. However, it would be wrong to place too much weight on the Mohan Pothi. The 600- and 448-page volumes do not even contain all the compositions of Guru Nanak. The group of hymns known as Asa di Var is missing from it, to cite only one important example. The Farid bani may have been in one of the other sources used by Guru Arjan. There is definite evidence that the first Guru knew at least some of the Sufi's poetry. One of his sabads occurs on page 794 of the Adi Granth.

> You could not make a raft at the time when you should have made it. When the sea is full and overflowing it is hard to cross. Do not touch the saffron flower with your hand, its colour will fade, my dear.
>
> First the bride herself is weak and in addition her husband's command is hard to bear. As the milk does not return to her breast so the soul does not enter the same body again.
>
> Says Farid, O my friends, when the spouse calls, the soul departs crestfallen and this body becomes a heap of ashes.

On page 729 is this verse of Guru Nanak's:

Make meditation on the Lord and self control the raft by which you cross the flowing stream. Your path shall be as comfortable as if there were no ocean or overflowing stream. Your name alone is the unfading madder with which my cloak is dyed. My beloved Lord, this colour is everlasting. The dear friends have departed, how shall they meet the Lord. If they are united in virtue the Lord will join them with himself. Once united the mortal does not separate again if the union is true. The true Lord puts an end to birth and rebirth.

She who removes self-centredness sews herself a garment to please her husband. By the Guru's instruction she obtained the fruit of the nectar of the Lord's word. Says Nanak, O my friends my spouse is very dear to me. We are the Lord's hand maidens. He is our true husband.

There are a number of obvious similarities of thought and the Guru can be seen to be replacing Farid's warnings against impermanence with positive commendations. In the original Gurmukhi there is a considerable identity of language.

The Mohan Pothi of Guru Amar Das was produced to meet three needs. First, the Sikh movement was expanding and the demand for copies of the hymns (pothis) of the First and Second Gurus was growing steadily. Second, the religion was now moving into its second generation, its leader was not someone who had been one of Guru Nanak's disciples. Men like Bhai Paira, who had copied pothis for the Second Guru, and Bhai Buddha were ageing. Soon their personal witness to the authenticity of the bani might be lost. Third, disgruntled sectarian groups were already beginning to assemble spurious collections of hymns attributed to Guru Nanak either for the purpose of promoting their own claims to be the true Sikhs or to bring the Guru into disrepute. The bani of Guru Amar Das contains a number of warnings against apostasy and false teachings:

All other teaching but that of the Sat Guru is false. False are those who utter it, false are those who hear it, false those who recite it and those who invent it. They utter the Lord's name with their tongue but do not understand what they say.   (AG 920)

It seems unlikely that a Guru who was himself under attack would have introduced non-Sikh material into the bani. Guru Angad was no innovator and therefore the conclusion would seem to be that Guru Nanak was responsible. The pothi was compiled by Guru Amar Das's grandson Sahansar Ram but the two volumes had passed into the hands of his father Baba Mohan by the time Guru Arjan decided to compile the Adi Granth, hence its name Mohan Pothi.

The Adi Granth of Guru Arjan was much more than yet another compilation. It was intended to be definitive and the Guru succeeded in this aim. As a result of considerable personal effort he gathered the best available manuscripts, even, it is said, going to the extent of singing Mohan's praises outside his window to obtain the loan of his collection of hymns. Mohan, the son of Amar Das, according to the same tradition, was disappointed when his father chose Ram Das to be Fourth Guru. Therefore, he was not inclined to behave in a very helpful manner towards Guru Ram Das's son. The song associated with the tale is to be found on page 248 of the Adi Granth. It does refer to Mohan but the context leaves no doubt that God is being addressed as 'the attractive one' (Mohan). The story's value lies in indicating Guru Arjan's concern to assemble the best available anthologies. He also borrowed a pothi in the possession of Datu, Guru Angad's son, but its contents are not known. In addition to these he had the help of Bhai Buddha, a surviving member of the Kartarpur community and therefore a valuable link with the living voice of Guru Nanak.

However, while fidelity to the bani and comprehensiveness were major concerns, Guru Arjan was not afraid to allow his own genius to express itself. He included his own compositions, almost equal in number to those contained in the pothis, but he also removed some verses of the bhagats, and simplified the language of others, for example the bani of Namdev. One sabad previously designated 'Kabir nama' he attributed to Namdev (AG 1252). Guru Arjan gave the Granth its distinctive form. The Book's arrangement is his, so is its final syntax, the poetry being accented in such a way as to make alteration difficult without going against its rhythm and musical setting. Mohan's pothi had fourteen divisions, the Adi Granth has thirty-one. These were made according to Indian musical measures, called rags. Generally speaking rags are composed to suit various moods. Some are appropriate to morning, others to evening, some to joy, others to grief. Guru Arjan indicated that faith should produce a balanced outlook, tempering both happiness and sadness so, for example, between pages 917 and 924 are found both the Anand, Guru Amar Das's hymn of joy, and Sunder's dirge on that Guru's death. The setting is Ramkali rag, which relates to the season of Besant in March shortly before harvest. The mood is one of yearning. The rag was often favoured by yogis. Another example is the inclusion of songs sung by ladies at wedding parties, and laments put on adjacent pages under Rag Wadhans (AG 575–81).

It is difficult to over-estimate Guru Arjan's achievement. Scrutinising the hymns of the earlier Gurus and the Hindu and Muslim poets had been the least of his difficulties. The quantity of their writings scarcely equalled his. To arrange the whole in an orderly manner and in such a way that the philosophy of the balanced life, including Sikhism, as the achieved ideal for which other faiths had been vainly striving was more difficult. No translation has yet managed to communicate the flavour of his success. Perhaps none ever will because of the sheer bulk of the material. It may be that a good translation of one of the major rags will serve to illustrate the point one day. So far no selection of passages from the Adi Granth has concentrated upon the complete examination of one particular rag.

The text of Guru Arjan's Adi Granth was considered to be the authorised version of the scripture. Two anecdotes illustrate the importance which was attached to it. The first has been mentioned earlier (see p. 32), and resulted in the name Ram Rai standing for apostasy among the Sikhs. The other incident occurred in the time of Guru Arjan himself. A disciple, Bhai Banno, made a copy of the Granth Sahib but when he came to the one line of the Bhagat Surdas which is to be found on page 1253 he added the rest of the verse. He also included a stanza by the woman poet Mira Bai at the end of Rag Maru. This Guru Arjan had deleted in the original manuscript by crossing it out. Bhai Banno's alterations may appear unimportant, but they were sufficient for the Guru to condemn the copy as 'bitter' in comparison with the 'sweet' authentic version.

To the Granth Sahib of Guru Arjan the Tenth Guru merely

added the hymns of his own father, Guru Tegh Bahadur. Also, before his death, he installed the scriptures as Guru thus completing a process which had been developing for well over a century. At Kartarpur it was the hymns of Guru Nanak which were given pride of place in the worship of the community, being already regarded as divinely inspired. At Amritsar the Fifth Guru housed the Adi Granth in the newly built Darbar Sahib and bowed before it. The recognition which the Tenth Guru gave the scripture made *de jure* what was in a sense already *de facto*. The distinction between the human Guru and the gurbani now became complete with his decision to appoint no human successor.

Close textual study of the Adi Granth is something which Sikh scholars have yet to undertake. The material for it exists. The Mohan Pothi survives, Guru Arjan's original manuscript is at Kartarpur in Jullundur district. The copy which Guru Gobind Singh used when he conferred guruship upon the scripture in 1708 was destroyed but copies made by Baba Deep Singh and Bhai Mani Singh survive. For that matter so does the Bhai Bhanno version and, at Dera Dun, the one used by Ram Rai. However, the analytical approach to scriptural texts which has concerned western scholars for the best part of two centuries seems not only unworthy but unimportant to many Asian scholars whose concern is for the message of the scripture. It could be that the next decade will see the publication of photocopies of the important texts mentioned above but if it does the enthusiasm for the venture will be greater among non-Sikhs than Sikhs, who will probably concentrate their efforts on presenting an understanding of the message of Sikhism to the western world.

The copies of the Guru Granth Sahib which may be found in any Gurdwara from California to Bangkok are identical. Each has 1430 pages. This standardisation of page length and numbering took place in the nineteenth century. The script used is called Gurmukhi and is used irrespective of whether the original hymn was composed in medieval Hindi, Punjabi or some other language. Apart from the Japji of Guru Nanak, Sodar, Sopurkh and the bedtime prayer Sohilla which follow it, plus seventy-eight pages at the end of the Adi Granth, the rest of the book is divided into thirty-one sections. The singing of the bani is called kirtan. It is intended to be simple and straightforward so that the congregation can participate and to prevent concentration upon the words becoming secondary to enjoying a musical feast. Usually in a gurdwara the musicians (ragis) will be three in number, one playing the portable harmonium (a result of eighteenth- or nineteenth-century European influence), another playing the drum, either the single instrument with parchment at both ends or two drums fastened together and with parchment at one end only. The third musician sings and explains the bani, and may play an instrument as well. A pair of steel tongs with rows of brass discs fixed along their length and the sarinda with its three strings which are played with a bow may be used as well as other stringed instruments, including the violin, an instrument which is not uncommon in southern India. Traditions in the singing of the gurbani change from time to time. The harmonium eventually found its way into the gurdwara despite resistance from the ragis of the Golden Temple. They have often been the mainstay of traditions and maintainers of standards, such men as the great Mahant Sham Singh Adanshahi who died in 1926 aged 123 years. Most of his seventy years as a ragi playing the sarinda and singing the bani had been spent in the Golden Temple. Now it seems that the Indian cinema may be influencing some younger musicians.

The structure of the Guru Granth Sahib is explained in Appendix 4. In this present section it is only necessary to note a few points. First, there is a major structure to the scripture. Pages 14 to 1352 are divided into thirty-one parts each named after the musical setting to which it should be sung. The compositions before page 14, the important hymns which Sikhs use in daily meditation, are given distinction by being excluded from the dominant form of arrangement. The last 78 pages contain hymns which are often so short that they could not be placed in the main body of the text satisfactorily.

Second, within the major structure there is a clear substructure. Each section begins with the writings of Guru Nanak followed by those of the Third, Fourth, Fifth and Ninth Gurus. After these are placed the non-Sikh compositions, beginning with those of Kabir. As the table in Appendix 4 indicates, not every author, even Guru Nanak, is represented in each section. Guru Angad's verses were few (sixty-two) and brief and have been attached to the hymns of other Gurus.

Finally, the Adi Granth is unique among the world's scriptures in its inclusion of non-Sikh hymns. Hindu and Muslim writings are included in what is called the bhagat bani.

Only speculative conclusions can be drawn to explain the inclusion of particular poets in the bhagat bani. It has already been suggested that some owed their place to Guru Nanak. The token presence of the bhagats seems to indicate Guru Arjan's desire to present Sikhism as the catholic faith. The inclusion of a hymn by a particular sant was not important in itself but for the acknowledgment which it made that he also proclaimed the sabd and for the claim that the right place for his devotees to be was within the fold of Sikhism.

Whatever the language in which a poet expressed himself, all the hymns of the Guru Granth have been recorded in the same script, that of the Punjabi language, called Gurmukhi. It is this name, not Punjabi, which should properly be used for written Punjabi, whether the reference is to a daily paper, a novel or the Adi Granth. Persian, Punjabi and Hindi are not written alike. The use of a uniform script by Guru Arjan despite the variety of languages and dialects may have been another way of asserting catholicity.

Revelation in the Guru Granth Sahib

When a Sikh describes the Adi Granth as the word of God he is making a statement which is both exclusive and inclusive. It is exclusive in the sense that it is the sacred book of his religion, it is the scripture which is to be found in the gurdwara and which forms the basis of his meditation, understanding of God and world-outlook. At the same time he would not confine the phrase 'word of God' to the Adi Granth. Not only would he wish to include the revealed scriptures of other religions, the Sikh would also wish to leave room for the words of living men and women, now and in the future, to be regarded as revelation. Godly people, having been enlightened by God, possess divine knowledge intuitively through meditation. 'God resides in the soul and the soul is contained in him' (AG 1153). The bani is the verbal expression of this. Revelation in the Adi Granth has as its heritage the rich concept of sabd in Indian thought, plus the belief that revelation is the expression of the experience of the truth which is God, in verbal form. The bani is God. Guru Amar Das said, 'The gurbani is God himself and it is through it that man obtained union with God' (AG 39). Guru Ram Das expressed the same thought in slightly different words, 'The gurbani is the Lord's name and this name I enshrine in my mind' (AG 1239). The compiler of the Adi Granth, Guru Arjan, said, 'The holy book is the abode of God' (AG 1226).

The Vedas are not condemned by the Sikh Gurus though the formalism arising from them is:

There are six Hindu schools of thought, each has its own guru and its own doctrine but the guru of all gurus is one, however many his manifestations. . . . As there is one sun and many seasons so there is one God though he has many forms.   (AG 357)

The principle of revelation is nowhere better demonstrated than by the inclusion of the bhagat bani, as the non-Sikh material is called, in the Adi Granth. It comprises about one-sixth of the total (938 sabads out of a total of 5894), thus exceeding the contribution of any one Guru other than Guru Arjan.

Of course the danger of false teachers exists. Accepting the view that God may speak through anyone leaves one open to the blandishments of any self-styled holy man, especially in the Indian village. The Sikh is advised to keep the fellowship of the sangat; in their company he will learn discretion. In practice he will test the teaching against the gurbani, the body of doctrine given by the Gurus.

Subject-matter and content

The form of the Guru Granth Sahib is poetry. Its major concern might be described as soteriological, though in the specific Sikh sense of enabling the reader, or originally the hearer, to realise the essential unity with God. There are no mythological narratives, though God is described in anthropomorphic terms and the Gurus are not afraid to use the imagery of family relationships to describe the union of God and man: 'A young wife sits at home. Her beloved is away. She continually thinks of him and pines for him. If her intentions are good their reunion shall not be delayed' (AG 594). The nearest the Guru Granth Sahib comes to narrative is the discourse between Guru Nanak and the yogis, Siddha Gosht. For the Sikh right living is the key to a proper relationship with God. Consequently the poems are full of references to individual conduct.

The most important themes are covered in the later sections of this book. At the end of the Adi Granth in a passage called Mandavani or the Seal, Guru Arjan explains the scripture in these words, comparing it to a dish of food:

In the platter are placed three things, truth, contentment and meditation. The nectar-name of the Lord, the support of all, has also been put therein. If someone eats this food, if someone relishes it, he is emancipated. This cannot be forsaken so keep it enshrined in your mind always. Falling down at the Lord's feet the dark world ocean is crossed. O Nanak, everything is an extension of the Lord.   (AG 1429)

The place of the Guru Granth Sahib in worship

The scripture is more than a visible focal point for Sikh devotions, though to sit for a time in a gurdwara, view its centrality and watch men and women bowing reverently in front of it is probably the best position from which to begin to understand its significance. The Guru Granth Sahib so dominates Sikh ritual and Sikh theology that it forms a recurrent theme in this book and therefore the reader is referred to other sections, especially those on the gurdwara, Sikh daily life, ceremonies, festivals, and the index. Here we shall confine ourselves to noting how the Guru Granth has taken the place of the living Gurus.

In 1920 an incident occurred which demonstrates the way in which the Adi Granth holds the position of Guru in another respect. The custom of consulting the scripture is common. At the end of a service the Adi Granth will be opened at random and a portion read. Many Sikhs do this daily, regarding the verses as word from God which they will find helpful during the day. This is called vak lao, taking advice. The 1920s was a period when large groups of Punjabi outcastes were becoming Sikhs or Christians in the hope of improving social status. Whilst commensality is practised by Sikhs, the question of allowing Untouchable converts to offer karah parshad presented a new issue as hitherto most Sikhs had been of a higher status. Members of the Singh Sabha reform movement advocated the right of the converts to offer karah parshad but organisations are as often influenced by traditions which have accrued as by the doctrine and in the nineteenth century Sikhism had often been introspective. In 1920 a large number of outcastes were initiated into the Khalsa and went to the Golden Temple to offer karah parshad. Traditionalists wished to refuse it; the reformers pressed the principle that karah parshad should be given by all Khalsa members. It was agreed that advice should be taken from the Guru and therefore a copy was opened at random. The passage which was turned up read:

> Upon the worthless he bestows his grace, brother, if they will serve the True Guru. Exalted is the service of the True Guru, brother, to hold in remembrance the divine name. God himself offers grace and mystic union. We are worthless sinners brother, yet the True Guru has drawn us to that blissful union.   (AG 638:3)

The words of Guru Amar Das clinched the issue. Clearly the Guru had accepted the converts. The sangat followed his direction and accepted karah parshad from the hands of Untouchables.

The Dasam Granth

Guru Gobind Singh was a prolific poet and seems to have been equally at home in Persian, Sanskrit or Punjabi. He included none of his writings in the Adi Granth and at the time of his death they were scattered in various parts of India. The Guru himself does not seem to have attempted to compile them into an anthology and certainly he would not have approved any suggestion that they might rival the Adi Granth. The corpus of Guru Gobind Singh's writings which bears the title Dasam Granth is the product of the devoted labours of Bhai Mani Singh and was not completed until twenty-six years after the Guru's death in 1734. It includes a number of compositions written by poets who were in the service of his court.

The Gurmukhi script is used throughout the book irrespective of whether the language be Sanskrit, Persian, Hindi or Punjabi. The form of verse and the type of poetry is as variable as the language.

There are more than 2,000 poems in the twelve sections of the
1428-page book. The first is the Jap, a meditative hymn reminiscent of the Japji of Guru Nanak. It begins,

God has no marks or symbols,
He is of no colour, of no caste,
He is not even of any lineage.
His form, hue, shape and garb
Cannot be described by anyone.
He is immovable, self-existent;
He shines in his own splendour;
No one can measure his might.
He is the king of kings, the lordly Indra,
Of countless Indras; the supreme Ruler
Of the three worlds of gods, men and demons,
Even the meadows and the woodlands
Cry in his praise, Infinite, Infinite!
O Lord who can tell the number of your names?
I will try to relate your names
According to your deeds.

In the second hymn, entitled Akal Ustat, the Praise of the
Lord, there are verses which indicate that the early spirit of
Sikhism still lived, which stated that behind the diversities of
religion lay the oneness of God:

By shaving his head a man
Hopes to become a holy monk.
Another sets up as a Yogi
Or as some other kind of ascetic.
Some call themselves Hindus,
Others call themselves Muslims.
Among these are Shiahs and also Sunnis,
Yet man is one race in all the world.
God as Creator and God as Good,
God in his Bounty and God in his Mercy
Is all one God. Even in our errors
We should not separate God from God!
Worship the one God,
The one divine Guru for all men.
All men have the same form,
All men have the same soul.

Some of the poems are very different. Vichitar Natak, the Wonderful Drama, outlines the Guru's family history, reforming mission and warlike exploits. The Zafarnama is a letter in Persian written to the Emperor Aurangzeb. In it the charge of deliberately provoking war is rejected but a doctrine of the just war is laid down:

When all efforts to restore peace prove useless and no
    words avail,
Lawful is the flash of steel, it is right to draw the sword.

Together with the thirty-three verses in praise of the Immortal One (Swayyas) the poems already mentioned probably constitute the best known and most important of the Guru's works. The Jap, some stanzas from the Akal Ustat and the thirty-three Swayyas are all used liturgically in the initiation ceremonies or other acts of worship and are to be found in the gutkas, small anthologies of hymns which many Sikhs possess and use for daily meditation.

In the Guru's own time other poems probably had a very strong appeal and significance but they fall into the class of occasional literature written to meet the needs of the day which once past makes their appeal diminish with time. Of such is Pakhian Charitra, a compendium of medieval legends and romances reinterpreted for use as the means of communicating homespun wisdom and ethical teaching, though a few passages from this 579-page section of over 400 stories are used in the amrit initiation ceremony. With Chaubis Avtar, based on the incarnation of Shiva, and Chandi Charitra, the exploits of Chandi, goddess of war, Pakhian Charitra is to be seen as a method which the Guru used to express Sikh ideas through the Hindu and local Punjabi culture. Instead of rejecting folk tales and myths out of hand he reinterpreted them hoping to wean those who had been brought up in them from the old traditions to the ideals of Sikhism. Sometimes in doing so he also explained mythological and historical references which are to be found in the Adi Granth. However, the unity of the Dasam Granth is only one of authorship and of the Gurmukhi script. Its language, purpose and form are diverse and it must not be regarded as anything more than an anthology.

CHAPTER FOUR

The Gurdwara and Sikh worship

Wherever there are Sikhs there will be a gurdwara. It may be a magnificent white ornate building rising high above the trees and houses of a Punjabi village, or it may be a plain flat-roofed building remarkable only for its size compared with the other houses nearby. In the UK it may be a terrace house or a former Christian church. Strictly speaking a gurdwara is any place where a copy of the Guru Granth Sahib is installed. The unique and distinguishing feature will always be the nishan sahib, a flagstaff with the yellow flag of Sikhism flying from it. This serves as a statement of the Sikh presence. It enables the traveller, whether he be Sikh or not, to know where hospitality is available. It is an assertion of authority, the principle of freedom of worship. For these reasons one will often see Sikhs bowing towards the nishan sahib, touching its base before they enter the building.

Gurdwaras fall into two groups, with the Golden Temple at Amritsar (the Darbar Sahib or Harmandir) distinct from either of them. First, there is the community gurdwara built by Sikhs to meet their religious and social needs. Then, better known, are the historic gurdwaras. These are buildings erected on sites which are important in the history of Sikhism. For example the Sis Ganj in Delhi marks the place where Guru Tegh Bahadur was martyred and the Keshgarh at Anandpur was erected over the spot where Guru Gobind Singh instituted the Khalsa. This practice seems to have begun with Guru Hargobind, to whom the first use of the word gurdwara is attributed. He visited places associated with his father or his predecessors, especially Guru Nanak, restored the buildings which he found, encouraging proper teaching and preaching to be given in them.

The name used for these structures was dharmsala, which can signify a rest-house for travellers in its normal Indian context but was used in the early days of Sikhism to denote a room or building used for devotional singing (kirtan) and prayers. Guru Nanak built a dharmsala at Kartarpur and Bhai Gurdas claims, possibly with some poetic licence, that,

> Centres of worship were established wherever Baba
> [Nanak] set foot.
> All the Siddh centres [i.e. religious centres] in the world
> became centres of Nanak's teaching.
> Every house became a dharmsala and kirtan was sung
> as if it were an unending Baisakhi festival.
>
> (Var 1, pauri 27)

It might well have been an early Sikh strategy to provide alternative meeting places to those of the other religions and cults present in north India. In the B40 Janam Sakhi God addresses the following words to Guru Nanak, 'As the Vaishnavas have their temples, the yogis their asan, and the Muslims their mosque, so your followers shall have their dharmsala.' So many passages in the janam sakhis end with the statement 'a dharmsala was built' that it seems to have been a provision introduced by the First Guru. Frequently the building was a gift from a devotee. The Hafizabad Janam Sakhi attributes the first dharmsala to a thag (a term which may denote a worshipper of Kali who practised ritual murder, or may merely mean a highway robber) named Sajjan who built it after his conversion. Another anecdote tells of a rich official who decided to drive Guru Nanak from the district. He mounted his horse but on the way it fell and he was unseated. As he returned home the people said that he had committed a dreadful sin and would have to go to the Guru for pardon. Next day he set out again but was overcome by blindness. The people explained that the Guru was an exalted person. 'You must go to him on foot with palms joined in humble submission,' they urged, 'and say "May my sins be forgiven".' He penitently made his way to the Guru, fell at his feet and was forgiven. Then he respectfully asked the Guru to accept a gift. At first Guru Nanak refused but eventually accepted a large area of land. On this a dharmsala was built. The remaining ground was cultivated and the income used to maintain the building and a common kitchen. It was buildings of such origins that Guru Hargobind restored. Some may have fallen into disuse as Sikhs moved from the district or reverted to the major Hindu tradition in the third or fourth generation. In the early seventeenth century the historical consciousness of the Sikhs grew and the work of the Sixth Guru matches the spirit of the age. The historic gurdwaras which are to be found in India and Pakistan today stand on the sites of those earlier times but are for the most part nineteenth- or twentieth-century constructions. They coincide not only with the peace of the British period but with the Singh Sabha movement which emerged as a response to Christian and Hindu missionary activity.

The architecture of the major gurdwaras is normally in the Mughal style of Shah Jehan which Sikhs find a congenial blend of Muslim and Hindu forms, though they have developed it in a peculiarly Sikh manner. Whatever the brick or stone used the finish is usually white. The chattris or kiosks which surmount the minarets of the Taj Mahal or the Lahore Gate of the Red Fort at Delhi are not only to be found at the four corners, as they are for example at the Diwan-i-Khaz of the Red Fort, but may be seen at many points along the parapet of a gurdwara. Sometimes the slender lantern-like kiosks of Aurangzeb's Pearl Mosque, also found in the Red Fort, have been incorporated. The other important characteristics are the oriel or bow windows and the domes. The windows have shallow elliptical cornices supported by brackets and the arches are frequently enriched by means of numerous foliations so that the gurdwara is reminiscent of the palaces of Udaipur. The domes of the gurdwaras may have a floral cap and spike (kalas) in common with the great mosques and Hindu temples of the last Mughal period, but they are distinctively fluted. Whereas the dome of a Hindu temple stands like a mountain over the sanctuary, the dome of a gurdwara is placed with architectural considerations alone in mind. If it is directly above the Guru Granth Sahib this is merely coincidental.

The Golden Temple at Amritsar, whilst distinctively Sikh, cannot be regarded as a typical gurdwara. Set in the centre of a rectangular artificial pool it is much more a house for the Guru Granth Sahib, where kirtan are sung all day and to which pilgrims come from 2 a.m. until late at night, than a place of congregational worship. Indeed both langar and diwan are held elsewhere than in the Golden Temple itself. However, the Harmandir does emphatically bring together the many facets of Sikh architecture including the inlay of semi-precious stones such as lapis lazuli and onyx on marble panels, as well as mirror-work inlay in some of the interior decoration, especially in the Shish Mahal or mirror room and the roof of the building. There are also murals depicting scenes from the life of Guru Nanak. Another feature of the interior is the inscription of verses from the Guru Granth Sahib in gilded lettering on some of the walls. A visitor to the Golden Temple may be reminded of Delhi's Red Fort, the lake palaces of Udaipur and the Taj Mahal but the Harmandir is ultimately more than the sum of these parts.

The function of the gurdwara is not unlike that of the dharmsala from which it evolved. From the B40 Janam Sakhi comes this account which provides some insight into early Sikh worship:

Below the raja's palace was the dharmsala where the Sikhs sang hymns and performed kirtan. Sitting there the raja would fix his attention on the music of whatever hymn the Sikhs were singing. One day the rani said to the raja, 'Raja, how is it no children have been born in our house? Let us go to the dharmsala and lay our petition before the congregation, for the Guru is present in the congregation.' 'An excellent idea!' replied the raja.

Next day the raja and the rani both joined the congregation. A large congregation was present. A hymn was being sung and all were sitting enthralled. The raja and the rani then presented their petition saying, 'You are the assembly of the Guru and whatever is sought from you is granted. May it please you to hear our intercession so that the Guru may grant a son.'

Those who were present in the congregation offered a prayer that the raja's faith might remain unshaken. Then they assured him, 'The Guru Baba will grant you a son.'

This description of a seventeenth-century act of worship not only shows the importance of kirtan, but it also emphasises the Guru Panth, the congregation met in the Guru's name. It is a tenet of the Sikh faith that where the company of believers (sangat) is, there the Guru is also:

> Attuned to you your devotees constantly sing your praises. You are the refuge in which they find deliverance, O Creator Lord. You unite them with yourself. . . . Without the True Guru there is no congregation and without the Name no one is ferried across the world ocean. He who utters the Lord's praise day and night merges his light with the supreme light. (AG 1068; 3rd Guru)

Therefore when a Sikh enters a gurdwara he believes he is entering the presence of the Guru. 'Gurdwara' means the home or abode of the Guru; wherever the Guru Granth Sahib is installed there is a gurdwara.

Entering a large gurdwara one will often encounter a complexity of rooms, for the building may also serve as a school where children are taught the rudiments of Sikhism, as well as a rest centre for travellers. Often there will be a kitchen where food can be prepared, though the langar itself might take place under an awning in the open air. Sometimes the gurdwara will also be used as a clinic. Its primary function is that of a place of worship and the main room will be that in which the Guru Granth Sahib is installed and where the community gathers for diwan. The focal point in this room will be the Book itself, placed upon cushions and underneath a canopy. Sometimes both cushions and canopy will be set inside a wooden frame called a takht (throne) or palki (akin to the word palanquin). Popular religious pictures sometimes show Guru Nanak sitting on his gaddi under a tree as those of Hinduism show Rama enthroned with Lakshman holding an umbrella (chattri) over him whilst Hanuman or Sita hold a wand or fan of peacock feathers. In the gurdwara the Guru Granth Sahib on its manji (bed) is the enthroned Guru, the canopy is the chattri denoting authority and the attendant waving the chauri (yak hairs embedded in a wooden or metal handle) is the devotee showing respect for authority. The room may otherwise be bare and even devoid of seats. The walls may be decorated with murals or Gurmukhi verses from the scripture. In brief the only requirement is the congregation and the Guru Granth Sahib. Without the Sikh community there would be no gurdwara in any real sense. The gurdwaras of Pakistan or Uganda are mere shrines as no Sikh communities remain to worship in them. On the other hand without a place where the gurbani may be heard and sung the Sikh sangat is incomplete.

Worship in the gurdwara

Worship may take place at any time and no quorum is required. It is customary for Sikhs to assemble for congregational worship early in the morning or, more especially, in the evening. This is in the tradition of Guru Nanak's community at Kartarpur but is also a recognition of the realities of the householder life. During the day most members of the community will be practising their faith at work. There is no fixed day for worship and even if some Sikhs living in the Punjab gather in greater numbers at Sangrand, the first day of the lunar calendar, this is only because in rural communities it is the moon cycle which plays a more important part in life than the Gregorian calendar. India's festivals like those of Islam or the dates of the Passover, Easter and Pentecost/Whitsuntide are for the most part determined by the moon. A Sangrand service may therefore include the Bara Mahan (Twelve Months) hymn of Guru Arjan with an explanation of its symbolic meaning, relating it to the stages of human life and the journey of the soul.

Before going to the gurdwara, whether it be in the morning or the evening, the Sikh will have bathed. In the morning he will also have recited some or all of the Japji. At the gurdwara he may bow and touch the flagstaff before climbing the steps into the gurdwara. As he mounts the steps he is likely to bend, touch the step with his hand and put his hand to his forehead: 'Wherever my Sat Guru goes and sits, that place is beautiful, O Lord King. The Guru's disciples seek that place and take and apply its dust to their foreheads' (AG 540; 4th Guru). It is customary to remove shoes before climbing the steps, or there may be a place to put them inside the building. Along village paths and roads it is common to walk barefoot, and a pump or channel of running water will be available at the gurdwara where those who

63

need to can wash their feet. The head is always covered and if a Sikh woman has been walking along the road with an uncovered head she will draw her scarf over it before entering the building.

Inside the gurdwara the Sikh will approach the dais upon which the Guru Granth Sahib rests, bow or prostrate fully and make an offering of money or food to be used in the kitchen. Careful not to turn the back on the Book the worshipper will then sit with the congregation on a bare floor or one which has been covered with a mat or carpet. (Chairs are not forbidden but in the subcontinent they are not found even in all Christian churches, despite the European influence. In the Punjab there are no gurdwaras with benches or chairs.) Men and women sit separately but this is a matter of convention, of custom not belief, similar to the practice in some Hindu temples or European churches. Worship need not begin with a litany or ceremony, but merely with the opening of the Book by any man or woman who can read it. Usually Sukhmani will be sung in the morning and often the time of evening worship is announced to the village by the granthi sounding a gong. At this service Rahiras will be the principal hymn.

Music, the singing of kirtan to the accompaniment of the drum and harmonium as well as other instruments, is an important part of worship. The Gurus encouraged music at their courts. Guru Arjan declared music to be 'an adornment of the tongue' and the third Guru said:

> The music and those songs are welcome
> Through which the mind is concentrated on him [God]
>   with ease.

(AG 849)

The singing of the Gurus' hymns (kirtan), exegesis, exhortation, mainly through stories of the Gurus and their most famous disciples, constitute the main parts of a service. Traditionally its length is not fixed. Some gurdwaras in Indian cities or in the west may now begin their service at set times and schedule them to last for ninety minutes or two hours. Such matters are decided by a committee. Sikhism has no priesthood, or ordained ministry. No human being may take the place of the Gurus or rival the Guru Granth Sahib. In some gurdwaras a man called a granthi may be paid a salary (sewa) to read the scriptures, conduct services and perform such ceremonies as marriages, but his role is purely functional. The appointment is not necessarily permanent. He is the servant of the community and his position has never become such that he might be compared to a priest or minister as normally understood.

Towards the conclusion of worship a liturgy emerges. The seated congregation will sing the Anand Sahib (the hymn of bliss of Guru Amar Das). In this the devotee rejoices that he has found the Sat Guru and is sustained by meditation on the Name. It ends:

> Listen to me my joy, my fortunate friends; all my desires have been fulfilled. I have reached God, the Supreme Spirit, and all my sorrows have vanished. My sorrows, afflictions and sufferings have departed by hearing the true Word. The saints and holy men are glad on hearing it from the perfect Guru. Pure are they who hear it; stainless are those who utter it, and the True Guru will fill their hearts. Nanak proclaims; for those who bow at the Guru's feet, heavenly trumpets will sound.   (AG 917)

The epilogue to the Japji Sahib of Guru Nanak will be read, which is a reminder of the liberating as well as awesome presence of God:

> Air, water and earth, of these are we made.
> Air like the Guru's word gives breath to life.
> To the babe born to the great mother sired of the waters.
> The day and the night our nurses be
> That watch us in our infancy;
> In their laps we play, the world is our playground.
> Our acts, right and wrong shall come to judgment at your
>   court.
> Some shall be seated near your seat, some shall always be
>   kept distant. The toils of those who have worshipped you
>   have ended,
> O Nanak, their faces are lit with joyful radiance,
> Many others are set free.
>
> (AG 8)

The sangat then stands to hear the verse 'Too Thakur tum pah ardas' composed by Guru Arjan:

Thou art the Master, to thee I pray.
My body and soul are thy gifts to start life with.
Thou art the Father, Thou art the Mother, and we Thy
children!
We drew manifold blessings from Thy grace.
None knows thine extent:
Thou art the highest of the high,
All creation is strung on thy will:
It has to accept all that comes from thee.
Thou alone knowest what informs Thy purposes.
I am ever and ever a sacrifice unto Thee.

(AG 268)

Then with hands clasped in front of the chest and head slightly bowed each member of the congregation stands silently whilst one of their number, it may be man or woman, who is a Khalsa Sikh, offers the prayer which is known by no other name than Ardas. (This important passage is printed as Appendix 2 and discussed fully at that point.) Everyone sings the final portion of Ardas after which the Guru Granth Sahib is opened at random and a brief verse of guidance (vak) read to the sangat. Diwan ends with a distribution of karah parshad. This sweet food is made of flour, sugar and clarified butter which has been cooked, and is served warm to everyone who is present. It symbolises universal brotherhood.

CHAPTER FIVE

Sikh religious thought

Introduction

Sikh theology possesses a coherence unique in the sant tradition. This brief outline is intended to convey something of this and so make the more detailed study which follows clearer by bringing out the inter-relatedness and interdependence of most of the beliefs. It has already been asserted that Sikhism grew out of the sant tradition and a general north-west Indian environment of religious variety in a basically Hindu cultural context. No attempt will be made in this section to examine the origins of the Sikh concepts unless it is considered necessary for the purpose of understanding them. We shall concentrate on describing and explaining them.

Sikhism is strictly monotheistic. So firmly is the oneness of God affirmed that it is arguably monistic. Ultimate reality is a unity, God is one without a second. Parmeshur (God) is essentially without qualities (nirguna). Consequently sat (truth) or akal (beyond time) or other negative terms such as ajuni (not becoming) are among the least inadequate descriptions. However, Parmeshur or Sat is also personal, manifest and possesses qualities (saguna), though his attributes are never physical, even though anthropomorphisms are used in the Adi Granth's poetry. In his manifest form his qualities, Sabd (word), Nam (personality or character) and Guru (enlightener) are communicative and creative. God is the creator, the universe emanates from him, its existence and its continuing survival depend upon his will (hukam) which is all powerful. Man is unique in this creation since he alone possesses the ability to discriminate and enter into a voluntary relationship of love with God. In his natural state man sees himself as creation's Lord disregarding the evidence of his own finiteness which mortality and nature's independence of him provide. He is characterised by self-reliance (haumai) and at best sees the world including himself erroneously as distinct from God. This duality leads to attachment to temporal values which is maya. The consequence is rebirth (samsara) on the basis of previous actions (karma). There is only one way of achieving liberation (mukti) – this is by conquering haumai, ceasing to be worldly-minded (man mukh) and become God-conscious and God-filled (gurmukh). This can only be done by becoming aware of the inner presence of God as Sabd, Guru and Nam and by coming completely under their influence. This in turn is only possible because God looks benignly (prasad, nadar) upon man's efforts and as Sabd, Guru and Nam makes himself known, enlightens and liberates the believer. Because God is within, rituals are unnecessary but right conduct is essential. The mark of the gurmukh is his life of service (sewa) in the world as a householder (grihastha), not a sannyasin (renouncer), because now in his state of jivan mukti (liberation whilst still in this corporeal existence) he perceives himself and the world as part of the one reality to which he is now consciously attached and in which, at death, he will be completely merged.

This brief outline, introducing the most important Sikh terms, is developed and explained in the sections which follow.

The concept of God

'God is the one, the only one', 'the one without a second'. These are the recurrent observations of the six Gurus whose hymns are contained in the Adi Granth and of Guru Gobind Singh. As a result there has been some discussion among scholars whether Sikhism is to be described as monistic or monotheistic. It is certainly monistic in the sense that the types of quotation

referred to above emphasise an ultimate unity of such a kind
that the world derives from God and will be reabsorbed in
him.

> When the Creator projected himself all
> creatures of the earth assumed various shapes.
> But when you draw creation within yourself,
> O Lord, all embodied beings are absorbed in you.
>
> (Guru Gobind Singh)

It is certainly true to say that Guru Nanak believed in a personal
God who could be worshipped and loved. This understanding
of God was derived from experience. When he was taken to God's
court, as he put it, he became aware of God as one, as personal
and as pervading the universe. He was given a cup of the
nectar of God's name to drink and was commanded to go into
the world to preach the divine name, but from then on he not
only found him within himself, he perceived God as 'pervading
all forms, all castes and all hearts' (AG 223). The Mool Mantra,
which is said to have been the Guru's first poetic utterance,
made soon after the Sultanpur experience, is a summary of the
beliefs. It reads:

> There is one God,
> Eternal truth is his name,
> Creator of all things and the all-pervading spirit.
> Fearless and without hatred,
> Timeless and formless.
> Beyond birth and death,
> Self-enlightened.
> By the grace of the Guru he is known.

The symbol representing 'Ik oankar', there is one God, is found
on the canopy above the Adi Granth in the gurdwara. It is an
immediate reminder of the symbol 'Om' which may be seen in a
similar position in Hindu temples, though here the canopy is
placed over pictures or statues of the deities. The coincidence is
intentional, Ik oankar (੧ੳ) like Om (ॐ) stands for the one
primal reality. Of Om the Katha Unpanishad states, 'That which
the Vedas declare, that which all austerities utter, that in desire
of which men become students, that word I tell you briefly is Om.

That word is even Brahman, the Supreme' (2.15). In the words of Guru Nanak,

> The one Lord [oankar] created Brahma,
> The one Lord fashioned the human mind,
> From the one Lord came mountains and ages. The one
> Lord created the Vedas.
>
> (AG 929)

This Lord may be experienced but he cannot be known by the mind, he is beyond comprehension. The Guru can only lament his inadequacy confronted with the ultimate reality of the all-pervading Lord; 'O mother, the attributes of God cannot be comprehended, and without actually seeing him one cannot say anything about him. How is he to be described, O mother?' (AG 1256). Strictly speaking God is pure being, without qualities (nirguna) and therefore Guru Nanak describes him as Sat (truth), 'Eternal truth is his name.' 'Only your functional names have I been able to describe. Your oldest name is Eternal Reality' (AG 1083). 'Sat' is itself a functional name significant for theology, personal belief and ethics, for life must be based on trust in God and truthfulness. Sikhs regard Sat as safer than other names given to God although these are found in the Adi Granth. Ram, Mohan (beautiful), Gobind (World Lord), Hari, even Allah or Khuda (Creator), taken from Hinduism and Islam, occur in the scriptures. For example, 'He is Allah, Alakh, Agam, Kadur, Karanhar, Karim' (AG 64). Manmohan Singh's translation reads, 'He is the unseen, inscrutable, inaccessible, omnipotent and bounteous creator', which hides the point that Guru Nanak was using Muslim names of God in such a way as to imply that all were acceptable but to be interpreted only as attributes of the One who is beyond names. However, each evokes some preconception, each can provide a stopping place which is short of ultimate, therefore the abstract term 'Sat' is preferred by Guru Nanak though occasionally God is addressed as 'Anami' (without a name). Because functional names can be applied to him, e.g. Sat Nam (name) and Sat Guru (True Guru), it may be said that God is saguna with attributes as well as nirguna, but Sikhism rejects the view that God ever assumes any physical form either animal or human.

The rest of the Mool Mantra is concerned with the functions of deity. First, God is creator, immanent in the universe. There are no creation stories, only the expression of a belief that the universe is an emanation of God produced because he willed its existence. The situation before time was as follows:

For millions of years there was nothing but darkness over the void. There was neither earth nor sky, only the Infinite Will.
There was neither night nor day, sun nor moon and the Lord was in a state of trance [samadhi].
The sources of creation did not exist, there was no speech, no air, no water, no birth, no death, no coming or going, no regions, no seven seas, no worlds above or below.
The trimurti of Brahma, Vishnu and Shiva did not exist. There was no other only the one Absolute Lord.
(AG 1035)

For reasons known only to himself, God decided to bring the universe into being. It was experience not metaphysics which concerned the Guru:

The Infinite Lord has enshrined his might within all.
He himself is detached and without limit or equal.
He created nature and inanimate nature came from the existing void. From his own Being [sunte] came air, water and the world, bodies and his spirit with them.
Your light, O Lord, is within fire, water and living beings and in your Absolute Self lies the power of creation.
From the Absolute Lord emanated Brahma, Vishnu and Shiva: from him came all the ages. . . .
All that springs from the Lord merges with him again.
By his play the Lord has created nature and by his word has manifested the wonder.
From himself he has made day and night.
From him came creation and destruction, pleasure and pain.
The godly-minded remain stable and detached from the effect of good or ill and find their home in God.
(AG 1037)

Sikhism has no difficulty in coming to terms with scientific theories of evolution, in fact they find them congenial to the belief in an expanding universe derived from the mind of God.

Their opposition is not to evolution but to a materialism which regards the universe as self-explanatory and self-existent. Those who hold such views are the victims of deception: 'The world without the True One is merely a dream' (AG 1274); they will waken to disillusionment, for 'God who is eternal, wise and omniscient is the master of destiny. The world, on the other hand, is fickle and inconstant' (AG 1109). The world is even described as his pastime (lila), but not in such a way that he is to be seen as fickle. Belief in God as Truth sees him as moral and the basis for morality, in the sense that it depends upon him for existence: 'Seated in the creation God looks on what he intended to be his pastime with delight' (AG 463).

The Lord is also described as fearless and without hatred. Man lives in constant dread of hunger, sickness or death; in Hindu mythology the gods are often afraid and frequently engage in vindictive wars, plots and deceitful tricks as they struggle for power. In the view of Guru Nanak a man should possess only awe in God's presence, not fear: 'To be possessed by any fear but God's is vain; all other fears are but phantoms of the mind' (AG 151). The Sikh should find his anxieties banished as he experiences union with God.

> The Guru's servants are pleasing to the Lord. He forgives them and they no longer fear death's courier. The Lord dispels the doubt of those who love him, and he unites them with himself. The Lord is free from fear, limitless and infinite. He, the creator, is pleased with truth.   (AG 1190)

The terms 'timeless, formless, beyond birth and death' must be considered together and one of them, 'beyond birth' (ajuni), has been given a chapter to itself, such is its importance. These words are to be understood by reference to their popular Hindu context. In the life of village India and its festivals Krishna, one of the principal deities, was born at Vrindavan, and his birthday is celebrated in late July or early August. In some myths the gods and goddesses die. It must be acknowledged that in the story of the Bhagavad Gita a much different view of incarnation is presented. It was not the profundities of this concept which the Guru had in mind, but the much more earthy anthropomorphic stories which led to what he regarded as futile superstition. An anthology of such stories is easily available in *Hindu Myths*,

(O'Flaherty, 1975). God is personal but not anthropomorphic; he does not grow old and is unwearied either by effort or supplication. Time is his servant not his master; changes are caused by him, God is not affected by them. Sometimes one Hindu god is enlightened by another. This is a way of arguing sectarian superiority, but in the teachings of Guru Nanak God is self-enlightened.

Finally, we come to that phrase of the Mool Mantra which states that God is known to man by the Guru's grace. The concept of grace will be discussed more fully elsewhere (p. 79). The immediate difficulty is the word 'Guru'. As the section on 'Guru' notes (see p. 100) the term may refer to a human preceptor or to God manifest as the word (sabd). There is no agreement among scholars as to which interpretation is correct here. It is suggested that the Guru is God himself for the following reasons. First, it would be uncharacteristic of Guru Nanak to assert his importance to the extent of suggesting that only through him or at his pleasure is God made known. Second, the Sikh view of revelation is one which insists that God is always revealing himself, that he has done so before and also beyond the teaching of the Gurus. Finally, the subject of the rest of the Mool Mantra is God and it seems logical to suppose that he is also the subject of this final phrase. The assertion would seem to be that just as God is self-enlightened so he is the enlightener. He cannot be discovered by philosophical study; austerities will not compel him to appear and incantations, or sacrifices or hymns of devotion cannot induce his manifestation: 'God does what pleases him. No one can say what he should do' (AG 2). The initiative is always God's.

Guru Nanak's concept of God apparently leaves little place for free will because there is no room for dualism. Everything that happens has been predetermined and occurs because he wills it. By his command (hukam) both good and evil happen: 'God drives all according to his will (hukam), his pen writes our deeds' (AG 1241); 'Through his will greatness is won, some become high and some low; some get joy and some pain; some are lost in transmigration and some are blest by you, O Lord' (AG 1). However, this is not the complete story. Right living cannot achieve release but it can lead to a better life in the next round of existence: 'Good actions may procure a better frame of life, but release comes only through his grace' (AG 2). Man is always free to accept the Guru's word or reject it even if the opportunity to hear it in the first place is given by God himself.

In keeping with the view that God is the only reality and self-revealing is the belief that when he discloses himself man discovers his immanence. Like Kabir, Lalla and many other sants, the idea of God residing 'at home' is very strong in the teaching of the Gurus. Consequently Guru Nanak recommended the householder stage of life as the one in which his followers should attain God-realisation and explore its meaning. Perhaps Guru Tegh Bahadur expressed the view most forcibly.

> Why do you go to the forest to find God? He lives in all and yet remains distinct. He dwells in you as well, as fragrance resides in a flower or the reflection in a mirror. God abides in everything. See him, therefore, in your own heart.
> (AG 684)

However, unlike some of the other mystics the Sikh asserts that a distinction between God and man does remain even after God-realisation. Guru Arjan wrote,

> God lives in everything,
> He dwells in every heart,
> Yet he is not blended with anything;
> He is a separate entity.
>
> (AG 700)

Despite this stress upon the immanence of God he is also transcendent. The passage quoted above insists on his separateness and frequently he is described as the Transcendent Lord. In the Japji Guru Nanak says 'God is great and his throne is very high. His name is higher than the highest' (AG 2). Ultimately although man discovers that God is within him he recognises that it is more correct to regard himself as existing within God. There is no place for pantheism in Sikh thought. The term panentheism is much more appropriate for everything owes its meaning to God and exists in him.

> O wise and all knowing God, you are the river. How can I, the fish within you measure your limits. Wherever I look I find no one but you and if ever I were to leave you I would perish.   (AG 25)

The enlightened, God-filled person experiences everything as existing within God and is also aware of God as immanent, but natural man is like a fish who is oblivious of the water in which he swims. It is to this state and his release from it that we must now turn.

Man

The starting-point for understanding the Sikh view of man must be the statement that 'all forms have come into existence according to his will' (AG 1). Man is not only the latest or highest product of an evolutionary process or the result of an accident, he is the consequence of God's intention. God alone knows why he made man or why man is in his natural state of separation from God, ignorant of his will and wandering like a lost elephant in a jungle crashing from dissatisfaction to bewilderment and despair. Concerned with experience, and man's condition as it is rather than speculation on the reason for the malady, Guru Nanak wrote,

> Man is born and then dies. Where did he come from? Say whence did he emerge and whither does he go? How is he bound to the round of coming and going (transmigration) and how is he released? How may he be united with the Eternal Lord?
> He who has the Lord's name in his heart and on his tongue becomes beyond desire, as the Lord himself is.
> Man comes and goes in the natural way [according to the law of Karma]. He is born because of the desires of his mind. The God-minded are emancipated and are not bound again for they dwell on the word [sabd] and attain deliverance through the Name.   (AG 152)

This passage does not take us back to the original mystery of the existence of man but it tells us all that needs to be known for practical purposes. The natural way of coming and going is caused by desire and may be ended by replacing natural attachments with devotion to God. The round of transmigration was described by Guru Arjan.

> For many births you have become a worm or moth, an elephant, a fish or a deer.

75

In several births you may have become a bird or a snake or
may have been yoked as a horse or an ox.
Meet the Lord of the universe. Now is the time to meet
him: after a long time you have been given human form.
In many births you were created in rocks and mountains,
produced as vegetation, even aborted from the womb.
You were made to wander among the eighty four hundred
thousand forms of existence.
By virtue of the fellowship of the saints (sangat) you have
achieved your present status so perform the Lord's
service, repeat his name guided by the Guru.   (AG 176)

No sequence from non-sentient life to fish or bird, to land animal
and then to man is suggested. Sikhism does not attempt to define
the progression but it does assert that human existence is the best
because man is unique. Among creation he alone possesses
discrimination and within him, though latent is a divine spark:
'O my soul, you have emanated from the light of God, know
your true essence' (AG 441). Guru Amar Das also said,

Man is brimful of the nectar of God's name. Through tasting
it its relish is known. They who taste it become free from
fear and find the Lord's elixir satisfies their needs.
He who is made to drink it by the Lord's grace is never
again afflicted by death.   (AG 1092)

Ignorance is the root of man's problems. Knowing neither his
true nature nor his destiny he is bound to come and go repeatedly.
The cry 'O man you are blessed by being born human, it is an
opportunity which you have been given to meet your Lord' (AG
378), falls on deaf ears.

Man is intelligent, he knows right from wrong, has the moral
law written in his heart, yet he misses the chance to meet his
Lord. There are several explanations for this failure. His birth
and environment may destroy the opportunity if he is born into a
family which is a thieves' kitchen or which inculcates the virtues
of self-reliance rather than dependence upon God. The general
term used to express failures which fall into this category is
karma, the law of cause and effect. 'One receives in accordance
to what one does. As one sows so one eats' (AG 662) is the
simplest way in which Guru Nanak expresses this concept. Our

present existence is determined by our former behaviour and our conduct now decides the manner in which we will return: 'Man's life proceeds as his accumulated actions determine it. He receives joy or sorrow in accordance with what his past deeds have earned. But all is good that comes from you' (AG 1107). However, our present failures, unlike those of the past, cannot be attributed to karma. They are the consequences of maya or haumai. The former term has been given a section to itself (see p. 82); very briefly it means holding a materialist view of the world and therefore living as though its values even its most praiseworthy such as moral rectitude were ends in themselves. Haumai is a difficult idea to render into English. Perhaps self-reliance is as satisfactory a term as any because though haumai results in pride this is not necessarily an immoral state. Self-reliance is often praised as a great human virtue, but for Guru Nanak it is a condition which blinds man to his dependence upon God, to the need for liberation and therefore to the hope of realising it. He even said 'Man degrades himself from the human order because of his haumai' (AG 466). Here we must remember that in Guru Nanak's teaching human birth was the first step on the road to liberation. It provides the opportunity for meeting God. The consequence of self-reliance is the rejection of this chance and a backward step to animal-like ignorance rather than progress to God-realisation:

In haumai man fails to perceive the true nature of liberation. In haumai there is worldly attachment [maya] and its shadow, doubt. By acting under the influence of haumai man causes himself to be born repeatedly. If he understands haumai he can find the door of liberation but otherwise he argues and disputes. Our karma is inscribed according to the divine will. He who sees the nature of the divine will perceives his haumai also.   (AG 466)

Dependence upon God and obedience to his will (hukam) is essential for liberation. By contradicting the former haumai denies the latter and is therefore, inevitably, subject to the law of karma.

The Gurus attach more importance to the impulses of haumai than do any of the other sants, including Kabir, for whereas a person has to accept the consequence of past actions, the present and therefore the future as well as his ultimate destiny are to a large degree in his own control. As long as haumai persists, however, it is a cloud blocking the light of the sun and there is no hope of release.

> In haumai he comes and in haumai he goes;
> In haumai he is born and in haumai he dies;
> In haumai he gives and in haumai he takes;
> In haumai he acquires and in haumai he casts away;
> In haumai he is truthful and in haumai he lies;
> In haumai he sometimes does good and at other times evil.
>
> (AG 466)

Although man can act morally, and many are of upright character, there is literally a world of difference between rebirth and liberation and this the man who is blinded by haumai fails to perceive. Suffering is the form which the condition of haumai takes. It is caused by wrong attachment, by regarding natural relationships as eternal or by substituting these for the one which cannot be broken, that between God and the devotee. Guru Tegh Bahadur must not be condemned as a cynic but recognised as a realist when he says,

> All worldly ties are only for this earthly life, be they those
>   of father, mother, sons, kinsmen or even a devoted wife.
> As soon as the soul leaves the body they cry 'Remove this
>   phantom'. No one keeps it even for an hour. It is hastily
>   taken from the house.
> Man, reflect on its fate. Consider the earthly creation a mirage.
>   Nanak says, contemplate God's name, this is how deliver-
>   ance is attained.   (AG 536)

According to Guru Nanak physical pain can be therapeutic if it disillusions the self-satisfied: 'Pain is the remedy and pleasure the sickness; where there is nothing but pleasure there is no yearning for God' (AG 469).

The search for God might be the consequence of dissatisfaction or of 'meeting the Guru'. Someone may succeed in the moral struggle, in the practice of asceticism, in visiting the pilgrimage centres or mastering the Vedas or the philosophical systems and yet be aware that something is still missing. Such striving is pleasing to God and may win his recognition. On the other hand it may be that without conscious effort, perhaps as the result of karma, someone hears the voice of God and the latent divinity is activated so that release is obtained. At this point we come to the difficult concept of the grace of God. The problem exists for the western reader because he is already aware that the word has a Christian context and even if he has not studied Pauline theology he knows something of the term because of its popular usage. A word used in the Adi Granth which is translated 'grace' is 'nadar' which has to do with 'sight'. Sikhism is above all else a particular kind of guru cult and it might help to consider a similar word to 'nadar', 'darshan', the Guru's glance, as we try to understand grace.

India is a land of villages, pilgrimage places and gurus. Almost every day there is some local festival, some holy man whose anniversary is being commemorated and in many villages there is a guru to whom people turn for enlightenment and guidance. Some of the gurus become famous beyond the locality and the roads to their teaching centres are busy with travellers. Others have only local reputations and are visited by a small but steady trickle of devotees. Outside the guru's home the faithful and the hopeful will sit and wait for him to appear. He may be away from the village in which case they will remain until his return. When he does appear there need be no words, merely a benign look of acceptance that is enough to convey a blessing. That glance is darshan. This Sikhism has in mind when it speaks of God's grace. He is the supreme Guru. Experience teaches that some people make the hard journey of asceticism or moral effort but do not receive this glance of acceptance. Others with but little struggle are not only smiled upon, they are initiated into the close fellowship of disciples. Acceptance or rejection is not arbitrary or the result of some quixotic impulse; the person who sought darshan and was refused it may be disappointed but the guru knows best. Even the disappointment is a pronouncement of some sort. It may be that the seeker must try harder, is being tested, is not yet ready for enlightenment. 'Baba knows everything'; even that the time for release may not be in this present life; perhaps the next birth will bring acceptance. One thing is certain, the hopeful pilgrim believes that the guru is necessary for liberation.

With this concept of guruship in mind it may be possible to understand such apparently harsh sayings as:

All bounties come from the Lord. No one can claim them as a matter of right. Some who are awake do not receive them, others he rouses from their slumbers to be blessed.

(AG 83)

Good actions may procure a better existence, but liberation comes only from his grace.   (AG 2)
God cannot be understood or realised through cleverness. (AG 221)

God cannot be won through rites or deeds. Learning cannot give help in comprehending him. The Vedas and the eighteen Puranas have also failed to reveal his mystery. Only the True Guru has revealed him to me.   (AG 155)

In Sikhism grace is the word which describes the way in which God focuses his attention upon a person. No one is ever beyond his care: 'He takes care of everything, though he remains invisible' (AG 7). Even to those who have not found him he is known through dissatisfaction: 'You are clearly present in the world, Lord, because all crave for your Name' (AG 71); Grace is the means by which this longing is met. It is the special notice which God takes of someone. It can even be a glance of disapproval but then its consequences are disastrous: 'A displeasing glance from God reduces even monarchs to straw' (AG 472). In the Japji Guru Nanak described five stages of human development. The first was the region or stage of piety (Dharam Khand). This is the realm into which all human beings are born. They may practise devotion and so reach the realm of knowledge (Gian Khand) in which they become aware of the vastness of the universe and the mystery of existence. The seeker may progress further, to the realm of effort (Saram Khand). In this stage mind and intellect become perfected or attuned to God. He has now gone as far as he can in developing his natural gifts. The stage of grace (Karam Khand) is only possible with the help of spiritual strength which comes from God. Help to enter this realm is willingly given by the loving God. Bhai Gurdas once said,

If man goes one step towards him
The Lord comes a thousand towards man.

It is the region in which only the great saints (bhagats) live in divine bliss.

> In the realm of grace spiritual power is supreme, nothing else avails. Brave and strong warriors in whom the Lord's spirit lives dwell there, those who are blended with him by singing his praises. Their beauty is beyond description, the Lord lives in their hearts. They do not die and are not deceived.
> The congregations of the blessed live there too. They dwell in bliss with the True One in their hearts.   (AG 8)

Grace in Sikhism has therefore a number of meanings. It is the glance which a Guru bestows upon the disciple denoting acceptance and conveying a blessing. It is also a glance which liberates the devotee in such a way that the efforts which were once undertaken to win recognition are now acts of loving service. Grace also transforms the disciple from being a hopeful seeker to being someone who has found the meaning of his existence. He is now at ease and at peace for he has realised God.

However, Karam Khand is not the last region, there is Sach Khand, the region of truth where God exists in his formless state. It cannot be described, only experienced by the liberated soul.

> In the realm of truth
> Dwells the formless One
> Who having created watches over his creation.
> He looks upon them with grace and his people are
>   in bliss.

> There is world upon world, form on form. All have their functions as God's will [hukam] ordains. The Lord sees his creation and seeing it rejoices. To describe it is hard, hard as steel to the hand.   (AG 8)

Guru Nanak was acutely aware of the paradoxes which are part of life, of seeking for God but not finding him, of striving but not being satisfied, of knowing that God is latent in everyone yet aware how few know him. The solution lay in the Indian concept of guruship which Guru Nanak accepted but interpreted in his own particular way (see p. 100). Two passages sum up both the paradox and the solution: 'Inside you is the king's throne, he himself dispenses justice. By the sabad we discover God's home, his palace is inside us' (AG 1092); 'Without the grace and guidance of the Guru we cannot know the essence of the truth: the unfathomable God lives in everyone' (AG 1093). Guru Nanak was also practical and we must turn not only to the concept of liberation but to the techniques which Sikhism advocates for attaining it. But first it is necessary to consider the term 'maya'.

Maya

Sikhism believes in the reality of the created universe. It accepts it and regards it seriously because it has been made by God. Therefore the world exists for man to use and enjoy, it is not to be shunned or regarded as evil. Maya is a term used to denote the temporal world in the broadest sense and attachment to it.

If we are realistic we have to admit that we cannot do without maya, when we mean by the word worldly possessions, food and clothing, land upon which to grow the necessities of life. In many of the passages which follow 'maya' is translated by the words 'wealth', 'nature' or their synonyms. Because God is the sole creator he is responsible for the existence of maya.

> Through his hidden omnipotence
> He has created the earth and the sky.
> Infusing his true might the Lord has
> sustained them without pillars.
> The Lord has created the three worlds
> and their binder, maya,
> of himself he creates and destroys.
>
> (AG 1037)

Thou thyself created the world and put it to work. Giving it the intoxicating herb of worldly love to eat thou hast thyself led it astray.   (AG 138)

The Giver has given man the intoxicating pill of falsehood. Drugged by it he has forgotten death and makes merry for four days.   (AG 15)

Here we encounter, in a Sikh form, one of the perplexities of monotheism, how the loving and beneficent creator of everything can be responsible for evil. With respect to maya the answer lies in two parts. First, despite the impression conveyed by the quotations already given, maya is not an objective reality. It is a subjective error resulting from a wrong point of view, a belief in duality rather than unity, so that like a mirage the world becomes an end in itself. Maya is anything which keeps a person from the truth and union with God. The word may therefore be used of love of family, patriotism, or the service of the gurdwara if devotion becomes so blind that the vision of higher goals is lost in the manner portrayed by the phrase 'my country right or wrong'. However, the usual forms ascribed to maya are the five evils of kam, lobh, moh, krodh and ahankar (lust, covetousness, attachment, wrath and pride), basically proper impulses which have got out of hand: 'Over the whole world is stretched the love of worldly values. Seeing a beautiful woman the lustful man covets her. With his sons and gold man increases his love. He deems everything as his own, he does not heed God' (AG 1342). Though God has given man the herb of worldly love this is not his only gift, and here we come to the second part of the Sikh answer. God has also given man power to discriminate and to assist him he has promised his bani and his grace.

The handcuff, the net, the snare, which are used as images for maya, need not result in permanent captivity though it is an imprisonment which is consequential upon birth. The Third Guru contemplated upon the matter in this way:

As is the fire of the womb within, so is the fire of worldliness without. The fires of worldly wealth and of the womb are all the same. The creator has set this play in action.

The child is born when it pleases him and the family is happy. Love of the Lord departs, greed attaches itself to the child and maya's writ begins to run. Such is maya, by which the Lord is forgotten, worldly love wells up and one becomes attached to the love of another. Says Nanak, they who enshrine love for the Lord by God's grace obtain the Lord in the midst of maya.   (AG 921)

Attachment to maya is to be replaced by attachment to God, the process of birth by which a person turns from his creator to the world must be reversed. This can be done through nam simran

83

(see p. 89) and through the company of the sat sangat, those who themselves have become gurmukh (God-filled):

> Poison and nectar, the creator has created both. To the world plant he has attached two fruits. The creator is himself doer and cause. He feeds whom he likes. On whomsoever he casts his gracious glance he bestows the nectar of his name. He removes his desire for attachment. This God himself performs. (AG 1172)

Both the disease is diagnosed and the cure prescribed at length by Guru Nanak in a long analysis containing a variety of examples. Part of it will serve as conclusion to this section:

> Mad duality has maddened man's mind. He has wasted his life in the error of greed. Duality clings to mortal man and no one has been able to overcome it. By implanting the name within, the Sat Guru saves man from it.
> Neither is the mind overpowered nor does maya die. He who has created everything, he alone understands this mystery. Contemplating the sabd one is ferried across the dreadful world ocean.

Amassing wealth (maya) kings become proud but the loved maya does not depart with the mortal. Maya is of many kinds, but only the name is a lasting friend and comrade. As is a man's own mind so he perceives another's to be. As is his desire so becomes his state of mind. As are one's deeds so is the tune one delights in, but only by seeking the Sat Guru's advice is the house of peace found. Singing and hearing temporal music man's mind is attached to duality. Deceit remains within him and he suffers great pain. Meeting with the Sat Guru he is blessed with right understanding and remains merged in love of the true name. Through the sabd he practises truth and sings the true bani and the Lord's praise which is eternal. Misunderstanding (maya) is destroyed through this discipline which makes him acceptable to God. (AG 1342)

Maya is not the cosmic illusion of classical Vedanta. It is a materialistic interpretation of reality, it is natural for unregenerate man to be ignorant of God or to view the world in a dualistic

(c) One of the panj
pyares sprinkling
amrit on the head
of a woman
initiate.

(d) Prayers and vows
being made when
the amrit has been
administered.

4 Amrit Pahul, Leeds
Gurdwara

(a) The Guru Granth
being read at the
beginning of the
ceremony.

(b) The mixing of
patashas and water
to make amrit.

3 Gurdwara at Birmingham UK (interior)
The place of the scripture in Sikhism can be seen as
similarities between it and Guru Nanak in the painting behind
it are noted. The mural by Hari Singh Bansal of Kenya shows
Guru Nanak with his two sons. Bhai Bala holds a chauri, and
Mardana his rebeck. The tree serves as a chattri.

1　The Golden Temple
Daily thousands of worshippers make their way to the Darbar
Sahib. This photograph was taken in April 1973 during kar
sewa, the manual cleaning of the tank, which is carried out
every fifty years by volunteers.

2　Gurdwara at Anandpur (exterior)
The architecture of gurdwaras is not fixed by any tradition but
often affinities with the Pearl Mosque of the Red Fort, Delhi,
or the Taj Mahal can easily be detected.

5 The Formation of the Khalsa
The panj pyares and Guru Gobind Singh watch two doves which, by drinking amrit, received sufficient strength to be able to kill hawks.

6 Langar at the Darbar Sahib
All visitors to the Golden Temple are expected to take food
in the langar as their predecessors did when they sought
darshan from the Gurus.

7 Hola Mohalla procession, Anandpur
In the Punjab important occasions are often accompanied by
open-air processions. This one commemorating the assembly
begun by Guru Gobind Singh is perhaps the most famous.

8 Wedding
The centrality of the Guru in Sikhism can be seen clearly
at a wedding.

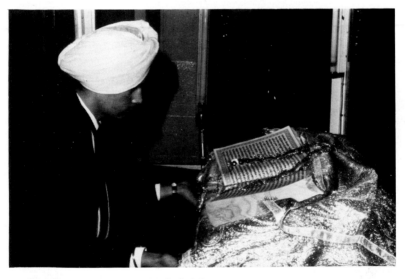

9 Reading the Guru Granth Sahib.

10 A page of the Guru Granth Sahib
Almost the entire Guru Granth Sahib is poetry but the lay-out
of a page gives no indication of this.

ੴ ਸਤਿਨਾਮੁ ਕਰਤਾਪੁਰਖੁ ਨਿਰਭਉ ਨਿਰਵੈਰੁ
ਅਕਾਲ ਮੂਰਤਿ ਅਜੂਨੀ ਸੈਭੰ ਗੁਰ ਪ੍ਸਾਦਿ ॥

11 The Mool Mantra written in the Gurmukhi script
See our English version on page 69.

way. When the One is perceived as the only reality the temporal will be merged in the eternal and maya will no longer exist.

Mukti – the path of liberation

Sacrifices, burnt offerings, charity given to acquire merit, austerities, even worship, are all worthless and the body continues to endure suffering. Without the name of God there is no release. He who, with the Guru's help, meditates on Nam finds liberation. Without God's Name birth into this world is fruitless. Without the Name one eats poison, speaks evil, dies meritless and so transmigrates. (AG 1127)

Liberation is release from the round of death and rebirth to the attainment of union with God. It can occur only when the soul has reached the stage of Saram Khand, the realm of effort, and is now in a position to enjoy God's kindly glance and so enter the realm of grace. Effort can take him no further and therefore such techniques as yoga or asceticism are rejected as futile:

Stubborn self torture only wears out the body, Fasting and penance do not soften the soul, Nothing is as efficacious as the Lord's Name; serve the Guru my soul, and keep the company of the servants of God.   (AG 905)

Only God in his manifest forms of sabd, nam and Sat Guru can take the soul further, to ultimate bliss. This fifth and final state Guru Nanak described as Sach Khand, the realm of truth. Another name is chautha pad, the fourth state which is beyond the three gunas or qualities which are believed to condition character. These are passion, which causes inertia and forgetfulness; desire, which stimulates ambition and produces restless activity, and peace, which is conducive to serenity but can degenerate into indifference. Chautha pad is attained by conquering the mind, for it is the key both to bondage and to liberation. The word 'personality' might be used to try to approach the one Punjabi term 'man' which refers to the combination of mind, heart and soul. In its natural state it is dominated by the three gunas. The consequence, as Guru Amar Das noted, is 'lack of equipoise [sahaj] and wandering in doubt' (AG 68).

Guru Nanak does not explain the fourth state of chautha pad but he does describe the results: 'Neither hope nor desire concern me and I have renounced longing for the three gunas. By seeking the refuge of the saints the God-minded attain the fourth state' (AG 356). The word used for 'God-minded' is 'gurmukh'. Literally it contrasts so-called liberation to natural personality (manmukh), which is actually bondage, with liberation to God-mindedness which is the true meaning of release from karma and haumai. Only the God-minded person is really free.

Sahaj is the word which Guru Nanak most frequently used for this state. It describes the equipoise and tranquillity which the soul enjoys beyond the reach of transmigration. The word was also popular with Kabir and the other sants. Turya avastha and param pad are tantric Buddhist terms which are given the same meaning as sahaj in Sikh teaching.

Almost by definition this state of bliss cannot be described, only experienced. The Gurus have the following things to say about it. Guru Arjan tried to express it through the idea of love. In the words of a bride he wrote: 'My friends met me and they asked me to describe my husband. I was so filled with the bliss of his love that I couldn't answer them!' (AG 459). All she can say is that when she lies in her husband's arms she experiences peace, joy and bliss. In another hymn he used more matter-of-fact language but the emphasis was much the same:

> The man who has the love of God's commands in his heart
> is said to be jivan mukt [liberated whilst in the body]. For
> him release is a present reality; joy and sorrow are both
> the same to him, his happiness is eternal and there is no
> separation from God.
> As is gold so is dust; as is nectar so is bitter poison. Honour
> and dishonour are the same. The pauper and the king
> are alike. He who regards success in this world as any
> enterprise-ordained by God, is said to be liberated whilst
> in the body.   (AG 275)

To be jivan mukt is possible because release is the supreme state of living in God's presence. The least acceptable of all unsatisfactory descriptions is that of being merged in the Absolute, even though the Gurus use the language of absorption in their attempt to express this experience of union with God.

As a million sparks rise from a single fire, separate and come
together again as they fall back into it:
As from a heap of dust grains are blown upwards, fill the
air and then drop back onto the heap:
As drops of water come from a single stream and return to it:
So inanimate and live creation emerges from God's form,
and since they arise from him they will return again.
(Akal Ustad)

Descriptions of heaven also make the point that bliss is being in
God's presence now or hereafter. 'Heaven is wherever God's
praise is sung' (AG 749), Guru Arjan said. 'The sixty-eight
places of pilgrimage are wherever the saints put their feet,
heaven is wherever they utter the Name' (AG 890). Hell, on the
other hand, is any place where deceit is found (AG 315). The
popular image of heaven as a place of comfort and pleasure is
rejected. Guru Nanak declared, 'The man who longs for God's
abode is unconcerned with heaven and hell' (AG 360), and the
Fifth Guru even dismissed the concept of mukti as freedom
from rebirth, replacing it with experiencing the presence of God:
'I desire neither worldly power nor mukti. My soul longs to
embrace your lotus feet. There are Brahma, Shiva, yogis and
sages as well as Indra but I desire nothing but seeing the Lord'
(AG 534). Heaven without God is not really heaven (AG 707),
it is merely a transitory state like the respite from rebirth which
some Hindu myths describe as the reward for asceticism. Once
the merit has been used up the soul has to return for it has
not found the abode of permanent release, the presence of
God.

Everyone longs for paradise [swarg], mukti and heaven
[baikundh] and rests all hope on them. Those who desire
the vision of God do not seek release, they are satisfied
and comforted by that sight alone.
The attachment of maya is powerful but the saints are
like the duck which sits on the pond but does not get its
wings wet.   (AG 1324)

There is a belief in judgment but this is a continuous process.
After death the soul appears before God and its future is decided
on the basis of actions while in the world. It may be reborn or

obtain some temporary respite or may remain in the presence of God, its development being complete.

Liberation is obtained by meeting the Guru, enjoying his grace and then adopting certain techniques. The most important of these is nam simran, meditation upon the name and nature of God, which is discussed in detail on pages 89–95. However, this should be accompanied by participation in the life of the sangat, the fellowship of believers. Good company is essential for godly living. 'In good company one becomes good,' said Guru Nanak (AG 414). The Fourth Guru saw it as having particular value for the weak: 'Just as the castor oil plant imbibes the scent of the nearby sandalwood so the fallen become emancipated through the company of the faithful' (AG 861). Both Nath yogis and Sufis as well as some north Indian Hindu sects lived in groups and saw the value of corporate religious life. This belief Guru Nanak and his successors clearly shared.

The sangat was the treasure house in which the Name was to be found, according to Guru Arjan. In it 'Birth and rebirth, worldly attachment and suffering vanish away' (AG 761). From the time of the Third Guru, who, it will be remembered, had the task of welding a second generation of believers into a coherent socio-religious group, the importance of the sangat in the hymns of the Gurus increases noticeably. Sometimes they express their own indebtedness to the fellowship of their disciples, as Guru Arjan did: 'Nanak's compassionate master is merciful to the meek. My burning has been cooled in the saint's fellowship' (AG 204).

In the fellowship of the sangat the life of effort continues but it is no longer a striving to reach the threshold of the stage of grace; it is sewa, the joyful service of the Lord. Its purpose is to obey God's will joyfully, not to attempt to win his grace. This has already been obtained. The effect is to become more God-like, for 'One becomes like the one he serves' (AG 224). The conse-quence of this devotion is that one becomes brahm-gyani, filled with the knowledge of God which is the ideal after which the Sikh strives. On death there is no returning but eternal life in God's presence, in that perfect fellowship of which the earthly sangat is the mirror.

There is one exception to this. It may be that God wishes a perfected being to return to earth in order to undertake some particular task which he desires to have accomplished. Such a person will already be brahm-gyani at birth. His entry into the world will be non-karmic, not the result of the law of karma but because of God's commandment (hukam). According to Bala Janam Sakhi accounts, Guru Nanak's entry into the world was of this type. Certainly this is the way in which Guru Gobind Singh regarded himself according to his autobiographical poem Vichitar Natak. Such a birth is not a cause for pride but an opportunity for sewa, and its purpose is to bring the light of God-realisation to other human beings. The concept of non-karmic rebirth is another illustration of the belief that there is a higher state than that of being released from transmigration; that of being in God's presence and service, which is a purely spiritual condition.

Nam simran

The easiest way to avoid oversimplifying one of the richest and most profound concepts of Sikhism, that of Nam, is to allow a number of quotations from the teachings of the Gurus to speak for themselves:

> Nam extends to all creation,
> There is no place where Nam is not.
>
> (AG 4; 1st Guru)

> Nam gives form to everything,
> Through Nam comes all wisdom and light.
>
> (AG 986; 1st Guru)

> Nam is the creator of everything,
> To be divorced from Nam is death.
>
> (AG 603; 3rd Guru)

> All creatures live by Nam,
> Nam supports the universe and its parts.
>
> (AG 284; 5th Guru)

From these passages it can be seen that Nam must be more than merely Name, its literal translation must in some way be synonymous with God. There are words of Guru Nanak's about God which make almost exactly the same statements as those expressed above:

89

The will of the one God alone pervaded all the world as creation is born of him.   (AG 233; 1st Guru)

The glories of the great God cannot be described. He is the creator, the almighty, and the beneficent one who provides sustenance to all living beings.   (AG 475; 1st Guru)

He alone lives in whom the Lord resides. No one else is really alive.   (AG 142; 1st Guru)

Perhaps this last verse provides a clue to the relationship between God and Nam. Above are the words of Guru Amar Das, 'To be divorced from Nam is death.' Yet there is also a basic teaching that the soul or jiva is immortal, though finite:

The body is mere earth in which air speaks. Tell me, O wiseman, what is it that dies? The life of pride and strife suffers death. But the soul that sees behind does not die. (AG 152; 1st Guru)

The body belongs to the material world, but the spirit or soul in it is in the essence of God.   (AG 695, Pipa)

The state of the unenlightened person is characterised by self-centredness (haumai) so that if he believes that God exists he thinks of him as a separate being and therefore man beyond his egoism is fearful of death, attached to the ephemera of life, and a victim of duality. The consequence is repeated comings and goings in the round of rebirth: 'He is born and dies because of egoism' (AG 466; 1st Guru).

Between the reality of one-ness and the consciousness of duality is the activity of Nam. Nam is God manifest, a God immanently active: 'The self-existent God manifested himself in Nam. Second came the creation of the universe. He pervades it and revels in his creation' (AG 463; 1st Guru); 'God, having made beings with souls, inscribed them with Nam, which is set up as a judge' (AG 463; 1st Guru). From this last verse Nam would seem to be conscience as well as the quality of divine pervasiveness.

Man, even in his unenlightened state, is a reasoning being. 'Man is blessed with the light of reason and discernment' (AG 913; 5th Guru). As an awakened person these qualities can be put to the service of God to produce right conduct.

By use of discernment or intellect one serves God.
By discernment one is honoured.
By discernment and understanding one understands things,
It is a sense of discernment that makes one charitable.
This is the right way. The rest are all wrong.

(AG 1245; 1st Guru)

Though Nam is God active in the universe and is latently present in everyone and may even be active in the form of reason and conscience, true awareness is only possible through enlightenment. This is the function of God as Guru or God speaking through the Vedas, Qur'an or one of the Sikh Gurus. He awakens man to his presence within him:

Nam the immaculate is unfathomable,
  how can it be known?
Nam is within us, how can it be reached?
It is Nam that works everywhere and
  permeates all space.
The perfect Guru awakens your heart to
  the vision of Nam.
It is by the grace of God that one meets
  such an enlightenment.

(AG 1242; 4th Guru)

However, Nam is more than the possession of a name or a verse. It is being God-filled. The transition from being self-centred to being God-centred is more than a perception of the truth intuitively grasped by the enlightened person that he is one with God. The perceived unity can only become daily experience in mortal existence through discipline. This is known as nam simran.

The main aspects of this discipline of meditation are as follows. First, as a child, the Sikh will become used to saying time and without number the word 'Waheguru', Wonderful Lord. This is not a term found in the writings of Guru Nanak and his successors; its first appearance in the Guru Granth Sahib is in the compositions of the bards (bhattas) who sang at Guru Arjan's court. Two quotations from their small contribution to the Guru Granth Sahib will serve as illustration: 'Our praiseworthy Waheguru, Waheguru, Waheguru, you are ever just and true, the abode of excellence, the primal person' (AG 1402); 'Uniting the elements

91

together you have created this great game and play of the world. Waheguru, all this is your creation' (AG 1404). Though this enthusiasm of the bards often results in them using language which almost makes the reader believe that they saw the Gurus as avatars in these passages, it is clear that Waheguru refers to God.

Though the word Waheguru is not used by any of the Gurus, in the scripture a word is found which may have prompted the bards and so may account for the existence of Waheguru. 'Wah, wah,' is a common Punjabi exclamation. Like the English word 'Ah!' it can signify amazement or wonder. Guru Amar Das applied it to God:

> Address wahe, wahe to him who is
> true, profound and unfathomable.
> Address wahe, wahe, to him who is
> the giver of virtue, knowledge and patience.
>
> (AG 515)

On the same page where the word 'wahe' occurs many times the Guru also says, 'The Guru's disciple who constantly utters wahe, wahe, attains his mind-desired fruit . . . wahe, wahe is the true Master [sahib] whose name is the immortalising nectar.' No wonder Bhai Gurdas wrote, 'Waheguru is the Guru's mantra' (Var 13, pauri 2), equating it with the Vedic mantra Om. It possessed the power to dispel self-centredness and fill the mind with God's presence: 'Waheguru is the Guru's mantra, by repeating it egoism is destroyed.'

'Repetition of the Name by the tongue will eventually produce the nectar,' Guru Nanak once said, but only if the mind is controlled in such a way that the mind becomes fixed on God. Guru Ram Das expanded this thought in these words:

> The name will percolate into the heart and give it a feeling of stability.
> Nam is the real elixir of the alchemist, The Lord pulls us out of the mire with his own hands.
> Holding us by the arms he removes all our deficiencies for us.
> In the garden of the heart plant, like a seed, the word of the Guru and water your garden with love, And all your orchards shall bear the precious fruit of the Holy Name of God.

Within your own body is the true pool of immortality.
Let your mind drink the nectar there.   (AG 997)

If the believer is to grow in his faith, he must soon recognise
that the goal cannot be reached by the mere saying of words.
Certain aids are needed if the state which Guru Nanak once
described in these words is to become a reality.

Listen my heart, love God ceaselessly, as the fish loves the
    water.
The deeper the water the happier and more tranquil the fish.
The greatest sickness of the soul is this, to forget for even a
    second the Beloved.   (AG 60)

The first aid is to rise early in the morning, in the ambrosial hour
before dawn (amrit vela), bathe and, before the cares, heat and
tumult of the Indian day have a chance to drive thoughts of
God from the mind, to repeat his name and meditate upon his
greatness: 'In the ambrosial hours of the dawn repeat the true
Name and meditate upon his greatness' (1 AG 2 Japji). The
devotee will recite and meditate upon the Japji, noting especially
how often the stanzas contain words of praise and refer to the
effect of hearing the word. The emphasis upon word and praise
in the scripture points to ways in which 'the fish may swim
deeper in the pool' and so gain greater peace. Although meditation can be individual, and often is, the believer is helped considerably by the company of others who share his faith and are
engaged in nam simran. It may appear obvious to say, as Guru
Nanak does, 'In good company one becomes good' (AG 414),
Indian religion has often emphasised individualism and each
man's choice of his own path on the journey to release. The
sangat, for the Sikh, is more than a brotherhood of like-minded
people, it possesses mystical qualities. The Guru lives in the
sangat, therefore Guru Ram Das could observe 'Just as the
castor oil plant imbibes the scent of the nearby sandalwood so
even the fallen are made free by the true sangat' (AG 861); 'In
good company we become true and develop love for nam' (AG
586). This points to the second aid to attaining the goal of nam
simran.

Through the bani and the sangat the devotee lives with God so
much in mind that ecstasy or bliss (vismad) and discretion are

attained. Vismad is a feeling of wonder and awe. Nature is seen to be the beautiful and harmonious product of the Creator. In humility the devotee looks beyond the world to God, sees it as an emanation or manifestation of his being and exclaims 'Waheguru'. The five evils, lust, anger, greed, attachment and pride, will continue to threaten those who practise nam simran but gradually they will be conquered and through God's grace the state of bliss will be reached. Sometimes this is called samadhi; Guru Nanak often used the word sahaj, and another word is liv. It is tempting to think of trance-like states but the normal condition is one of ajapa japa, spontaneous remembrance. This is a state in which the mind is so completely attuned to God that the person becomes merged with him as it thinks of him every moment of the day: 'The hungry soul will find its fulfilment if by praising his virtue it is absorbed by him' (AG 147; 2nd Guru).

The result is a life of service to others: 'Those who meditate on him do good to others' (AG 263; 5th Guru). Through nam simran personality becomes complete, not lost. God-conscious-ness is becoming what one really is. The deluded man is the one who cannot perceive God or who fails to recognise his ultimate unity with God. The grihastha stage is not left behind, it too is completed as the true spouse, father or mother is found in God.

Nam simran is not a saying of words but it is a transforming of personality through practice. As Namdev once said, it is like a girl carrying a pitcher of water on her head; eventually she is able to walk almost oblivious of it. Though Sikhs may use a mala (woollen rosary) when they say 'Waheguru' it should be clear by now that nam simran is a serious spiritual discipline. Guru Nanak himself warned against formal, meaningless incan-tations:

> By mere utterance with the tongue
> Your bonds are not loosed,
> For egoism and doubt do not leave you.
>
> (AG 353)

> Through utterance one does not mount to God,
> When, by grace, the Lord is enshrined in the mind,
> then alone is the fruit harvested.
>
> (AG 491)

The discipline of nam simran is not easy. Many Sikhs do not attain perfection but the ideal of jivan mukti is possible and worth striving to achieve.

> By prayer I live, without it I die,
> The name of the True one is hard to say.
>
> (AG 349; 1st Guru)

Ajuni – one who does not take birth

The Mool Mantra statement that God is ajuni, one who does not take birth, would be unnecessary but for the fact that Sikhism was born and grew up in a predominantly Hindu environment which held the doctrine of avatar. Perhaps the belief is best expressed by Krishna in the Bhagavad Gita:

> For wherever the law of righteousness withers away and lawlessness arises, then do I generate myself [on earth].
> For the protection of the good, for the destruction of evil-doers, for the setting up of the law of righteousness I come into being age after age. (R. C. Zaehner, *The Bhagavad-Gita*, Oxford, 1969, p. 184)

Sikhs reject the view that God descends into the world and takes bodily form either animal or human. They do not believe that this happens repeatedly, occasionally or even uniquely because God is essentially nirguna, without qualities. When he manifests himself it is not in a physical way but as truth, as word, as name. Second, their concept of revelation is one which holds that God is continuously expressing himself. Belief in avatar would suggest to Sikhs not a caring God who restores order when the need arises but a casual one who lets things slide and then is compelled reluctantly to intervene. As God is the one without a second upon whom creation and all life depends for their moment by moment existence he must be constantly active: 'His bounties are so great that the giver keeps on giving but receivers grow weary in receiving. It is not only now but in every age that man has been living in his bounty' (AG 2). In the same way he is constantly communicative, so neither occasional prophecy nor incarnation is acceptable.

This does not mean that God has not revealed himself through Moses, Jesus or Muhammad as well as through the Gurus. It is

95

an assertion that none, not even the Gurus, was special or final. The bani is the word addressed to man since his creation. It is still to be spoken directly to the heart of individuals, for godliness is latent in everyone. God pervades all forms, all castes and all hearts (AG 223). Therefore Guru Nanak could say, 'Of Brahma, Vishnu, Shiva and Indra and all seers, sages, ascetics and medicants, whoever obeys the command of God is honoured at his court' (AG 992).

Any tendency to exceed the view that God pervades all hearts but that his light might be seen most clearly in certain men and women who had attained the liberated state whilst in the flesh (jivan mukt) is repudiated vehemently especially by the later Gurus. Guru Arjan said, 'May the mouth burn by which it is said that the Lord becomes incarnate, He neither comes to nor departs from this earth. The God of Nanak is all-absorbing and ever-present' (AG 1136).

Guru Gobind Singh writes in the Swayyas, which have important devotional significance and are probably better known than any other of his compositions to the average Sikh:

> Only the creator is deathless, who keeps creating and destroying to the end and is of endless existence. He for whom praise and disparagement are the same, who has no friends or enemies, What compelled him to become Arjuna's charioteer? The saviour who has no father or mother and no children, why should he come into the world to be called Devaki's son? He who created gods and demons and pervades every direction and all corners of the world – to call him the destroyer of Mur the demon is no offering of praise!

In one of his poems, Parasnath Avatar, he takes up the same theme.

> Say, if Krishna were the ocean of mercy, why should the hunter's arrow have struck him? If he can save other families why did he destroy his own? Tell me why he who called himself the eternal and the unconceived entered Devaki's womb? Why did he who is without parentage call Vasudev his father? Why call Shiva God? Why speak of Brahma as God? God is not Ram Chandra, Krishna or Vishnu whom you suppose to be lords of the world. Shukdev, Parasar and

Vyas erred in abandoning the one God and worshipping many. All have set up false religions. In every way, believe that there is but one God.

Guru Nanak was also scathing of avatar mythology in a passage which Guru Gobind Singh might well have had in mind:

God created air and brought together fire and water and placed earth in their midst. The foolhardy ten-headed demon brought about his own destruction. To call God the slayer of Ravana does not add to his greatness. How can I praise you? Your devotees see you as all pervading. He created all things and keeps them under his own control. To say that he strung the nostrils of the serpent Kalee does not make him greater. You are no one's husband, whom can we call your wife? You pervade everything. Brahma who sprang from the lotus and was thus blessed began to explore creation. He could not find its limits. The slaying of Kansa does not increase God's glory. Nanak says that in God's creation there is not one Brahma but many, not one Krishna or Shiva but a countless number – so why worship them, his creations? (AG 350)

Sikhism denies that God takes birth, but it has its own doctrine of avatar. It reduces the gods to legendary human figures and is then able to regard them as men through whom God has worked. They have a place alongside Kabir, Muhammad, Jesus, Gandhi and the Gurus as bringers of light. As Guru Arjan put it, 'God appoints holy men as witnesses to show us that he is not far from us' (AG 933). This transformation of the concept of Guru is developed most fully and most daringly in the epic Vichitar Natak (the Wonderful Drama) by Guru Gobind Singh. In it he traces his own family, the Sodhis, to one son of Rama and Sita, Lav, and Guru Nanak's family, the Bedis, to their other son Kushu. He also describes a prophecy in which a Guru will appear from the Kushu branch but in the fourth generation his panth will be led by a Sodhi. Eventually in the epic the Guru comes to his own birth:

When I was performing austerities and meditating on Kali and Maha Kal on lofty Hemkunt in the high Himalayas, I became absorbed in the Immortal One and was one with the

97

Lord because of the devotion of my mother and father [Guru Tegh Bahadur]. I did not wish it, but the order came for me to take birth in the Kal Yug [the present Evil Age]. The Immortal One told me how the demons were created, but they trusted in their own army and so were destroyed. Then the gods were created but they became proud [worshipped their own strength] and called themselves Parmeshur [Supreme God]. Maha Dev [Shiva] called himself the Imperishable: Vishnu appointed himself Parmeshur; Brahma stated he was Par Brahm [Supreme Brahma]; but none of them knew the True Lord. Then the Lord created the right witnesses [the basic elements of nature] but people began to worship them. Some people worshipped water, and others became ensnared in egoism. The Siddhas and the Sadhus likewise founded their own Panths and went astray in quarrels and pride. When I created Datta Traia, he only let his finger nails grow long and matted his hair, but he failed to meditate on the love of Hari. Gorakh made disciples of great Rajas but only taught them to split their ears and put in earrings. Ramanand became a Bairagi and wore a wooden necklace, but forgot the Lord. All the great souls only founded their own sects. Muhammad was ordained king of Arabia by the Lord but he only taught circumcision to his devotees. He caused his own name to be repeated and he did not proclaim the True Name. So the Immortal said to me,

I have blessed you as my son, I have created you to proclaim the Panth. Go spread the faith and restrain the people from folly.

I stood up, made obeisance and said, 'This Panth will spread in the world when you give assistance.' For this reason the Lord sent me, then I took birth and came into the world. What he spoke that I speak, and I bear no enmity to anyone. Those who call me Parmeshur shall fall into the pit of hell. Know me as his slave only, have no doubt of that. I am the slave of the Supreme Being and have come to behold the spectacle of the world. What the Lord told me that I tell the world and I will not remain silent through fear of mortals.

Superficially it might seem that Guru Gobind Singh is raising himself to the level of Vishnu or Shiva but he is in fact reducing them to the level of himself and using them together with Gorakhnath, Ramanand and Muhammad as example in a cautionary tale. Each forgot the Lord, according to the Guru, and offered mankind some false substitute for the truth which they had been chosen to proclaim. There were those around him who might proclaim him as avatar in the traditional Hindu sense. To them he addressed his warning, 'Those who call me Parmeshur shall fall into the pit of hell. Know me as God's servant only – have not the least doubt of that.' Every man and woman was potentially an avatar in the Guru's eyes, one who, as a God-filled person, could witness to the truth. The details of the story need not concern us over-much. We need not regard it as evidence for a knowledge of a former existence and the Sodhi and Bedi links with the family of Rama are not intended for close literal scrutiny! Nevertheless there is an inescapable similarity between Krishna of the Bhagavad Gita, the avatar par excellence and Guru Gobind Singh. Each differs from other men in remembering a previous existence or pre-earthly state. In the Gita Krishna says, 'Many a birth have I passed through as you have, I know them all, you remember none' (45). Neither is born because of the consequence of karma. In the Gita we read, 'For whenever the law of righteousness withers away and lawlessness raises its head, then do I generate Myself [on earth]' (47). Later in Vichitar Natak the Guru uses some words which are very reminiscent of those from the Gita quoted at the beginning of this section. He writes:

For this purpose I have come into the world, for the sake of the faith the divine Guru sent us: 'Wherever you extend the faith seek and hurl down evil deceivers.' For this purpose I have taken birth, to spread the faith, to protect the saints and to destroy evildoers. Let the saints understand this.

Few Muslims were becoming Sikhs at this time. Guru Gobind Singh was recruiting his followers from the fold of Hinduism. Audaciously he was speaking to them through Hindu mythology but he was not betraying the fundamental principles of Sikhism in the process. His mission was a response to the divine command and his duty and that of the panth was to proclaim not dharma in the sense of the Hindu social order but the truth which brings liberation through union with God. Sonship in the context of this poem has to do with the blessing which anyone can obtain through obedience to God, significantly the very next phrase God says, 'I have created you'. A clear distinction between the human Guru and Parmeshur is maintained throughout the poem. If Guru Gobind Singh is Krishna he is the human charioteer only; God's servant and nothing more.

The poem Vichitar Natak was intended to encourage the Sikhs in a time of crisis when they were engaged in a bitter struggle with the Mughal armies. Its method was to represent Sikhism as the true faith of the present age. This it did by showing that although the Guru had been performing austerities of a Shaivite nature he was chosen, because of his parents' devotion to the truth, to proclaim the Sikh faith. As God's ordained he was a man of destiny and his followers were encouraged to see themselves as sharers in that destiny, members of a panth created by God to witness to the truth and restrain the people from the folly of false religion. By implication he is God's messenger and deliverer in the Kal Yug (the present evil age). He was not the first to suggest this. The idea is strongly present in the first Var of Bhai Gurdas:

> Hearing mankind's cry the Benificent Lord sent Guru Nanak into the world. Although Guru he performed the humble service of foot washing and provided nectar for his own disciple to drink. In this Dark Age [Kal Yug] he revealed that there is one supreme God. . . . Baba Nanak ferried the Dark Age across the Ocean of Existence by proclaiming the mantra of the True Name.   (Var 1, pauri 23)

The idea is also found in the Var of Rai Balwand and Satta (AG 967–9) in which the word avatar is actually applied to Guru Amar Das indicating that eighty years before Vichitar Natak was written Sikhism felt confident enough to employ this important Hindu term.

The nature and role of the Guru *

The Sikh Gurus have much in common with other preceptors in the Indian tradition but their history and contribution is also

---

* This important subject is examined in detail in W. O. Cole, 'The Guru in Sikhism', an unpublished thesis in Leeds University Library.

distinctive. They were not Brahmins, they did not see their calling to be that of expounding the Vedas. They taught in the vernacular not Sanskrit and their message was for everyone. They were ten in number, each remaining faithful to the teachings of Guru Nanak, and when the line was ended by a conscious decision of Guru Gobind Singh succession was invested in a collection of teachings which was given the title Guru Granth Sahib. This is now the Guru of the Sikhs.

The first requirement of the Guru is that he should be enlightened. Only in the case of Guru Nanak himself is the story of his experience available. It has already been described (p. 9). At the court of God he received a vision, a message of truth and a charge to preach that message to mankind and create a fellowship which would remain faithful to it. Guru Amar Das described his enlightenment, saying, 'My soul is ecstatic on hearing my Lord's coming. Sing songs of rejoicing my friends to welcome my spouse. My house has now become my Lord's mansion' (AG 921). The same metaphor is used by Guru Arjan, 'Blessed, blessed is my destiny, my spouse has come into my home' (AG 847). In his biographical epic, Vichitar Natak, Guru Gobind Singh briefly but significantly makes the same assertion: 'What he [God] spoke, that I speak.' The message was not that of the Ten Gurus but God's.

Guru Nanak and his successors were conscious that they were operating on two levels. They were Gurus but they were only messengers of God whom they frequently call 'Sat Guru' to an extent that makes it difficult to understand to whom the particular scriptural passages refer. As Gurus they enjoyed considerable prestige. Guru Nanak was granted an audience with the Emperor Babur after his imprisonment in 1521 at Saidpur and obtained the release of himself and other captives. Hindu gurus and Sufi pirs were influential in a manner which the modern western mind can scarcely appreciate. Certainly from the time of Guru Amar Das the Gurus knew the Mughal Emperors personally or their activities were carefully watched by the state. On the other hand they were God's servants. 'A bard of low birth, unemployed until God gave him a tune to sing', was Guru Nanak's description of himself. 'Know me as God's slave only', was the command of the tenth master whilst his father Guru Tegh Bahadur wrote scarcely a sabad without uttering some word of self-deprecation.

An important characteristic of the teaching of the Sikh Gurus is their emphasis upon the message, the bani. It is this stress which made possible the transfer of guruship to the scripture. When Guru Nanak was asked by the Nath yogis to name his guru he replied, 'The word [sabd] is my Guru and the meditating mind the disciple. By dwelling on him I remain detached. Nanak, all the ages through, God the cherisher of the world is my Guru' (AG 943). The message is not only the word of God, it is God, it is the form he takes to manifest himself to humanity: 'From the Primal One has emanated the gurbani, and it has effaced all anxiety' (AG 628). In the words of Guru Amar Das, 'The gurbani is God himself, and it is through it that man becomes united with God' (AG 39). The human Gurus were the instrument through whom the voice of God became audible. In the words of Guru Nanak, 'As the word of the Lord comes to me so do I utter it' (AG 722), so he is also compelled to plead, 'Be merciful to me, for only then can I repeat your name' (AG 566). When passages which speak of the necessity of the Guru are read it must be with these other beliefs in mind. Unless God discloses himself man can never know the truth and be united with him. God's self-disclosure is his word communicated through chosen men and women:

> Without the Sat Guru no one has become one with the Lord.
>   In the Sat Guru the Lord has placed himself. I openly declare this and proclaim it.
> Liberation is obtained eternally by meeting the Sat Guru who has banished the worldly love which is within. (AG 466)

> As the water remains confined in the jug but the jug cannot be shaped without water so the mind which is controlled by divine knowledge is restrained, but without the Guru there can be no knowledge.   (AG 469)

The inclusion of hymns composed by Hindus and Muslims of the pre-Sikh times is the best demonstration of the belief that the Gurus never claimed to be the exclusive spokesmen of God's word.

When he refers to serving the Guru, Guru Nanak is again pointing to God: 'The attendant who performs the Guru's service, remains attached to the Guru's hymns and who accepts both good and bad with equanimity will, in this way, become absorbed in the Lord' (AG 432); but the affirmation could easily become a word which encouraged service to the human Guru. Thus Lehna showed himself to be such a humble man that he was designated Guru Nanak's successor, and Amar Das carried water from the river for Guru Angad's morning bath. For Sikhs today the service of the gurdwara, scrubbing its floors, washing dishes and preparing food in the kitchen, is the equivalent form of humble service.

The many stories which are told of the readiness of disciples to serve the Gurus sometimes in humiliating conditions and by dying for them are reminders that the Guru in Sikhism is a human being and the Sikh theory of guruship explains the spiritual relationship which existed between ten men. The theory is usually expressed in the words of the bards Balwand and Satta: 'The divine light is the same, the life form is the same. The king has merely changed his body' (AG 966). Bhai Gurdas used similar language:

> Before he died Guru Nanak installed Lehna and set the Guru's canopy over his head. Merging light in light the Satguru changed his form. None could comprehend this mystery; he revealed a wonder of wonders. Changing his body he made Lehna's body his own! (Var 1, pauri 45)

In the Puratan Janam Sakhi Guru Nanak says, 'From this day you are the Guru while I am your disciple. From this day you will sit on the gaddi and initiate disciples while I remain a disciple.' The changing of Lehna's name to Angad (my limb) was a very simple way by which Guru Nanak gave expression to the theory. Sikh artists demonstrate it visually by giving each Guru identical dress and remarkable facial similarities whilst preserving certain human distinctions, for example Guru Har Krishan is always portrayed as a child, Guru Hargobind wears two swords and Guru Amar Das and Guru Nanak have white beards. The turban is also a symbol of unity not only of Guru but also of Guru and Sikh.

Balwand and Satta describe Lehna's installation with words which are similar to Bhai Gurdas's but provide two important additions. They write:

Nanak placed the Guru's canopy over Angad's head and they drank nectar [nam amrit] by singing the Lord's praise. He placed the soul-illuminating, all powerful sword of the gurbani in his mind. He put the tilak mark of authority on his forehead. During his lifetime Guru Nanak made obeisance to his disciple.   (AG 966)

The ability to express the gurbani was transferred from Guru to disciple who then became a disciple by bowing at Angad's feet. The choice of successor was never intended to be democratic. There is a tradition that each Guru nominated his successor even if he could not physically install him. By this device of public affirmation it was intended that leadership disputes should be averted.

The installation ceremony developed over the years and it is not possible to state when particular elements came into evidence or whether they were used on all occasions. For example, there is the tradition that Guru Nanak gave Lehna a book of sabads. There is no reference to such a gift when Bhai Buddha installed Guru Hargobind, as the Adi Granth was now in existence. The practice of placing five coins and a coconut in front of the nominee cannot be said with certainty to have happened on every occasion. Of the significance of the symbols more comment can be made.

The pothi of hymns showed that the Guru had been made custodian of the bani. With the compilation of the Adi Granth the bani came to possess a measure of independent existence and it may be that later Gurus followed the example of Guru Arjan who bowed before the copy which he installed at the Darbar Sahib. The coconut is said to represent the natural universe, the hair upon it representing vegetation. The five coins signify either the five elements, air, earth, fire, water and ether, or, being artefacts, human industry. Placed before the Guru they represent his custody of the creations of God and men. Guru Nanak wore a seli, a woollen cord, the Sufi's mark of renunciation. This was given to each of his successors until Guru Hargobind took it from Bhai Buddha and had it put away for safekeeping, choosing to wear a sword instead. The seli denoted detachment not withdrawal as each Guru was a married man, except for the boy Guru Har Krishan. With the accession of Guru Hargobind the political and temporal concerns which had occupied his father in the last years of his life became such that the seli was no longer an appropriate insignia for the Guru to wear. Bhai Buddha who installed the four masters from Guru Amar Das to Guru Hargobind also put the tilak mark upon their foreheads. In Hindu worship this mark is often put upon statues, pictures and the foreheads of devotees. It is a symbol of blessing. In the installation of a Guru it was a public affirmation of election. This was the significance also of the small low stool (chawki) upon which the Guru was seated. This was the Guru's throne, in fact a teaching seat. Sometimes this is called a gaddi but in correct usage 'gaddi' is a concept of authority not a physical object, at least in Sikhism. If the gaddi of Guru Amar Das was at Goindwal this means that it was there that the Guru had his headquarters and from there exercised his authority. The umbrella or 'Guru's canopy' was the object which would more than anything else indicate to a stranger who the Guru was.

Guru Arjan paved the way for a guruship of considerable temporal significance and his son Hargobind and grandson Gobind Singh made the concept a reality. Nevertheless sight was not lost of the primary concern for providing spiritual enlightenment and so the disciple was made the spiritual equal of his master. Guru Amar Das declared, 'The Guru is the Sikh and the Sikh is the Guru. Both preach God's mission which is God's name and placing the sabd in men's hearts' (AG 444). Guru Gobind Singh said, 'The Khalsa is my other self. In them I live and have my being.'

Ultimately the function of the Sikh Gurus was not to be world rulers but world enlighteners. This the Tenth Guru recognised at his death when, asking to be set in front of the Granth Sahib, he said, 'Take me to the presence of the Primal Guru. When he had bowed before it he said,

A Sikh who wants to see me should look at the Granth. One who wishes to talk to me should read the Granth and think over it. One who wishes to listen to my talk should read the Granth and listen to its recitation with attention. Consider the Granth as my own self, have not the least doubt about it.   (Quoted from Gupta, 1973, p. 238)

CHAPTER SIX

Daily life, ceremonies and festivals

Introduction

The word 'Sikh' has two meanings. In this book it generally refers to a person who holds certain beliefs, lives according to these and takes part in certain rites associated with them. However, it may also denote someone who comes from a Sikh family, perhaps wears a turban, speaks Punjabi and is in a cultural sense a Sikh but has ceased to practise the religion. He is a Sikh in terms of identity only. This is important for him, but for the student of Sikhism he may be misleading, conveying a casualness to beef-eating (see below, p. 141), turban-wearing, the cutting of hair or smoking which is not orthodox. The model for this chapter will be the person who is attempting to regulate life according to the Code of Conduct which is set out in Appendix 1.

The Sikh is heir to an Indian tradition which stresses physical cleanliness and the importance of appearance. Indian saddhus, Buddhist bhikkus and Gandhi have all used dress to make some important point, and the Five K's and the turban are employed by Sikhs in the same way. Their particular meaning will be discussed later in the chapter. Most rituals are preceded by a bath and this is also how the day should begin. The tedium of repeatedly referring to this practice will be avoided as each particular rite is discussed but it should be understood that three considerations combine to make bathing important, the Indian tradition, the Indian climate and hygienic common sense. Bathing is not a ritual and the idea of pollution should have no place in Sikhism. If perfume is used or a Sikh woman puts a mark (bindi) on her forehead the purpose is purely cosmetic. When shoes are taken off before entering a gurdwara it is Indian tradition which is being followed, one which some Indian Christians are now accepting. Respect for the Guru Granth Sahib and not carrying the dirt of the streets into the clean room would be reasons Sikhs would give for removing their shoes. The horror they can express if someone should carry his shoes through the gurdwara is related to a feeling of insult that the scripture has been treated impiously, not to a belief in pollution.

A Sikh is a person who abides by the gurmatt, the teaching of the Gurus, and keeps it constantly in mind. 'Learning the Guru's discipline I have discovered that the merciful master ferries his servant across [the world ocean]' (AG 465; 1st Guru). Bhai Gurdas spoke of 'Gurdiksha', pledging oneself to the Guru (Var 3, pauri 11). The daily routine should follow the precepts laid down in some verses of Guru Ram Das. The practice he describes is as old as the Kartarpur community and the model is Guru Nanak himself:

> He who call himself a Sikh of the great Sat Guru should rise early and meditate on God's name. He should rise early, take a bath and make an effort to wash himself clean in the Pool of Nectar. By repeating God's name according to the Guru's instruction all his evil deeds and mistakes will be washed away. Afterwards, at sun rise he sings the gurbani and throughout the busy day he should discipline his mind to live in God's presence.
>
> The Guru's disciple [Gursikh] who with each breath and every morsel of food contemplates my Lord God becomes pleasing to the Guru's mind.   (AG 305; 4th Guru)

First a Sikh will take a bath in running water. At dawn he should meditate by reciting the Japji, the Jap of Guru Gobind Singh and his Swayyas, before or after breakfast, but before the day's work is begun he should sing the gurbani in the gurdwara. God should not leave his thoughts as he engages in the day's work and in the evening he should return to worship reciting the

Rahiras (the Holy Path) at dusk and the Sohilla before going to bed. Of course the ideal is not always possible. To bathe and meditate is an individual responsibility which a child learns from the example of parents or grandparents. In the towns gurdwaras open at an early hour and a Sikh can listen to or participate in kirtan on the way to work. Sikh schools and colleges have their religious assemblies. However, not every village has a gurdwara and where there is one there may be no provision for daily congregational worship. Often the granthi will merely open the Guru Granth Sahib with a prayer and villagers enter as they pass during the day, to worship by bowing before the scripture or perhaps reading a passage from it. Often they will take a gift, in kind in the villages, a cup of flour or a bowl of milk, but usually of money in the town. It will be used by the granthi and his family.

'Every work is noble if performed in the right way,' said Guru Amar Das. Earlier Guru Nanak had remarked, 'He alone has found the right way who eats what he has earned through toil and shares his earnings with others' (AG 1245). It is almost a popular expression of everyday life to say that a true Sikh must lose kirt, kul, karm and dharm. Kul is pride in high birth or shame in low birth, karm is attaching importance to ritualism, and dharm is having a communal outlook rather than a universal one. Kirt is possessing a wrong notion about work, regarding some tasks as ignoble, not in keeping with one's social status. Guru Nanak's sons showed themselves unfit to lead the community because of kirt. Sikhs are also reminded of Bhai Lalo, the poor village carpenter, who was one of the Guru's favourite companions. They are also told of the way in which Guru Gobind Singh once refused a cup of water from a young man whose soft hands showed that he had never done a hard day's work. Guru Nanak was a farmer at Kartarpur. Manual work is a high form of worship in Sikh eyes. No task is ignoble but some work is unworthy. For universally accepted ethical reasons a Sikh should not run a gambling club, become a dancer (frequently the work of a courtesan), or a prostitute. Many religions would frown on these forms of employment but there are others where the prohibition is more peculiarly Sikh, for example growing or selling tobacco, or trading in alcoholic drinks. No Sikh should earn his living by begging, though the poor and needy, as opposed to professional beggars, are always to be helped whether they be Sikhs, Muslims or Christians. Buddhist bhikkus are included in this category. Pilgrims from Tibet to the Buddhist shrines were given hospitality at gurdwaras as they passed through the Punjab in the days before the Chinese annexation. In opposition to the four attitudes which must be rejected three should be cultivated, nam japna, kirt karna and vand chakna, meditation resulting in being God-filled, honest work, and giving to charity. These are the principles which should determine daily life. Because the stress is upon daily religious observances and the Guru's rejected belief in auspicious days Sikhs have no weekly holy day. A tendency to observe the first day of the month (new moon day) has a secular rather than religious significance.

Dress

North India was dominated by a Muslim outlook for two or three centuries even though Islam never became the major religion in terms of numbers. Sikh women have tended to wear the shalwar-kameeze even though there is no religious reason for them to do so. It might be regarded as a regional dress in the Punjab – the trousers, shalwar, are comfortable and functional. The tunic, kameeze, is the natural other part of this garment. The sari is becoming increasingly popular. It should be worn with a full blouse which covers the midriff, so that the injunction is obeyed which warns against 'wearing clothes which cause pain to the body or breed lustful thoughts' (AG 16). Around their shoulders or over their heads women will wear a muslin scarf (dupatta or chuni). In the presence of men or when entering the gurdwara, they will pull it respectfully over their hair. Sometimes it is pulled down so far that it hides the face. This may be noticed more among brides than any other group, though occasionally a young woman in a village will cover her face if she sees a stranger.

Purdah, the social separation of men and women, has no place in Sikhism, but there is a cultural tradition in India for men and women not to eat or socialise together. In a Punjabi peasant's home, irrespective of religion, this separateness is likely to be found, though a male visitor may meet the female members of the family. In the gurdwara men and women will worship together and a woman can lead the worship, but in the langar men and women will not eat together though men play a full part in preparing and serving food. Western dress has influenced Sikh men more than women. In the towns most will be seen wearing western-style trousers and suits and shirts buttoned at the collar, though the tie has never become popular. The tight-legged pyjama with hanging-out shirt has never disappeared in the village, where good sense as well as conservatism favours it, and some older sants prefer them. The short trouser, kaccha, are sometimes worn as an outer garment by men, but usually constitute the underwear of men and women.

THE TURBAN

The turban is the most notable feature of men's clothing. It is worn by other men in the Indo-Pakistan subcontinent, is mentioned in the Old Testament, and has often been a feature of Muslim dress, but it has become almost synonymous with Sikhism. In Britain disputes with transport authorities in Wolverhampton, Manchester and Leeds and the legislation exempting turbanned Sikhs from wearing crash helmets when riding motor cycles or scooters would make it appear to be the hallmark of a true Sikh. This it is. Pictures of the Gurus show them wearing a Pathan or Rajput type of turban. The one commonly seen today is a development which may be traced to the Sikh princes at Ranjit Singh's court. Style is unimportant, so is colour, but for every male Sikh, once he knows how to tie it, the turban is essential. The reasons are various. There is the example of the Gurus who raised their disciples to their own level and commanded them to be like them. The injunction to imitate referred to faith and conduct but did not exclude appearance. 'The Guru and the disciple are one' (AG 444) most completely when they are indistinguishable from one another. The turban also serves as a uniform. In the Punjab, East Africa or London it makes the Sikhs stand out visibly from other men. When the Gurus encouraged the wearing of the turban they did it partly to prevent non-Sikhs being picked upon and treated as Sikhs in time of local persecution and they did it also to prevent the less courageous of their followers deserting and merging with the crowd when the going became hard. A person known to hold certain beliefs is more likely to live by them; the Sikh who publicly demonstrates his allegiance by wearing a turban will be more likely to remain loyal to the gurmatt than one who dispenses with it and cuts his hair. The turban has often been associated with the uncut hair, as in this quotation from Guru Arjan which encourages a man to maintain his natural appearance and not shave:

Let living in his presence,
With the mind rid of impurities be your discipline. Keep
the God-given form intact, let the complete body be the
turban on your head.   (AG 1084; 3rd Guru)

Those being addressed are Muslims not Sikhs and the emphasis of the whole passage is upon the attributes of a true Muslim. The five prayers are described as God's praise, contentment, humility, alms-giving and self-restraint. True ablution is abstinence from evil deeds and the one dietary law is – eat food which has been earned honestly. The practice of circumcision is rejected and so may be the sectarian use of the turban by the injunction 'let the complete [or natural] body be the turban on your head'. Clearly this particular verse is not a safe one upon which to urge the necessity of the turban; it could even be used as a counter-argument.

The Codes of Conduct are unequivocally to be regarded as possessing the authority of the Gurus. In that of Bhai Nand Lal, dating from the time of Guru Gobind Singh, the command is given 'A Sikh must comb his hair twice a day and tie his turban smartly.' Ultimately, however, the turban issue is not one which can be understood by quoting passages from this source or that. It can only be appreciated by those who recognise that the Sikhs believe themselves to be a community called to walk in the ways of the Gurus and to take their identity and purpose upon themselves.

The turban's function has to do wholly with religious and social identity and cohesion. Its purpose is symbolic not functional. The uncut hair is kept tidy by the comb. In everyday life the symbolism of the turban is seen when turban lengths of cloth are exchanged at marriage ceremonies or when the head of a family has died. On this occasion relatives may bring turban lengths to his successor who will tie his turban in public so that the family and the village may know the identity of the person in whom authority is ultimately vested. A bald-headed Sikh should still wear a turban!

Sikh ceremonies

In the life of the Sikh there are three domestic rites, naming, marriage and cremation, and one specifically religious ceremony, initiation into the Khalsa.

NAME GIVING

The birth of any child, boy or girl, should be welcomed equally as a gift of God. When the mother is well enough the family will visit the gurdwara to give thanks. An offering of one-and-a-quarter rupees (sava) is the traditional gift to pay for making karah parshad, but this now buys little and an extra amount is usually added. In the villages women of the family will often make karah parshad themselves and take it to the gurdwara. Also a romalla, a piece of brocade or silk about a metre square, is often given to the Guru Granth Sahib. Thanksgiving sabads will be read, one being that which Guru Arjan composed on the birth of his son Hargobind (see above, p. 27) and the other also by the Fifth Guru:

> The supreme Lord has given me his support, the abode of distress and disease is demolished. Men and women alike make merry as God, the Lord master has extended his mercy to them. O saints, now there is peace everywhere.
> (AG 628; 5th Guru)

Sometimes the visit will coincide with the end of a complete reading of the Adi Granth which the family has requested. Devout families will ask that the baby shall be given amrit, the nectar made by dissolving patashas (sugar crystals) in water. The granthi will recite the first five verses (pauris) of the Japji as he stirs the water with a short two-edged sword (khanda). He will then put the tip of a kirpan in the amrit and touch the baby's tongue with it. The mother will drink what is left. The Guru Granth Sahib will now be consulted by being opened at random and the first word of the left-hand page will be read to the parents. They will then decide upon a name beginning with this initial and the granthi will announce it publicly, adding Kaur for a girl or Singh for a boy. He will then cry 'Jo bole so nihal' and the congregation will give its approval by replying 'Sat sri akal'. The first five and the last pauris of the Anand will be read, the prayer Ardas will be offered, karah parshad will be shared and the ceremony is over. Where there is no gurdwara, or the mother and child are not well enough to make the journey, or during a season of bad weather, naming may take place in the home. Amrit will be prepared by an elderly person and a gutka, a small collection of hymns, will be used instead of the Adi Granth.

Birth is attended by a number of social customs. Where the joint family system operates the baby will be born in the husband's home. The wife's parents will visit their daughter taking clothes and similar gifts for her and the mother-in-law and a turban for the father-in-law and their son-in-law. The mother will also make a preparation of ghee, sultanas, almonds and gram flour (dabra), to help her daughter recover her strength. Sweets will also be taken. Money gifts may be sent as substitutes by relatives living at a distance. The baby may be given a gold kara (wrist band). Prescribed gifts – saris, shalwar-kameeze for women, turban lengths and shirts for men – are given to relatives by the child's father. Tradition dictates the amount and the span across the joint family. These or other presents will be given to friends. He may also invite five respected men to his home to pray for the child. They will be given a meal and a token present of a turban length and some money. A langar may be arranged for the poor and gifts may be made to poor widows or charitable causes.

Many names are common to boys and girls. There are also fashionable name endings, '-want', '-jit', or '-inder'. Jaswant, Amarjit and Harminder may be male or female, hence the appended common name Kaur or Singh is essential. Though these names are associated with the foundation of the Khalsa they are used by all Sikhs and do not imply initiation. Sikhs also show a great delight in coining names – as one put it, they can provide a name for every occasion. Some families also enjoy giving their children names beginning with the same initial – Harbans,

Harjinder, Hardeep. At present the use of names which describe divine qualities – Parkash (enlightenment), Santosh (content-ment), Gurmukh (God-minded) – does not seem fashionable.

The appended names Singh or Kaur, meaning lion and princess respectively, date back to the establishment of the Khalsa and give practical effect to the idea of a brotherhood in which all distinctions of birth cease to have any value. Nevertheless, surnames have not disappeared because they are useful, as any teacher with eight Singhs and five Kaurs in the class will know! They denote the sub-caste of the family, e.g. Grewal (Jat), Bansal or Kalsi (Ramgarhia), Jas, Chand or Rasila (Bhatra), or its home village (e.g. Gill, Mirpuri). Sometimes nicknames have become surnames, e.g. Ainki, one who wears spectacles, Dhiddal, with a paunch. The proper prefix of address is Sardar (Mr) and Sardarni (Mrs). When speaking to a man whose name is not known it is usual to call him 'Sardarji'.

MARRIAGE

Except among some westernised subgroups in the larger Indian cities social mixing between the sexes is restricted, even in co-educational schools. Also, the joint or extended family system is still the Indian norm. It is in this context, which can only be referred to in passing in this book, that Sikh marriage must be understood. Marriage is not a private matter between two persons. Through the couple two families become closely connected and into one family group comes a stranger, the wife. She has therefore to be compatible not only with her husband but with his parents, brothers, their wives and his unmarried sisters. Ideally the marriage is based upon love, the love of both families for their children. Social status and monetary advantage, if they play a part, should be subordinate considerations. Assisted marriage rather than arranged marriage is the phrase Sikhs would prefer to describe the procedure of choosing a husband or wife. The decision to marry is itself a joint one, though custom also plays its part. Among some groups there may be a tradition of marriage at fourteen or fifteen. Child marriage in the traditional Indian sense has always been repudiated by Sikhs and a fourteen-year-old in India can be shouldering considerable adult re-sponsibilities. The legal limit in India now is eighteen for women and twenty-one for men, and Sikhs accept the law of the country in which they live.

The decision to seek marriage may be influenced by a number of considerations. Normally the older daughter should marry before her sisters. If the young person is undergoing higher education marriage will be deferred till after graduation. An older brother whose father has died waits until his younger brothers and sisters have received an education or training and the girls have been married. The emphasis upon family life as that which God has ordained is such that few Sikhs remain single.

The family assists in finding a partner. Suitability should have as its criteria virtuous qualities, temperament and age. Then, if they have any place, social status and economic position. A final factor will be caste consideration. A Jat is likely to marry a Jat, an Arora an Arora, a Ramgarhia a Ramgarhia, but there are many exceptions. It is most important that a Sikh marries a Sikh. The true life of discipleship to the teaching of the Gurus can most completely be carried out in the householder (grihastha) state and it is important that it is expressed in a united family. Mixed marriages are not successful in normal experience, whether the tensions be caused by conflict between town and village, wealth and poverty, laxity and piety. Kinship has a negative influence. Sikhs should not marry someone whose caste name is the same at the distance of the four grandparents.

It is unusual for the couple whose marriage is being assisted not to meet before a decision is made. They will not come together in private (dating is a practice which is disapproved) but they may meet on a number of occasions in company and each will be fully informed about the interests and lifestyle of the other.

A betrothal ceremony may precede marriage but it is not essential and not religious. The wedding is both a social and religious occasion. It can take place on any day. The monsoon season influences arrangements but the belief that some days and some seasons are more auspicious than others should not, for Sikhs repudiate it. The wedding will normally take place at the bride's village and may be celebrated on the flat rooftop, in a courtyard, garden or in the gurdwara – anywhere so long as the Guru Granth Sahib is present. The groom's party (braat) will have arrived in the village on the previous evening and the formal meeting (milani) of the two families will have taken place. The wedding is celebrated early in the morning. The congregation gathers as if for a normal service and when Asa di Var, the morning hymn, has been sung the groom comes forward and takes his place at the foot of the Adi Granth. The bride then joins the congregation and sits at the left side of the groom attended by a friend. Whoever is conducting the marriage asks the couple and their parents to stand whilst he or she prays that God will bless the marriage. A short hymn is sung which contains general advice:

> Before undertaking anything seek the grace of God. By the grace of the true Guru who in the company of the saints expounds the truth, success is attained. It is with the true Guru that we taste ambrosia. O thou destroyer of fear, embodiment of mercy, bestow thy grace on thy servant. Nanak says by praising God we apprehend the infinite. (AG 91)

The concept of Sikh marriage is explained by one of the ragis or by the officiant. Marriage is not a social contract but aims at the fusion of two souls into one. It is analogous to the union of God and man which is the goal of Sikh piety. Various hymns give advice on marriage:

> The bride should know no other man except her husband, so the Guru ordains. She alone is of a good family, she alone shines with light who is adorned with the love of her husband. There is only one way to the heart of the beloved, to be humble and true and to do his bidding. Only thus is true union attained. They are not man and wife who have physical contact only. Only they are truly wedded who have one spirit in two bodies.   (AG 788)

> Ask the happy one by what ways they have won the beloved. They will answer, by sweetness of speech and the beauty of contentment. A loaf of dry bread and a bed of bare earth is full of happiness in the company of the beloved. Let humility be the word, contentment the offering, the tongue be the mint of sweet speech. Adopt these habits dear sister, then you have him in your power.   (AG 1384)

Another person's property, another man's wife, talking ill of another, these are poisons. The touch of another man's wife is like a poisonous snake.   (AG 403)

The bride and groom publicly assent to the marriage by bowing towards the Guru Granth Sahib. When they have sat down again the bride's father comes forward, to garland the Guru Granth Sahib, his daughter and the groom and tie the end of his daughter's dupatta to the muslin scarf which hangs from the groom's shoulders. Another hymn is sung: 'Praise and blame I forsake both. I seize the edge of your garment. All else I let pass. All relationships I have found false. I cling to thee, O my Lord' (AG 963). The officiant now opens the Guru Granth Sahib at the Lavan of Guru Ram Das (AG 773), a hymn which he composed for his daughter's wedding. The first verse is read and then sung by the ragis as the couple walk slowly round the Guru Granth Sahib in a clockwise direction, the groom leading. They return to their places and sit down while the second verse is read and then the circling is repeated. This happens four times. The last is often a signal for the throwing of flower petals. The service concludes with the singing of the first five and the last stanzas of the Anand followed by the prayer Ardas. The Guru's counsel (vak) is taken by opening the scripture at random and the congregation is served with karah parshad. After further celebrations at the bride's home the marriage party (dholi) will leave for the groom's home in the late afternoon. There, as a member of his family, the bride will begin her new life.

The four verses of the Lavan (circling) hymn have a double significance. They provide the couple with advice but they place the union within the deeper context of union with God. The first verse reads,

By the first circling the Guru has shown the duties of the householder life. Sing the bani instead of the Vedas and hold fast to the faith which they reveal so that God may free you from evil inclinations. Hold fast to righteousness and contemplate the name of God. Fix the smirti in your mind, they too contain God's word. Devote yourself to the true Guru and all evil will depart. Those minds are blessed indeed which are filled with the sweetness of his name. To them bliss comes without effort.

God's servant, Nanak, proclaims that in the first circling the marriage rite had begun.

The significance of the verse is first the affirmation that the householder (grihastha) stage of the four Hindu ways of life is the proper one for the Sikh. In it he can become liberated through being filled with the knowledge of God (Brahm gyani), which must be the basis of family life, without passing along the progressive path laid down for Hindus from student through householder to ascetic and recluse. Second, this is done through meditating upon nam and knowing the bani which is clearly set out in this verse as the teaching of the Guru and the undefined 'smirti' or devotional books to the specific exclusion of the Vedas. The verse may therefore be regarded as constituting part of the third and fourth Guru's attempt to establish a coherent Sikh community. Here it is being done not only through the provision of an alternative form of marriage to that of Hindu tradition but by including in it injunctions which are specifically Sikh.

In the second stanza the God, the true Guru, is commended as the dispeller of fear, the soul of the universe, all-pervading but particularly present in the sangat:

In the second circling you are to recognise that God has caused you to meet the true Guru. By holding him in reverent awe and singing his praises self-centredness is washed away. I stand in his presence, face to face, with reverence. The Lord God is soul of the universe, there is nothing he does not pervade. He is both within us and outside us, the only one. Songs of rejoicing are heard in the company of the saints. The slave, Nanak, proclaims that in the second round the divine music is heard.

In the third circling longing for the Lord and for detachment from the world wells up. By our good fortune, in the company of the saints, we encounter the Lord. He is found in all his parity through praising him and singing his hymns. Good fortune has brought us into the saints' fellowship in which the story of the ineffable Lord is told. The Lord's love fills our minds and absorbs us, as we have been blessed with a good destiny which is recorded on our foreheads. In the third circling, the slave Nanak says, God's love is awakened in the heart.

In the third stage of life a Hindu detaches himself from his householder obligations and business interests to attach himself to God. The third circling reminds the Sikh of detachment but it is found through fellowship, the company of the sangat. This fellowship meant a great deal to the Fourth Guru who did much to weld the Sikhs into a cohesive panth. Here he suggests they should be grateful for a birth and destiny which has resulted in them coming within the sound of gurbani so that the longing for eternal bliss is awakened.

The final verse describes the conclusion of the journey of the soul to God. The devotee becomes filled with divine knowledge (Brahm gyani) so that sahaj, perfect bliss, is attained. The word is difficult to explain. Its Sikh meaning is brought out by this stanza better than any prosaic discussion. Guru Ram Das, commending married life, is quite prepared to regard it as analogous with the relationship between God and the devotee, one which in this life outwardly seems that of two distinct souls but one in which the devotee is aware of a deeper union which death will perfect:

> In the fourth round the mind attains divine knowledge and union with God becomes complete. Through the Guru's grace this blissful state is attained. The sweetness of the beloved pervades our souls and bodies. The Lord is dear to me and I am pleasing to him. Day and night my mind is fixed on him. By exalting the Lord I have attained him, my heart's desire. The beloved has completed the union. The bride's mind has blossomed with the Lord's name. The Lord is united with his holy bride.

Says the slave Nanak, in the fourth circling I have become one with the eternal Lord.

DEATH

Sikhs share the view of many inhabitants of hot climates that the funeral should take place quickly, normally on the day after death. They also practise cremation. Burial at sea is permitted and inhumation is not considered wrong but cremation has been the tradition of five hundred years and any other method of disposing of the dead is psychologically undesirable. The ashes may be buried – this has obviously happened in the cases of many sants as their shrines (samadhis) testify – but normally the remains are put into the nearest river. The building of funeral monuments is not regarded as properly in keeping with Sikh beliefs. The Gurus forbade them in the case of themselves, though the sites are now the locations of gurdwaras.

The cremation ceremony is a family occasion. The body will have been washed and clothed by members of the family who have been careful to ensure that it is wearing the symbols of the faith (the Five K's). It is then taken to the cremation ground outside the village in a solemn procession. During the journey the mourners sing hymns. The funeral pyre is lit by a close relative and the evening hymn (Sohilla) sung during the cremation. Prayers, concluding with the Ardas, are offered.

When they return to the home of the deceased the mourners wash their hands and faces and it is customary for the complete reading of the Guru Granth to begin, though on this occasion it is more likely to be done intermittently over a period of about ten days rather than continuously for forty-eight hours. Before taking leave of the bereaved family mourners will receive karah parshad. The sharing of food at this time is particularly meaningful. It symbolises the continuity of social life and normal activities as opposed to isolation from human contacts, fasting and other ritual manifestations of grief.

Birth into the Sikh faith is the result of a good karma. It has provided the soul with an opportunity to come within the sound of gurbani and so to receive liberation. Death is the removal of the last obstacle to complete union with God, if one has been a sincere believer. It is common for Guru Arjan's Sukhmani (Hymn of Peace) or a similar sabad to be read in the presence of the dying person. From such words as these everyone derives encouragement:

Let your heart sing praises of the formless One; this should be your righteous course. Keep your tongue pure by the touch of his nectar-name; it will give you peace of mind. With your eyes behold the splendour of God's presence. The company of the faithful will banish every other presence from your sight. Walk in the way of God. With every step you take you will be treading down evil inclinations. With your hands do God's work and with your ears listen to his instruction. Thus your life will be rounded off by God's approval which will be reflected in your face.   (AG 281)

Death is a very strong and frequently recurring theme in the hymns of Guru Nanak and his successors. This is not because of morbidity nor yet because death has always been a very noticeable aspect of the Indian scene. It is because death is the reminder par excellence of man's self-centredness:

His step has become ugly, his feet and hands slip, the skin of his body has shrivelled up. Eyes have become dim, ears deaf, but the self-centred man still does not know the Name. What have you gained by coming into this world, blind man? You have neither enshrined God in your heart nor have you served the Guru. You are departing having lost even the accumulation of good works which you have brought into the world.   (AG 1126)

Death does not wait for auspicious days or ask whether it is the light or dark side of the month. Some people are harshly treated, others are well cared for. Some leave armies and mansions to the sound of drums. Nanak the heap of dust is returning to dust.   (AG 1244)

In food, drink, enjoyment and sleep death is forgotten. Forgetting the Lord is to make life a heap of ruins. There is nothing that can survive from such a life.   (AG 1254)

Sikhism's emphasis upon finding God through the householder life could well explain the warnings in the Adi Granth against clinging to the world:

Affections are dead, love is dead, hatred and wrangling are dead too. Colour has faded, beauty is gone and the body rolls in agony. Whence did he come, where did he go, what wasn't he, what was he? The self-centred talked incessantly and enjoyed their pleasures enthusiastically. But, says Nanak, without the true Name their honour is split from head to foot.   (AG 1287)

They cry 'alas, alas', and wail for the dead. They beat their cheeks and pull out their hair. Did they but cherish the name and practise it, Nanak, it would be a sacrifice for them. (AG 1410)

The Sikh is called upon to remember that

The dawn of a new day
Is the herald of a sunset.
Earth is not your permanent home.

(AG 793)

The vesper hymn, which many know by heart, encourages them to use the opportunity well of being able to hear the gurbani: 'Know the real purpose of being here and gather up the treasure under the guidance of the Sat Guru. Make your mind God's home. If he abides with you undisturbed you will not be reborn' (AG 13). The passing of an old person who is believed to have lived according to these precepts is no cause for grief. The cortege may be accompanied by a brass band and the rites followed by a feast. Presents may be given to the grandchildren. Whether the deceased be old or young relatives will usually make gifts to the poor, to the gurdwara or to a charity.

SIKH INITIATION

Having described the family ceremonies we now turn to the one specifically religious rite, initiation. It is not birth which makes a Sikh but illumination, and in consequence a way of life which Bhai Gurdas defined thus:

Dead to the world a Sikh lives in the spirit of the Guru. A man does not become a Sikh by merely paying him lip service. A Sikh dispels all doubts and fears and lives a life of deep patience and faith. He is truly a living sacrifice, a loving slave of the Lord.

He does what the Lord wills. He forgets hunger and sleep in his love. His hands are busy helping the needy and comforting the weary. His hands are busy washing their feet. Magnanimous, tolerant, and serene he lives to serve mankind.

In glory a Sikh does not laugh. In suffering he does not weep. He is a seer living in God's presence; he is a devotee imbued by love. He steadily grows into perfection and is blessed and adored like the new moon on the Muslim day of Eid.   (Var 3, pauri 18)

Initiation into the Sikh panth was by charn amrit received from the Guru himself from the days of Guru Nanak until 1699: 'Only on receiving initiation from the Guru [gurdikhia] can a disciple call himself a Sikh' (Bhai Gurdas, Var 11, pauri 3). Charn amrit literally means foot-nectar and was prepared by pouring water over the Guru's feet and catching it in a bowl. The nectar was then drunk by those wishing to receive initiation. The Indian practice of showing respect to a person by clasping or kissing his feet is very ancient. Touching the feet of a saintly person is considered to be a way of receiving a blessing and one calls to mind the footprint of the Buddha at Bodh Gaya and the sandals of people such as Kabir which are preserved as relics. The survival of the practice of charn amrit or charn pahul (literally foot-bleaching) into the time of Guru Gobind Singh and its replacement by khande ka pahul is witnessed to in a story in which a young Sikh paid homage to Guru Gobind Singh and said, 'O true King, I am the son of Manula. We are both initiated Sikhs. My father became a Sikh by charn pahul while I was initiated by the double edged sword [khande-di-pahul]' (Sau Sakhi 25). There is also an account of Rattan Rai, an Assamese prince, receiving charn pahul from the Tenth Guru.

Details of the early form of initiation are not available but the new members must have taken certain vows on joining the panth. Again Bhai Gurdas provides the evidence: 'He initiated his disciples with charn amrit, water sanctified by the touch of his lotus feet, and gave a new code of conduct as the highway to the path of truth' (Var. 23). From an examination of the Vars, a convenient quarry, these would seem to have included spiritual and moral injunctions as well as community rules. Sikhs were told to bathe daily early in the morning and then spend time in meditation. They were encouraged to treasure seeing the Guru (darshan) and opportunities of touching his feet, but more important was obedience to his teaching. They were to read the gurbani with understanding and preach it. Presumably this is the origin of a Sikh concern for literacy and education; to see the Guru and hear him was not enough, they should be able to read his hymns and be sufficiently conversant with the faith in order to be able to communicate it to others. At this time, early in the seventeenth century, Sikhism would seem to have been a missionary faith. 'Gurpurbs' are also mentioned; these are festivals associated with anniversaries of the Gurus' birth and death. These were now being observed as well as Baisakhi and Diwali which the disciple was ordered to keep in the Sikh as opposed to the Hindu way, that is by assembling wherever the Guru happened to be. Despite this command Bhai Gurdas says the six systems of Hinduism should be regarded as one and should be seen as emanating from the one light. The advocate of Sikhism should not attack the fundamentals of other faiths, and a scrutiny of the Adi Granth shows that it is ritualism and claims to exclusiveness, which are seen to obscure the principles of Islam and Hinduism even in its yogic form, which come in for criticism rather than their basic concepts. The sacred thread and the Vaishnavite hair lock are specifically rejected. Renunciation is commended but defined as being like the lotus in water; worldly activities should be pursued but with detachment. Thus the Sikh should work hard and earn an honest living but also be generous and give to charity. Celibacy is similarly commended and defined. He is celibate who is married to one wife only and treats all other women as sisters and daughters. Both these important aspects of Hinduism are thus reinterpreted in the context of the householder (grihastha) form of life. Respect for another person's possessions is inculcated in a telling metaphor, 'as beef is to the Hindu and pork to the Muslim so other people's property should be to a Sikh' (Var 6, pauri 8). From Bhai Gurdas it is even possible to discover the approved Sikh form of greeting; disciples should bow low to one another and touch each others' feet, so demonstrating humility and respect. This greeting was changed by Guru Gobind Singh to 'Waheguru ji ka Khalas', to which the other person replied 'Waheguru ji ki fateh' ('The Khalsa are the chosen of God, the victory is God's').

The contributions of Bhai Gurdas can be augmented by a few pieces of information from a book written in praise of the Sixth Guru entitled 'Guru Blas'. The Sikh writer says that Guru Hargobind commanded Sikhs to read the Adi Granth when someone died (this would seem to be the origin of the path) and not to think of auspicious days. 'When you wish to embark upon an undertaking, pray about it and then get on with it!' Finally, he upheld the belief that death is not final but that which completes the soul's liberation, saying, 'It is my order that you should not lament and wail when I die but you should sing God's praise.'

Bhai Gurdas and 'Guru Blas' provide an insight into some of the main precepts of Sikhism at the time of Guru Hargobind. These derive from the Gurus themselves and echo many passages which can be found in the Adi Granth. The Code of Discipline laid down for the Khalsa, to which we shall turn after describing initiation into the Khalsa, should be seen as supplementing not nullifying the instructions of the earlier Gurus.

The normal Baisakhi assembly of 1699 took place at Anandpur. The date was 30 March by European reckoning because the Gregorian calendar had not yet been introduced. Unknown to his followers the Guru had devised a new means of obtaining personal loyalty to overcome the rivalry of the regional commanders and spiritual viceregents the masands. It took the form of a new method of initiation, by nectar made from dissolving sugar crystals in water by stirring them with a double-edged sword. The precise events of that Baisakhi day may now be uncertain. It has been suggested that the Code of Discipline attributed to that occasion evolved during the eighteenth and early nineteenth centuries (J. S. Grewal, 1972, ch. 12; McLeod, 1976, pp. 51–3). What concerns us here is not rehearsal or evaluation of this evidence but an attempt to explain the significance of the khande ka pahul ceremony of initiation. We shall therefore examine the rite as it is performed today.

Initiation may take place at any time of year, though Baisakhi is a popular season. Strictly speaking the initiates should be over fourteen years of age but there is ample evidence of young children being initiated in the Punjab. The rite is the same for Sikhs and non-Sikhs but some Codes of Discipline require a three-year period as a catechumen before admission. The person who asks to become a Khalsa Sikh must be in possession of the Five K's, should be tidily dressed and be known to be attempting to follow the Sikh way of life as well as accepting the doctrines of Sikhism. The rite must be performed by five people, men or women, to re-enact the original ceremony, and these must possess the Five K's and be physically complete as well as devout members of the community. Both outwardly and inwardly they should represent the perfect human form. As long as the place where the ceremony is held is one where there is a certain amount of privacy there is no restriction upon the location or on the numbers taking part. Lapsed Sikhs who have broken the Code of Discipline may undergo the ceremony a second or even a third time. Such Sikhs, who have perhaps cut the hair or discarded the turban, are sometimes called sahajdaris, those who are slipshod or easy in their attitude to the faith, as opposed to those who are earnest and who can most easily be observed by their unshorn hair and are hence called keshdaris, those who have adopted the kesh. Originally sahajdari did not denote someone who had lapsed but a person who had not yet made the step of becoming a Sikh. The correct word for a Sikh who has discarded the kesh is patit (apostate).

The beginning of the ceremony is marked by the opening of the Guru Granth Sahib. One of the five conducting the ceremony then explains the principles of the Sikh faith and asks those about to be initiated whether they accept them. A prayer for the preparation of amrit is offered and a sixth person, acting as granthi, reads a passage from the scriptures. The five (panj pyares) kneel around an iron bowl (batta) on a pedestal (sonera) with their right knee on the ground and the left raised. They place sugar crystals (patashas) in the bowl and one by one stir it with a short double-edged sword (khanda) as they recite the Japji of Guru Nanak, the Jap and ten Swayyas of Guru Gobind Singh, the Chaupai, which is part of the evening hymn, and the first five and last stanzas of the Anand. These constitute an excellent precis of the Sikh faith in the words of the Gurus and their recitation takes almost two hours. When the nectar is ready the panj pyares lift up the bowl and one of them offers another prayer.

During this impressive preparation the candidates have been sitting or standing while they listen to the gurbani. Now they come forward one by one and kneel in the same manner as the panj pyares. Each one is asked to say 'Waheguru ji ka Khalsa, sri Waheguru ji ki fateh' ('The Khalsa is of God, the victory is to God') and then is given a handful of amrit to drink before nectar is sprinkled five times on their eyes and hair. Any amrit which is left is drunk by the initiates who sip it from the batta.

Repetition of the Mool Mantra five times by the panj pyares, echoed on each occasion by the initiates, begins the third part of the ceremony. The senior member of the five then tells the new members of the Khalsa that they are children of the same family whose parents are Guru Gobind Singh and his wife Mata Sahib Kaur. They must set aside all other religious beliefs and practices and cling only to the teachings of the Gurus. They must offer daily prayers, pay tithes and keep the Five K's. He then lists the rules of conduct which they have vowed to observe. The first four are major prohibitions (kurahts): failure to avoid them would result in a severe penalty, perhaps a fine or a requirement to perform some act of menial service over a long period of time, and reinitiation. They are, cutting of the hair, eating meat slaughtered in the Muslim manner, adultery, and the use of tobacco. The lesser prohibitions (tankhahs) are: joining any of the breakaway sects or the company of lapsed Sikhs; eating with non-Khalsa or apostate Sikhs; dyeing or plucking out grey hairs; arranging a son's or daughter's marriage for financial gain; using narcotics or intoxicants; performing any ceremony which breaches Sikh principles; breaking the vows taken at initiation.

The service ends with the Ardas, the reading of a randomly chosen passage from the Adi Granth, and the sharing of karah parshad which all initiates eat from the same dish. Anyone who has come new to Sikhism will be given a name following the procedure for naming a child before karah parshad is distributed.

Guru Gobind Singh's purpose in introducing this new form of initiation has already been mentioned. It was to focus the loyalty of Sikhs who were already soldiers upon himself. It may be that from 1699 the norm is the warrior Sikh but he was only completing a process which begins with Guru Hargobind in Sikh history. The Sixth Guru was probably harnessing existing Jat energies and his grandson was now giving them discipline and coherence. McLeod (see especially McLeod, 1976, ch. 3) has argued strongly that the Code of Discipline and the Five K's indicate Jat influence and that this Punjabi agrarian caste exerted strong pressure upon the Gurus in the seventeenth century and were largely responsible for its development as a militant faith. It is certain that the view which sees the change from the pacifism of Guru Nanak to the militarism of Guru Gobind Singh as taking place suddenly in 1699 is over-simple and historically incorrect. In passing it may be remarked that the belief that the early Gurus were consciously pacifist is open to question. The apparent contrast may owe more to change of conditions than to change of attitudes and to a current inclination to see Guru Nanak as a sixteenth-century Gandhi.

Particular injunctions in the kurahts and tankhahs may be explained as having origins in Punjabi culture or some special significance in the seventeenth and eighteenth centuries. The rejection of meat slaughtered by Muslim methods in favour of that killed by one blow (jhatka) may be a positive acceptance of the Punjabi custom as well as a rejection of Muslim practice. Opposition to narcotics might simply seem to be common sense if physical fitness and spiritual enlightenment are to be realised.

The Kanphat yogis were often accused of addiction to drugs and drink (Briggs, 1938) and it may be their influence and that of Shaivite sects in the Shavilik hills which the prohibition had in mind. Both drugs and wine are repeatedly condemned in the Adi Granth from the time of Guru Nanak. The Portuguese brought tobacco to Goa by 1508, it reached north India in Akbar's reign and his son Jehangir condemned it as an evil weed. It was popular in Afghanistan and the Sikh condemnation of smoking might belong to the eighteenth century when soldiers would come in contact with the 'vices' of their opponents. The emphatic condemnation of adultery is regarded as more than a moral injunction; it is an explicit rejection of the view that women could be regarded as legitimate spoils of war. For the same reason, respect for women, it was forbidden that marriage should become an auction.

The remaining prohibitions have to do with the Five K's (panj kakke) which are the kesh (uncut hair), kangha (comb), kirpan (sword), kara (steel wrist band) and kacch (a pair of breeches which must not reach below the knee). Both the kacch and the kirpan may belong to the Jat tradition in the Punjab, as did the custom of not cutting the hair, but from whatever sources the Five K's were derived they were given new meanings with Sikh belief. The kesh was worn by rishis and some yogi groups but often in a matted and unkept manner. The Sikh is ordered to be tidy in appearance, to wash the hair regularly and comb it twice a day. The comb is therefore partner of the kesh and with it symbolises orderly spirituality. The kacch signify modesty, moral restraint and continence. Constraint is also present in the kara, which is worn on the right wrist. Sikhs commonly say this may have been a protection against the bowstring. More likely perhaps it was a protection on the sword arm, but the circle is also of symbolic importance in Indian thought, for example the wheel of dharma in Buddhism. In common usage a kara is the metal hoop which binds a barrel. It reminds the Sikh of his unity with God and with the Khalsa and consequently of vows and beliefs in nam and service which should control his use of the kirpan. The sword signifies dignity and self-respect, a readiness to fight but only in self defence or in the protection of the weak and oppressed.

The panj kakke with the turban constitutes a uniform which made the Khalsa an easily identifiable group but the complete initiation rite may have a more profound meaning. J. P. Singh Oberoi (Harbans Singh, 1975) has expressed the view that the rite contains a marked theme of inversion. The sannyasi at initiation has the head shaved and declares, 'I am no one and no one is mine'; the Sikh accepts the Guru and his wife as his parents. The yogi vowed never to touch weapons; the Sikh wears the kirpan. He is also initiated by a group, not by a single initiator and the mantra instead of being secretly whispered is audibly expressed. Tidiness in appearance, an orderly code of life, and commitment to a life of service and world-acceptance complete the explicit rejection of yogi and sannyasin outlooks. This interpretation has much to commend it, but in pairing kesh and kangha, kara and kirpan, kacch and uncircumcised member he may be pressing his argument too far.

Sikh festivals (melas)

Since the time of Guru Amar Das it had been customary for Sikhs to assemble before their Guru on two of the most important Hindu festival occasions, Baisakhi and Diwali. To these Guru Gobind Singh added Holi.

Baisakhi is New Year's Day in the Punjab and falls on 13 April. The date is fixed, being based on a solar calendar, though once every thirty-six years it occurs on 14 April. Guru Amar Das's purpose in assembling the Sikhs was to wean them from Hinduism. As Bhai Gurdas expressed it, 'Non-Sikh festivals should not be celebrated. Even if we observe the same day we do it in our own way.' At Baisakhi instead of offering barley and grian to the Brahmins from the crops about to be harvested they gave worship to God and listened to the teaching of the Guru. With the passage of time Baisakhi assemblies have acquired an historic significance. Guru Gobind Singh at the gathering in 1699 formed the Khalsa brotherhood. In the eighteenth century the Sikhs began to assemble at Amritsar for Baisakhi and this town now became their focal point in the absence of a human Guru. On Baisakhi 1747 they decided to construct a permanent fortress at Amritsar, threatening communications between Lahore and Delhi. A few years later in 1762 Hindu Brahmins came to the assembly and laid a complaint against the Afghan Usman Khan who had forcibly abducted the wife of one of them and converted her to Islam. The Sikhs consulted the Guru Granth Sahib and decided to take up their cause. More famous is the story of Baisakhi 1919 when General Dyer, acting on the orders of the Lieutenant Governor of the Punjab Sir Michael O'Dwyer, tried to resist history by preventing the Sikh assembly, regarding it as part of Gandhi's home rule campaign. The Sikhs met and in a small enclosure called Jallianwala Bagh they were fired on by the army. Three hundred and thirty seven men, forty-one boys and a baby were shot and the British hopes of saving India suffered a severe setback at the same time. Today Baisakhi in Amritsar is a political, religious and social occasion. Long before dawn pilgrims make their way to the Golden Temple and the stream of people crossing the causeway and bathing in the pool continues far into the evening. A few hundred metres away Jallianwala Bagh is the scene of political rallies in the afternoon, and a little to the east of the town a large animal fair is held at which working animals of every kind from camels to goats are bought and sold. For the people of the outlying villages this festival is a last opportunity for relaxing before beginning to harvest the corn. Elsewhere the occasion is often a time for initiating new Khalsa members by the pahul ceremony, though this may be held at any time of the year. More prosaically, it is the season for holding elections to the gurdwara executive committee!

The second mela, Diwali, is also a New Year celebration which is celebrated during the dark half of the lunar months of Asvina and ends on the second day of the month of Kartik. For Hindus it is a festival of light and deliverance and for Sikhs it has something of the same significance. Gurdwaras are illuminated with coloured electric lights or small wick-lamps, and children receive presents, but the story which is told is about Guru Hargobind not Rama and Sita. The Sixth Guru, Hargobind, was imprisoned by officers of the Emperor Jehangir in the Gwalior Fort for non-payment of the fine imposed on his father and the officers became suspicious that he was committing treason by raising an army against the Mughal rulers. Eventually Jehangir examined the case personally and ordered the Guru's release. Sharing his imprisonment were fifty-two Hindu princes who were not offered their liberty. Guru Hargobind said that he would accept his freedom only if they also were allowed to leave the prison. The reply was that as many princes as could pass through the narrow passage holding on to his clothes could go free. The Guru ordered a cloak to be brought which had long tassel-like ends. The rajas walked to freedom holding on to his train.

At Amritsar during Diwali the Golden Temple is illuminated and there are firework displays and a general gala atmosphere pervades the town. Treasures accumulated during the Sikh raj are put on display for a brief period of two hours.

Holi for Hindus is a Krishna festival marking the beginning of spring. It falls in the bright half of Phalguna (February–March). In the Punjab the air is becoming noticeably warmer and the sharp chill in the early morning air disappears. Rather than encourage his Sikhs to expend their energies in what he regarded as the purposeless and often degrading excesses of Holi, Guru Gobind Singh summoned them to Anandpur for a new festival, Hola Mohalla. Guru Hargobind had created a standing army, his grandson decided that this should be the occasion when it should assemble to perform mock battles and military exercises in his presence and that of the Sikh community as a whole. The most satisfactory translation which can be given to the festival's name is probably 'manoeuvres'. When Guru Gobind Singh ordered his followers to assemble in 1680 he was providing an alternative to the Krishna festival and regularising the training of his army. The high spot of the two-day festival was a mock battle in which the Guru led an attack on a fortress which had been specially erected for the occasion. However, there were also archery and wrestling contests as well as more pacific music and poetry competitions. The general emphasis was clearly military and the festival was a means of expressing the belief that every Sikh is a Kshatriya before the Khalsa had been formed.

Anandpur remains the principal location of this mela. There is a fair, pilgrims visit local shrines and gurdwaras, especially that which commemorates Gurditta, Guru Hargobind's son and father of the Seventh Guru. The festival culminates in a carnival procession behind the flags (nishan sahibs) of the gurdwaras. All facilities – banking, ambulance stations and langar – are available but the descendants of Guru Gobind Singh, the Sodhis, on their elephants have now become a spectacle which is only a memory.

GURPURBS

All over the world three important anniversaries are celebrated. These are the birthdays of Guru Nanak and Guru Gobind Singh and the martyrdom day of the Fifth Guru. Such occasions are called gurpurbs, the syllable 'pur' signifying a holiday. In India these festivals are usually observed by carrying the Guru Granth Sahib in procession through the village or city. It will be placed on a float or van strewn with flowers and will have an armed guard, five of whom will head the procession and represent the panj pyares. Collections will have been organised to hire most of the local bands and to bring prominent speakers long distances to lecture the crowds or to pay for the posters announcing the festival and the prizes for competitions which may have been organised, and to provide the langar.

Many of the gurpurbs are local events celebrated only where the original event took place, except in a centenary year. Between the universal gurpurbs already named and the purely local come the martyrdom day of Guru Tegh Bahadur and those days which commemorate the martyrdom of the four sons of Guru Gobind Singh.

A full list of Sikh gurpurbs and melas as they fall within the Gregorian calendar is as follows:

| January | Maghi Fair at Muktsar near Ferozepore. Commemorates the battle of Muktsar fought by Guru Gobind Singh. |

January	Baba Deep Singh, scribe of the Sikh scriptures and martyr, who died attempting to recover the Darbar Sahib from the Mughals in 1760. Commemorated at Amritsar.
January	Chheharta Sahib fair (near Amritsar) where Guru Arjan sank six wells to supply the needs of the district.
February–March	Hola Mohalla mela.
March	Mela at Dera Baba Nanak Gurdwara, an historical site for a long time in the possession of the Bedi family. Opposite Kartarpur where Guru Nanak spent the last years of his life.
13 April	Baisakhi mela (once every thirty-six years, as in 1975, this festival falls on 14 April).
May–June	Martyrdom of Guru Arjan. Universally commemorated.
June	Death of Maharaja Ranjit Singh, celebrated in various towns associated with his reign, until 1947 principally at Lahore.
July	Birthday of Guru Har Krishan, celebrated at Delhi.
August	Mela Baba Bakale. Held at Bakale near Amritsar where Tegh Bahadur was proclaimed Guru.
September	Goindwal fair to commemorate the death (Immersion into the Eternal Light) of Guru Amar Das.
September	Anniversary of the installation of the Adi Granth (1604). Amritsar festival.
October–November	Diwali mela.
November	Guru Nanak's birthday, universally celebrated.
November	Achal Sahib Batala fair (Gurdaspur) where Guru Nanak disputed with the yogis.

December	Birthday of Guru Gobind Singh, universally celebrated.
December	Martyrdom of Zorawar Singh and Fateh Singh the young sons of Guru Gobind Singh, observed especially at Fategarh Sahib near Sirhind.
December	Martyrdom of Ajit Singh and Jujhar Singh, sons of Guru Gobind Singh, observed especially at Chamkaur Sahib where they died.
December	Martyrdom day of Guru Tegh Bahadur, observed at Delhi.

Most festivals and gurpurbs are fixed by the lunar calendar and may vary within the limit of about fifteen days.

It will be observed that the date already given for Guru Nanak's birthday was 15 April 1469 but that the gurpurb is celebrated in November (Kartik). The difference is explained by most Sikh scholars now preferring the first date which is given by many of the janam sakhis whilst the Bala tradition provided the November alternative. It appears that writings based upon the popular Bala Janam Sakhi in the nineteenth century had the effect of encouraging the celebration of the gurpurbs in November. Macauliffe (1963, vol. i, pp. lxxxiv–vi) states that this date was chosen to draw Sikhs away from a Hindu fair held at Ram Tirath on the full moon of Kartik.

A feature of many gurpurbs is an akhand path. This is the name given to an unbroken reading of the Guru Granth Sahib. It takes approximately forty-eight hours and will begin in the morning two days before the gurpurb so that completion will occur before dawn on the anniversary. Formalities commence with the preparing of karah parshad, the reading of six verses from the Anand Sahib and the offering of Ardas, which includes asking a blessing upon the reading. Then the scripture is opened at random for guidance and a verse is read, after which the akhand path begins with the Japji. During the two days members of the community will visit the gurdwara when they can, therefore karah parshad must always be available to give them and someone must be present to give it to the worshippers. Relays of readers are organised so that each person does a stint of no more than two hours at a time. Someone is always present to take over in the event of a reader being taken ill. The conclusion (bhog) of an akhand path is the occasion for everyone who can to assemble. It begins at page 1426 with the sloks of the Ninth Guru and continues to the end of the scripture. Sometimes the first five verses of the Japji will be read, then six pauris of the Anand Sahib. Ardas will be offered and karah parshad shared.

Besides being a prelude to important anniversaries, akhand paths may be arranged before weddings, after funerals and at any time of family or community importance. At the principal gurdwaras one bhog ceremony is immediately followed by the start of the next continuous reading. On domestic occasions, for practical reasons, a sahaj path is more common. This is a broken reading taken in a more leisurely manner at times when the family can gather together. It may occupy a week or ten days. The bhog ceremony will be as described above, however, and is never broken. A description of an akhand path is a fitting way to conclude this section for it emphasises the centrality of the Guru Granth Sahib not only in worship but in community and domestic life.

CHAPTER SEVEN

Ethics

Sikh ethics are based upon three fundamental concepts – first, that the principles kirt karo, nam japo and vand cako, work, worship and charity, should dominate one's complete life. Second, that self-reliance (haumai) is the great enemy of God-realisation and that it manifests itself in lust, anger, greed, materialism and pride. Activities which result from any of these vices should be avoided. This is best done by practising the virtues of contentment, patience, the service of others and humility which is considered to be the lynch pin of them all. Guru Nanak once remarked, 'Sweetness and humility are the essence of all virtues' (AG 470). Finally, it is as a householder (grihastha), a member of a family, not as one who has withdrawn from the world either to become a student or a hermit, that a Sikh should explore the meaning of God-realisation. Again the Guru said, 'The householder who gives all he can afford to charity is as pure as the water of the Ganges' (AG 952).

Putting the principles into practice is difficult because the requirement to live like a lotus in a dirty pond, to be in the world but not attached to it, to radiate beauty and remain pure, is hard. It is easier to turn away from the city, but asceticism and re-nunciation are rejected. Instead Guru Nanak commanded:

Remain in towns and near the main high roads, but be alert.

Do not covet your neighbour's possessions. Without the
Name we cannot attain inner peace nor still our inner
hunger. The Guru has shown me the real life of the city, the
real life of its shops, it is the inner life. We must be traders in
truth, moderate in our eating and sleeping. This is true
yogism.   (AG 939)

The predominant Hindu culture in a Mughal imperial context
determined which social concerns should dominate Sikh teaching.
Consequently caste and the status of women assume considerable
attention in the teachings of the Gurus. The religious implica-
tions of the caste system were rejected by the very fact that the
Gurus were Kshatriyas not Brahmins. Whilst they had a right and
responsibility to know the Vedas they had no business to teach
them. In fact they replaced vedic knowledge with their own and
asserted a divine initiation into guruship. Using the vernacular
instead of Sanskrit they went even further against the Brahminic
tradition as set out in the Laws of Manu by preaching to the low-
est castes and accepting them into the Sikh panth. The Harmandir
at Amritsar was given four doors to be open to all four castes and
Guru Arjan said of the Adi Granth, 'This divine teaching is for
everyone, Brahmin, Kshatriya, Vaishya and Sudra. Whoever
utters the Name which lives in all hearts, under the Guru's
instruction, is delivered from the Dark Age [Kal Yug]' (AG 747).
The caste system was condemned primarily because it was a
practical denial that God is one and the creator and sustainer of
all life: 'God's light pervades every creature and every creature
is contained in his light' (AG 469). The consequence of this, as
the Guru discovered, was that the Sudra as well as the Brahmin
could attain God-realisation. Many of the lower caste might
receive enlightenment, for they were already of humble status
and haumai was unlikely to stand in their way. Man came from
one clay, at death he would return to the same dust be he priest
or cobbler and 'In the hereafter caste and power do not count,
for every soul appears there in its true colours' (AG 469). As the
aim of the God-realised person was to live on earth as he would
live beyond death in the presence of God so he was instructed:
'Know people by the light which illumines them, and do not
ask what their caste is. In the hereafter no one is distinguishable
by caste' (AG 349). Guru Nanak's primary reason for attacking

the caste system was theological rather than social. Although all the Gurus attacked it and the adoption of the names Singh and Kaur as well as the institution of the langar (common kitchen) were successful attempts to remove caste distinction within the panth, the message of Sikhism is concerned with liberating the atman more than ameliorating social conditions. The elimination of caste even within the community has only been partial. Though Sikhs will eat together in the langar, worship together and share karah parshad, marriages are still usually arranged between members of the same subgroup be it Arora, Ramgarhia or Jat.

The doctrine of non-violence (ahimsa) permeates India as strongly as the social phenomenon of caste. It is usual to read that Guru Nanak was a pacifist and that Guru Gobind Singh changed the religion by creating the militant Khalsa. Elsewhere we have already noted that the transformation began with Guru Hargobind acting upon the advice of his father to arm himself and his followers. Here it is necessary to question the view that the early Gurus were pacifist. The fact of the matter seems to be that pacifism was not an issue. Guru Nanak was a spiritual preceptor who also told those who became his disciples how to order their lives. His immediate successors were responsible for spreading the same message and establishing the community. After Babur's invasion in the early sixteenth century, the Punjab enjoyed peace until Emperor Akbar's death and better government and security than it had known for several centuries. Only later when Mughal policy alienated the Sikhs as well as other indigenous groups was there violent unrest. When Guru Arjan told his son to arm the Sikhs he does not seem to have considered himself to be creating a new doctrine and rejecting an established tradition but merely responding to the changed needs of the time. He was also rejecting the Mughal regulation that only Muslims and Rajputs should be allowed to bear arms.

Guru Nanak's encounter with the invading Mughals at Saidpur in 1521 provides an interesting insight into his approach to violence. The town was taken and plundered by Babur's army from Khurasan and the Guru was taken captive. As he tramped along in the company of other men, women and children whose lives had been spared he composed a hymn, part of which reads,

It is your will, O Lord! Honour and dishonour both are your gifts. You bestow one or the other at your pleasure. People, if you had thought of him in time and taken heed this retribution would not have fallen on your heads. Kings, if you hadn't lost all wisdom amid self-indulgence and pleasure this misery wouldn't have befallen the land. Now the armies of Babur are spreading across the country. No one can eat in peace. How hard it is for the captives. The times of worship and prayer pass by unused. These Indian women have nowhere to sit and cook, to bathe or anoint themselves by putting the frontal mark on their foreheads. They never gave God a thought, now they have no leisure in which to remember him.   (AG 417)

His tone is that of the prophet declaring that Babur's invasion is the chastisement of God. In fact a few verses later he makes this explicit:

Today Khurasan seems to be yours, Lord, why not India? Why have you made that land yours and terrified this by the terrible threat of retribution? Are you pitiless, Creator of all? You have sent Yama [god of death] disguised as the Mughal.

He questions God: 'Did you feel no pity for what happened, for the screams of those who cried in agony?' He concludes by saying that all, victor and victim, should remember that they are in his sight and that hope lies only in serving God:

Lord, you see even the smallest crawling creatures and the worm that nibbles the corn. He alone can win merit who has accepted death in life, who has put down his lower nature and lives hourly in the spirit and who, moment by moment, loves, serves and remembers God.   (AG 360)

In keeping with his teaching the Guru provided spiritual comfort for the prisoners. He also asked Babur for their release, charging him to rule India wisely and with justice, but he left no one in doubt that political solutions were inadequate for what were ultimately spiritual problems.

What little attention the early Gurus give to politics in their hymns does not seem to be pacifist. Guru Nanak condemned the

Kshatriya (politician) caste for neglecting their duties: 'The Kshatriya have abjured their dharma and taken to an alien one. The whole world has assumed the same caste and the rule of righteousness has lapsed' (AG 663). The caste all had adopted was that of self-interest. Guru Amar Das characterised the true Kshatriya as follows: 'He alone is a Kshatriya who is brave in good deeds. He yokes himself to charity and alms giving. Within the field bounded by the protecting fence of justice he sows seed which benefits everyone' (AG 1411).

During the period of Guru Gobind Singh the struggle against Mughal authority which had continued intermittently for two generations became a crusade. Among his other writings the Guru sent an admonitory letter to the Emperor Aurangzeb, known as the Zafarnama. In this he took the Emperor to task for the perjury of his officials who had attacked the Guru's forces after a peaceful withdrawal from Anandpur had been arranged in 1704. He also blamed Aurangzeb for his misuse of power and his unholy alliance with idol-worshipping rajas when he described himself as an idol-breaker! In this Letter of Admonition he named him not bhut shikan (idol breaker) but paiman shikan (oath breaker).

The Guru accepted the idea of the just war and enunciated it in a famous couplet.

> When all efforts to restore peace prove useless and no
> words avail,
> Lawful is the flash of steel, it is right to draw the sword.

His verses differ from those of his predecessors most significantly in their use of military metaphors and their references to the struggle against tyranny. Nevertheless he taught that besides only being undertaken as a last resort, it should always be defensive, for the protection of the oppressed and the cause of liberty. The Sikh should never be the first to draw the sword. An epitaph upon his life and a conclusion to the discussion of the Sikh attitude to violence might be the epilogue to one of his own epics, the Story of Chandi (the goddess Durga):

> Grant me this boon,
> O God, from your bounty,
> May I never refrain from righteous acts.

May I fight every foe in life's battle without fear and claim
the victory with confidence and courage.
May my greatest ambition be to sing your praises and may
your glory be engrained in my mind.
When this mortal life reaches its end may I die fighting with
limitless courage.

Vegetarianism is another form in which the Hindu doctrine of
non-violence is expressed. Here the position of Sikhism is far
from clear. Many Sikhs will not eat any form of meat, rejecting
fish as well as eggs. For some the cow is the only forbidden
animal and some do eat beef. In the langar, however, meat is not
served and no visitor is embarrassed in consequence. The practice
of the Gurus is uncertain. Guru Amar Das ate only rice and
lentils but his abstemiousness cannot be regarded as evidence of
vegetarianism, only of simple living. Guru Nanak seems to have
eaten venison or goat, depending upon different janam sakhi
versions of a meal which he cooked at Kurukshetra which evoked
the criticism of Brahmins. Pages 1289 and 1290 contain a number
of verses which can only be read as a rejection of the belief that
flesh-eating is polluting and should be avoided. 'Man is born
from flesh, his atman [spirit] lives in flesh', is the refrain. 'When
he is taken from the womb of flesh he takes a mouthful of milk
from teats of flesh.' He refers to myths in which the gods sacrifice animals and asserts that meat-eating is permitted in the
Hindu Puranas and the Qur'an, and has been accepted in all the
four ages of the Hindu time cycle. 'Fools quarrel over flesh,' he
says, 'but they do not know God and do not meditate upon him.'
    One of the commandments laid upon a Khalsa member is that
of not eating meat slaughtered according to Muslim practice.
Sikh vegetarians see this as a rejection of a particular method of
slaughter not a permission to eat meat killed in some other way.
However, we consider that the prohibition must be seen as
permitting the eating of meat killed at a stroke and not bled to
death. Vegetarianism is not a universal Hindu custom and the
Jats and other groups in the Punjab were meat-eaters. For the
Sikh of today vegetarianism must be a matter of personal conscience.
    The status of women has always been the concern of a religion
which asserted the equality of mankind. To condemn caste

distinction and condone widows being burned on their husbands' funeral pyres or having little place in religious or social life seemed hypocritical. The corollary of Guru Nanak's command, 'Call everyone noble, none is lowborn: there is only one potter, God, and he has fashioned everyone alike. His is the one light that pervades all creation' (AG 62), was respect for women. Yet often they were despised, menstruation and childbirth were polluting, celibacy was preferable to marriage, a widow brought ill-luck upon those with whom she came in contact. Often death on the funeral pyre could be more attractive than the ordeal of loneliness and isolation that lay before her. Guru Nanak denounced the prevalent Hindu attitude:

> It is through woman, the despised one, that we are conceived and from her that we are born. It is to woman that we get engaged and then married. She is our life-long friend and the survival of our race depends on her. On her death a man seeks another wife. Through woman we establish our social ties. Why denounce her, the one from whom even kings are born? (AG 473)

Women served as missionaries during the fifteenth century and when Guru Gobind Singh introduced the new initiation rite in 1699 it was significant that his wife should place the sugar crystals in the water. According to Hindu thought she could have defiled and nullified the ceremony.

Sikhs are monogamous and marriage is a religious ceremony not a civil contract. It takes place in public in the presence of the Guru Granth Sahib. When Raja Hari Chand and his queen visited Guru Amar Das he gave her a pair of shoes to indicate that the ideal life is that in which man and woman become one, a pair, each essential to the other. The whole basis of the Sikh householder life depends upon the strength of the marriage partnership. Divorce is discouraged, but possible. The remarriage of widows is accepted but when they remain unmarried widows are to be respected and allowed their full place in the life of the family and the community. They may, in fact, hold the position of head of family, the eldest son being the executor of his mother's decisions.

Other aspects of Sikh ethics need only be mentioned in passing, but the western reader should note that the janam sakhis record many cases of Guru Nanak healing lepers and other sick people. The Guru established a leprosarium at Taran Taran and medical work and the care of the needy have always been regarded as important forms of charitable service (sewa).

India and many other nations of south-east Asia do not have welfare states or social care programmes. This must be borne in mind in considering Sikh charitable work. Wherever there are Sikhs, in Cambodia or Thailand, Madras, Bombay or the Punjab, hospitals, schools or smaller ways of helping their own community and the cities in which they live are to be found. Sikh denominational schools are open to pupils of all faiths and bursaries are available to help poor children obtain an education in them. Hospitals, orphanages and similar institutions cater for anyone who needs their services. A number of establishments are famous throughout the Sikh world and receive donations from Sikhs living in the rich western hemisphere. Some of them are regularly mentioned in the *Sikh Review* and similar journals. One such institution is the Guru Nanak Niketan at Calcutta. Early in the 1970s, like many other Indian charities, it gave generous help to refugees from Bangla Desh. At more normal times it is a base for midwives, medical teams and self-help projects using Gandhian principles. Also in eastern India, in Bihar, is found the Guru Nanak Hospital for Handicapped Children. It is one of the many institutions set up to mark the quincentenary of the First Guru. Donations which enabled 500 blind people to have operations which restored their sight were another way of celebrating this anniversary. Amritsar is naturally the focal point of Sikh charitable work. Among the many examples may be named the Guru Ram Das Hospital and the Central Orphanage which was set up at the beginning of this century. Near the bus station is the Pingalwara, a centre run by an elderly Sikh named Puran Singh which provides a home for hopeless cases whose families cannot support them, for the chronic sick and the destitute. The Pingalwara is staffed by volunteers and depends on the charity of Sikhs, Hindus and some Christians in many parts of the world. A feature of many Gurdwaras in India is the dispensary, which may be traced back to the Seventh Guru's interest in medicine. On one occasion he helped cure Emperor Shah Jehan's son, Prince Dara. Most gurdwaras also have sarais, lodging houses where pilgrims and travellers may stay.

The list of charitable work could be extended further and we must remember to include such ordinary everyday individual expressions of sewa as helping build or repair gurdwaras, fanning the congregation when the temperature is 90 degrees F in the shade, carrying water to quench the thirst of pilgrims or preparing food for the langar at the Golden Temple. These recall the simple but necessary forms which sewa often took in the days of the Gurus.

Many of the social and ethical ideals of Sikhism are summed up in the life of the gurdwara and the langar. The sangat is a democratic community. There are no priests or ordained ministers. The village granthi who is responsible for opening the Adi Granth in the morning, closing it in the evening, attending it during the day and performing teaching duties, is a paid officer and his personality may give him considerable influence, but he is only the community's servant. When the sangat meets men, women and children assemble together as theoretical equals at the feet of the Guru Granth Sahib. Decisions should be made by all its members. In the langar the different castes will work together preparing food and they will sit together to eat it. The sangat and its individual members are expected to strive for the ideal which Guru Nanak stated in his conversations with the yogis: 'As the lotus in the pool and the water fowl in the stream remain dry; so a man should live, untouched by the world. He should repeat and meditate on the name of the Supreme Lord' (AG 938). It is sometimes summed up in discussion by a Sikh saying he should be a Brahmin in his piety, a Kshatriya in his defence of truth and the oppressed, a Vaishya in business acumen and hard work and a Sudra in serving his fellow men. A Sikh should be all castes in one person who should be above caste.

CHAPTER EIGHT

The attitude of Sikhism towards other religions

Guru Nanak's first words after his enlightenment experience at Sultanpur were, 'There is neither Hindu nor Mussulman so whose path shall I follow? I shall follow God's path. God is neither Hindu nor Mussulman and the path I follow is God's.' This chapter might be regarded as a commentary upon these words. They could easily be regarded as a condemnation of the two major religions with which Guru Nanak was in everyday contact. His criticisms of the religious practices of his day were many and fill many pages of the janam sakhis. A number of examples have already been given; we will confine ourselves to adding two more.

A raja, Jagat Rai, who had been deposed from his kingdom, asked the Guru to help him regain it by his prayers and his blessing. The Guru asked him to prepare some food and distribute it to the poor. The raja was penniless and could only provide a deer which he had killed. When he proceeded to cook this a group of Brahmins began to criticise Guru Nanak for permitting it. Not only was he calling in question their beliefs in vegetarianism, he was also preparing meat during a solar eclipse on the sacred ground of Kurukshetra, where the legendary battle between the Kauravas and Pandavas had been fought. This was in flagrant opposition to well established tradition. The Guru reminded them that horses and other animals had been sacrificed during the Vedic age and that Brahmins had shared the meat. He also told them that they were the worst meat-eaters of all, exploiters of their fellow men, bloodsuckers:

> In ancient days Hindus killed rhinoceros and offered its flesh as oblations on the sacrificial fires. Today Brahmin Hindus have become maneaters; they suck the blood of the innocent masses through cruel and pitiless exploitation. Yet, at the very sight of meat they hold their noses and show their contempt. They are morally and spiritually blind who cannot see the right and act upon it.   (AG 1289)

At Puri is the famous temple of Jagganath which is sacred to Krishna. Guru Nanak visited Puri and joined the congregation for the evening act of worship with lamps (aarti). When everyone else stood to take part in this service he remained seated, murmuring quietly something which could not be heard above the tinkling of the bells, the dancing of the devotees and the chanting of the priests. When puja had ended a number of priests demanded an explanation of his conduct. 'Why didn't you stand when aarti was being performed before Jagganath, Lord of the Universe? What kind of holy man are you?' 'I was performing aarti before the Lord of the Universe,' the Guru replied, 'and the whole of creation, the whole firmament joined me. Your hearts and minds, alone, were turned against it. I worshipped the supreme light. You worshipped a stone image. I contemplated the eternal word [sabd]. You chanted mantras without understanding them. My mind was enchanted by the unstruck music and the universe and by God's presence in it. Yours was deluded by the noise of temple bells, feigned ecstasy of the dancers and the smell of incense.' He then sang his own aarti, part of which states, 'In every heart there is the same light, the light of God. It illumines every soul and gives light to everyone. Through the Guru's word this light is revealed within the soul' (AG 663).

These two anecdotes show what Guru Nanak condemned was superficiality, externalism and religious hypocrisy. The Brahmins at Kurukshetra were wrong because they were more concerned about the polluting of the place than they were about the hungry who would benefit. Their scruples rendered them horror-struck at the thought of eating meat but did not prevent them living as parasites upon humanity. At Puri the Guru perceived that the ceremonial attached to the statue now prevented the God who lay beyond it being seen and worshipped. Ritualism of any form Guru Nanak condemned or ridiculed by action and in words because, he said, 'Rituals and ceremonies are chains of the mind' (AG 635).

However, the attitudes of the Gurus towards Hinduism and Islam were far more complex than these and similar stories would have us suppose. The many anecdotes include an element of desire to turn those with whom the Guru was in conflict from futility to the truth. His purpose was not merely to condemn. Certainly he did not regard Hinduism and Islam as futile. Of Hindus he said,

> The Hindus have strayed from the Primal Lord and are going the wrong way. They worship idols made of stone, not realising that these stones which themselves sink cannot carry others across the world ocean. (AG 556)

> A Hindu goes to the house of another Hindu, chants verses and places the sacred thread around his neck. Despite wearing it he does wrong and therefore, is not approved by God. Thus all his ceremonies and ablutions go to waste. (AG 951)

Neither of these quotations is totally condemnatory. By indicating that Hindus have gone astray the first passage suggests that Hinduism was once a path of truth. Unfortunately trust has been placed in stones and sacred threads. Islam is a major subject of one of the Guru's hymns on the general theme of true religion. It is to be found between pages 137 and 143 of the Adi Granth. Addressing a Muslim he says, 'Let compassion be your mosque, faith your prayer carpet and righteousness your Qur'an. Let modesty be your circumcision and uprightness your fasting. Thus you will become a true Muslim.' He further describes the true Muslim as follows: 'If he willingly submits to God's will and, believing the creator to be supreme, loses himself; if he is also merciful to all creatures, he will be worthy of being called a Muslim.' In a manner reminiscent of Sufi teachers he spiritualises the five daily prayers without denying their worth:

> There are five prayers, five times and five names assigned to

them. Let truthfulness be the first, honest living the second and charity in the name of God the third. Let your fourth be purity of mind and good intentions, and the fifth the praise and adoration of God. Let good deeds be your article of faith. Thus you may be called a true Muslim.

In the same hymn the Guru refers to another group:

Some roam about wearing ochre robes, pretending to be yogis or sannyasins. Within them all is desire and they long for clothes and food. They waste their lives in vain. They are neither householders nor world renouncers. The round of birth and death [transmigration] has not ceased to hover over their heads.

However, even the yogis can find liberation, though only if yoga is practised together with contemplation of the name of God (AG 946) and equipoise is taken to the point that yoga no longer consists of mere talk but of looking upon all human beings as possessing dignity and considering them as equals (AG 730). Exclusiveness and pride tended to characterise the way of yogism. Guru Nanak wished to encourage the yogi to gain more than self-satisfaction from his techniques:

Let contentment be your ear-rings, industry your begging bowl and meditation the ashes you smear on your body. Let thought of death be your patched clothes, chastity your path and faith in God the staff you lean on. Let universal brotherhood be the highest aspiration of your religious order, and know that by subduing your mind you will be able to subdue the world about you.   (AG 6)

The later Gurus are regarded as sharing Guru Nanak's insights and attitudes to other religions. Mian Mir, one of the most famous Indian Sufis of his day, laid the foundation stone of the Darbar Sahib at Amritsar. At Sri Hargobindpur the Sixth Guru provided money for the building of a mosque and a Hindu temple. Guru Tegh Bahadur died as much for the religious liberty of Hindus as he did for his Sikh faith. Guru Gobind Singh said:

Hindus and Muslims are one. The same Lord is creator and nourisher of all. Recognise no distinction between them.

The temple and the mosque are the same. Puja and namaz are the same. All men are one, it is through error that they appear different ... Allah and Abhek are the same, the Puranas and the Qur'an are the same. They are all the creation of the One.   (Akal Ustat)

In Maharaja Ranjit Singh's secular state of the early nineteenth century respect was given to all faiths and Muslims, Sikhs and Hindus shared in the government of his empire.

When we turn to the views which the Gurus expressed about the scriptures of other faiths we discover an interesting and consistent attitude of respect. Sikhism, a religion of the word (sabd), perceives the word of God in the Vedas, Puranas and Qur'an. Its quarrel with Hinduism and Islam is that the word has been ousted by things not only of secondary importance but by distractions so that the voice of God cannot be heard for the tinkling of temple bells or concern for washing properly before saying namaz: 'The Vedas, the shashtras and holy men cry out, but the deaf do not hear them' (AG 408). In this case Guru Arjan blames avarice, passion and the desire to exploit others for drowning the sound of God's voice. Guru Nanak also expressed his belief in the ancient texts of Hinduism as containing God's word: 'The Vedas preach the sermon of devotional service to God. Whoever continually hears and believes them beholds the Lord's light' (AG 143). In another verse on the same page he says, 'The shastras and smirti impress meditation of the Name.' The scriptures contain the truth, therefore he says, 'Anyone who speaks the truth establishes a link with the scriptures [Vedas]' (AG 143). He compares their effect upon the mind to that of lighting a lamp: 'When the lamp is lit darkness is dispelled. Similarly by reading the religious books [Vedas] evil-mindedness is destroyed' (AG 791). Although these two quotations refer explicitly to the Vedas it is usual to regard them as referring generally to sacred literature. In words which Guru Gobind Singh may have had in mind when composing the verse from Akal Ustat quoted earlier, Guru Nanak said:

There are six Hindu schools of thought, each with its own founder and teacher. The Guru of gurus is one but his manifestations are many. In whatever school the glories of the Creator are sung, accept it as your own. As there is one sun but time is divided into many seasons, hours and minutes so there is one God though he has many forms. (AG 357)

The Gurus were opposed to an exclusive claim which a particular religion might make. Guru Amar Das prayed, 'O Lord, out of your mercy save this burning world, and save it through whichever way it can be saved' (AG 853). Guru Gobind Singh said, 'Salute him who is without the label of a religion.' They believed that there was only one religion, God's religion (AG 360): 'For anyone who is determined to practise truth there is only one religion, the religion of truth. One knows, through the Guru's wisdom, that the perfect One remains the same age after age' (AG 1188). Therefore he told the Brahmin, 'Do not be proud of your caste, only he is a Brahmin who knows his lord' (AG 1128). To the yogi he said:

> Religion does not lie in patched garments and a staff, or in smearing the body with ashes. Religion does not lie in suspending large rings from split ears, in shaving the head or blowing a conch shell.
> To live uncontaminated amid worldly temptations is to find the secret of religion. It does not consist of empty words: he is religious who regards all men as equals.   (AG 730)

Having examined the many aspects of the Gurus' teaching about other religions it may be said that they did not consider them to be futile but they did reject their rituals and their claims to possess exclusive truth. Usually it is at the levels of belief that religions clash but in the early days of the Sikh tradition, as seen from a study of the janam sakhis, the reaction was not against ideas but practices and conduct. Eventually Sikhism itself emerged as a religion in the institutional sense, possessing an exclusiveness which seems contrary to its spirit. Passages from the Code of Discipline, the Rehat Maryada, which forms Appendix 1 in this book demonstrates something of this exclusiveness. One or two comments may be made about this. First, it seems to be the natural consequence of the institutionalising of any system of politics or belief. As human beings group together they tend to express their identity by requiring allegiance to the community. In the case of Sikhism the Five K's, the turban, the vows taken at initiation and the emergence of a distinctive culture have been the result. However, when Guru Arjan said:

> I do not keep the Hindu fast nor the Muslim ramadan. I serve only him who will save me in the end. The one Lord of the world is my God. He ministers justice to both Hindus and Muslims. I do not go on pilgrimage to Mecca or worship at the holy places.
> My body and soul belong to him who is called Allah by Muslims and Ram by Hindus.   (AG 1136)

it must be remembered that it was he who also, finally, placed the hymns of Hindu and Muslim bards in the Adi Granth. Numerically he may have only been making a token gesture but he was also making the affirmation that through Trilochan, Namdev, Ramanand and the rest God had spoken. It is unlikely that Sikhism will reject its own sectarian marks; it will argue that a Sikh should remain a Sikh and a Muslim a Muslim. At the practical level it sees difficulties in mixed marriages and in people leaving one culture to embrace another, for this is what conversion to a different religion usually requires. It is strongly opposed to any tendencies to hop from one religion to another, for this is merely a temptation to find satisfaction in novelty and the superficiality of growing a beard, or wearing a turban. Let each remain within his own faith, would be the advice of Sikhism. All religions come from God, deep down they reveal God, let the devotee look inside his own home for the truth, he will find it there. At its best Sikhism does not condemn other faiths, it does not claim exclusive possession of the truth, it does not wish to evangelise. It still regards its mission as being identical with that of the Gurus, to witness to the truth. So the Ardas, at the conclusion of a Sikh service, ends, 'May the glory of your Name increase and may the whole world be blessed by your grace.'

CHAPTER NINE

Sikhism 1708 to 1976

1708 saw the death of Guru Gobind Singh, with which the line of human Gurus came to an end. The fundamental basis of Sikhism had been completed with the inauguration of the Khalsa in 1699 and the installation of the Adi Granth as Guru in 1708. There is a natural tendency among Sikhs to regard the religion as it is practised in the late twentieth century as that which might have been found in Amritsar or in a Punjabi village at the end of the Guru period. However, a careful examination of the Rehat Maryada (Appendix 1) shows when read in the light of this present chapter that the centuries which have elapsed since 1708 have had a considerable influence upon Sikh worship and attitudes, especially towards the rituals of other religions.

From the Sikh point of view their history during the eighteenth century was a painful but eventually successful attempt to implement the slogan 'Raj kare ga Khalsa', 'the Khalsa shall rule'. These words are associated with Banda Singh's capture of Sirhind, a town in the Punjab, in 1710. The city's governor was killed in the battle outside the town and until Banda Singh was captured and executed in 1716 the Punjab was intermittently under Sikh control. Banda Singh had been one of Guru Gobind Singh's companions at Nander. When the Guru died he returned to the Punjab and organised his temporarily successful revolt.

Its immediate consequence was a conscious attempt to exterminate Sikhs. In December 1710 an edict was passed that all 'disciples of Nanak' were to be killed wherever they were found. It also strengthened the Sikh resolution to survive as a people possessing a distinctive identity. For a generation their homes were their saddles. Somehow they maintained not only a steady opposition to the Mughals but also allegiance to the teachings of the Gurus. It seems to have been during the first half of the eighteenth century that the practice of akhand path, the continuous reading of the Guru Granth Sahib, developed to sustain small armies of Sikhs, including their women and children, constantly on the move from one refuge to another. Sikh power grew as Mughal rule weakened partly because of Afghan-Mughal wars but also because central government was weakening and local governors alone could not impose their authority on subjects whose sympathies lay with the Sikhs. In 1765 the Sikhs were able to organise themselves into twelve misls or military groups covering most of the Punjab. Their initial organisation was republican but before long an hereditary principle evolved. Each Baisakhi and Diwali they assembled at Amritsar. A leader of one of these misls was Ranjit Singh. He was born in 1780 and captured Lahore in 1799. The city, which had fallen to the Sikhs several times during the last thirty years, now became his capital, the political focal point of the Sikh Raj lasting until the British annexation of the Punjab in 1849 after the battle of Chillianwala. Though Maharaja Ranjit Singh was a Sikh his rule was tolerant, and no religion was given preference. His chief minister, personal physician and police administrator of Lahore were Muslims as were some of his chief army officers. The chamberlain of the palace was a Hindu. The fifty-year period of domestic peace and prosperity, although the state was frequently at war, resulted in the building of gurdwaras and the restoration of such shrines as the Golden Temple. The number of Sikhs declined sharply after the period of independence. One estimate gives the numbers as ten millions during the Maharaja's reign, dwindling to 1,141,848 in 1868 and rising to 1,716,114 in 1881 (*Spokesman*, Republic Day Issue, 1974, p. 11; the 1881 census figures are given in Appendix 3, p. 184). An explanation for this decline is perhaps found in the eclectic nature of Hinduism. Most Sikhs were of Hindu origin. Even in the Punjab Sikhs did not constitute a majority of the population and in normal, peaceful circumstances there was a natural tendency to revert to the major tradition whilst still revering many of the Guru's teachings. The codes of discipline were not well known or generally observed. Many Sikhs were 'Nanak panthis', that is believers in Guru Nanak's teaching, rather than turban-wearing Khalsa members. The strong distinctive culture and identity which is associated with the word 'Sikh' in the 1970s, whatever its origins, is really the consequence of movements which developed after the British annexation of the Punjab. Even today the Khalsa Sikh who forms the model for this book, because he is the norm, can be matched by many whose identity is Sikh but who vary from the ideal in belief and practice though they would deny that they were in any way 'patit' (lapsed). Before the end of the Sikh Raj Christian missionaries had entered the Punjab. In 1834 the first, an American protestant, arrived at Ludhiana. His account is an interesting contemporary portrait (if misguided in some respects). He writes:

He [Guru Nanak] appears to have been a man of genius and originality of character, and intent upon awakening a spirit of devotion among his countrymen. . . . In process of time Guroo Govind became the leader of the sect, and acquired greater fame and veneration than any of his predecessors. . . . This people are distinguished for their excesses in the use of ardent spirits, opium and other intoxicating drugs; and some other vices are probably no less prevalent among them than the tribes of southern India. As soldiers they are active, cheerful and brave, and in their general character they are more open and sincere than the Mahratas; less fierce and cruel than the Afghans, and more indulgent to the female sex than any other people in India. (Quoted, *Punjab Past and Present*, April 1973, p. 181)

The same article by Dr Loehlin also gives this assessment by Sir Donald McLeod, writing in 1872: '[Amritsar] is the acknowledged chief centre of Sikhism, and thus the headquarters of what I believe to be the most interesting, most accessible, and least bigoted race in the Punjab, as well as the most rigorous and manly' (p. 182). The two passages contain a number of interesting observations which might be discussed at length. The specific points here are the references to being open and accessible and 'least bigoted'. The consequences of these characteristics were that the Sikhs not only lapsed into Hinduism they also converted to Christianity. In the last decades of the nineteenth century they were also preached to by missionaries of the conservative Hindu Arya Samaj reform movement. The latter, however, had less success than they might have had. Their founder Dayananda was welcomed by some Sikh leaders, and Lahore came to eclipse Bombay as the main centre of the movement, but in 1888 some Arya Samaj leaders spoke against the Ten Gurus and tenets of the Sikh faith and Sikhs withdrew from the organisation.

The first Sikh reform movement preceded the annexation. In 1853 the annual report of the Lodiana (Ludhiana) Mission referred to a religious sect which had already been in existence for eight or nine years 'but during the Sikh reign, fear kept them quiet'. It goes on to give this description of them:

> They professedly reject idolatry and all reverence and respect for whatever is held sacred by Sikhs or Hindus except Nanak and his Granth. The Hindus complain that they even abuse the cow. . . . They are called Nirankaris from their belief in God, as a spirit without physical form. The next great fundamental principle of their religion is, that salvation is to be obtained by meditation on God. They regard Nanak as their saviour, in as much as he taught the way of salvation. Of their peculiar practices only two things are learnt. First, they assemble every morning for worship, which consists of bowing the head to the ground before the Granth, making offerings and in hearing the Granth read by one of their members, and explained also if their leader be present. Second, they do not burn their dead because that would assimilate them to the Hindus; nor bury them, because that would make them too much like Christians and Musalmans, but throw them into the river. (Quoted, *Punjab Past and Present* April 1973, pp. 1 and 2)

Baba Dayal (1783–1854) was the founder of this movement. Though he was born at Peshawar and died at Rawalpindi the census figures for 1891 registered 8,703 of his disciples at Amritsar, 2,358 at Patiala and 1,268 at Ambala, an indication that by no means all the 60,000 followers were confined to the western Punjab. The enlightenment of Baba Dayal took place when he was only eighteen years old. One day when he was waving the chauri over the Guru Granth Sahib he went into deep meditation and heard a voice saying

'Give up this ritualistic practice. You have been commissioned to expel the darkness of ignorance, superstition and falsehood from the minds of the people; illuminate their path by the true spiritual knowledge, propagate meditation of Nam-Nirankar. . . . You are a true Nirankari as you are a believer of God as spirit, without bodily form.'

The slogan of his mission, which often provoked considerable opposition, was 'Jappo piario dhann Nirankar. Jo deh dhari sab khuar', 'All glory to the Formless One, god corporeal you must shun.' During the reign of Maharaja Ranjit Singh the Nirankari movement met strong opposition because it was a threat to the religious harmony and tolerance which the ruler treasured. When Christian and Arya Samajist agitators entered the Punjab it became popular, being seen as a parallel but indigenous agent of reformation. Many gurdwaras were purged of Hindu practices which had crept into their worship but its main lasting contribution was to win acceptance for Anand marriage, the practice of being married in the presence of the Guru Granth Sahib to the singing of the Lavan of Guru Amar Das. Nirankaris are often called Nanak panthis because they reject the institution of the Khalsa, which they regard as an accretion introduced by the Tenth Guru. Their headquarters was Dyal Sar near Peshawar. At partition in 1947 they lost access to it and the Nirankaris as a separate group have now almost disappeared, being reabsorbed into the Sikh fold.

The second reform movement of this period still maintains its distinctiveness. This group is called the Namdharis, from the insistence which their most famous teacher Baba Ram Singh placed upon the practice of Nam. The name was introduced by Ram Singh himself. Kuka (Shouter) is another name they have been given because their acts of worship often resulted in states of ecstasy in which they would dance and cry out (kuk). The movement came to prominence under Baba Ram Singh (1816–84) who was as much a social reformer as a leader who, like Baba Dayal, wished to purge Sikhism of non-Sikh religious practices. Especially strong was his rejection of purdah, girl infanticide, child marriage, the financial basis of arranged marriages, and his support for the right of widows to remarry. In his congregation men and women worshipped together. He encouraged the use of a white woollen mala (rosary) in meditation and his male followers adopted a white sidhi pag, straight turban, laid flat across the front of the head. Baba Ram Singh also encouraged vegetarianism and forbade alcohol or drug taking. A strong and important reform movement, it eventually acquired a political characteristic, by accident rather than design. A group of Kukas attacked and killed the butchers of Amritsar who had provocatively set up a slaughter house near the Lahori Gate. Some butchers were killed. When Baba Ram Singh heard of the incident and that innocent people had been arrested he summoned the men to him and told them, 'Go to the court and confess your guilt so that the innocent may be saved.' This they did and were executed. A second incident took place at Raikot in the Ludhiana district in July 1871, but the final act was the attack on a slaughter house at Maler Kotla on 15 January 1872 by about 125 Namdharis. Many of them were caught and arrested and 65 men were blown to pieces by being tied to the mouth of canons. Although Baba Ram Singh was not implicated he was deported to Rangoon. Unfortunately the authority of the Akal Takht was used to denounce the Namdharis as non-Sikhs and the opportunity to prevent the movement acquiring permanence was lost. Kukas were regarded as members of an illegal organisation until 1922 when they were recognised by the government in order to play them off against orthodox Sikhs in the struggle for gurdwara control. In the meantime, however, the Namdharis had acquired two characteristics. First they had developed a consciousness of themselves as part of the Indian independence movement. The Maler Kotla Namdharis were the first large group of Indians to be executed by the British after 1857 and the British had exiled their leader. Second, they developed an alternative theory of guruship to that of the Ten Gurus and the Guru Granth Sahib. Namdharis believe that Guru Gobind Singh did not die at Nander but became a recluse. He eventually installed Baba Balak Singh as Guru and in 1841 Ram Singh came under his influence. In 1862 Ram Singh became the Twelfth Guru. Kukas believe that Guru Ram Singh still lives and will one day reappear. Meanwhile, first his brother Hari Singh, then his nephew, Partap Singh, from 1906 to 1959 became viceregent Guru. In 1959 his son, the present Guru, Jagjit Singh, was installed as leader of the movement. Baba Ram Singh was a Ramgarhia and it is among this social group that most Namdharis are to be found. They are hospitable people but refuse food which has been prepared by anyone who is not a Namdhari. They do sometimes intermarry with orthodox Sikh families but their place within the Sikh community is ambiguous. Their reforming heritage wins respect and ties of kinship still bind many of them to the larger Sikh community. However, they not only reject the authority of the Guru Granth Sahib, they believe in a living Guru who, though he is happy to be described as the 'viceregent' of Guru Ram Singh, is nevertheless spiritual head of something like 700,000 followers. Their places of worship are called dharmsalas, the word gurdwara being reserved for a building actually visited by one of the Gurus.

We have not discussed the Radhasoami movement in this book because it is not part of Sikhism. However, some of the Association's leaders have been Sikhs and this has clearly influenced its theology. The similarities and differences can be observed from reading Philip H. Ashby's chapter on the Radhasoami Satsang in *Modern Trends in Hinduism*, Columbia University Press, 1974, in conjunction with this present volume.

The concern of the Nirankaris and Namdharis was primarily with practical issues but the method of Christians and Arya Samajists was often to appeal to the mind. The Sikh reaction to this threat came in the form of the Singh Sabha Movement, named after the society (sabha) which was formed in 1873 at Amritsar. This long overdue response was provoked by the decision of four Sikh students at Amritsar Mission College to be baptised into the Christian faith and by Sharda Ram Phillauri's writings and lectures on Sikhism which misrepresented the teachings of the Gurus. In 1879 another Singh Sabha was founded at Lahore and attempts were made to unite the two Sabhas. This failed initially because Lahore stood for radicalism, for example the opening of gurdwaras to Untouchables at all times, whilst the Amritsar group was more conservative. In effect the Lahore group was nearer to the principles of the Gurus than the conservatives. However, the growing success of the Arya Samaj movement brought the two together again, this time in the successful attempt to found an educational establishment, the Khalsa College, Amritsar, in 1892. The aims of the society were to restore Sikhism to its original purity as seen in the Khalsa ideal; to promote education; to publish books and periodicals on Sikhism; and to win the support of the English for these aims. The governor of the Punjab, Sir Robert Egerton, became the movement's patron and the viceroy, Lord Lansdowne, gave his support. The Sikhs were still under suspicion – the Singh Sabha movement began only a year after the Maler Kotla disturbance – and they wished to emphasise their loyalty to the crown. This was almost taken to a ridiculous length in the suggestion that the new college should be called the Loyal Lyall Khalsa College. (Sir James Lyall was the governor who in 1892 laid the foundation stone. He himself seems to have been responsible for averting the catastrophe.) Its first principal was an Englishman. The Singh Sabha movement's interest developed in two other directions. At village level it copied the Arya Samajists who sent teams to recall the peasantry to the pure Hindu faith. This quickly highlighted the fact that many gurdwaras were now in the hands of non-Sikhs. Reform could not proceed very far if some of the most important shrines were in the possession of Hindus. In 1905 the reformers succeeded in removing Hindu statues from the precincts of the Golden Temple. Whilst on the one hand, therefore, Sikhs founded the political Chief Khalsa Diwan in 1902, to 'cultivate loyalty to the crown', a grassroots movement was developing which would jeopardise this loyalty. The First World War pushed the struggle into the background, but in 1920 a proclamation was made from the Akal Takht, Amritsar, that a committee was to be set up to manage all Sikh shrines. This was known as the Shiromani Gurdwara Parbandhak Committee (Central Gurdwara Management Committee), usually referred to by its initials SGPC. Sikhs organised themselves into a volunteer brigade, the Akali Dal (army of immortals) dedicated to wrestling gurdwaras from their custodians (mahants). The recruitment of nihangs, men dressed in blue, heavily armed and sworn to defend gurdwaras to the death, increased. A class of men who had been left over from the eighteenth century once more assumed relevance. There were clashes with the army. The Akali Dal was declared illegal but in 1925 the Sikh Gurdwaras Act was passed. This listed the gurdwaras and placed them in the custody of the SGPC and locally elected committees. It also defined a Sikh as 'one who believes in the ten Gurus and the Granth Sahib and is not a patit [apostate]'. Eventually a separation in function and interest developed and the Akali movement became a political party in the Punjab whilst the SGPC confined itself to religious and educational matters. Its membership has, however, been dominated by the Akali Party.

The Sikh renaissance followed the reformation which began with the Nirankaris and Namdharis and culminated in the Gurdwara Act. It owes much to the consequences of independence. In 1947 the Punjab was partitioned and with this event came the movement of some two and a half million Sikhs into India from those areas which had become part of Pakistan. Hopes of an independent Sikh state were finally dashed, but the special needs of Sikhs were recognised by the central government, especially after the political successes of the Akali Dal in defeating the Congress Party in the Punjab. In 1962 the Punjabi University was established at Patiala and similar institutions have been set up at Chandigarh and Amritsar. As the Secondary Sources section shows, beginning with the *Spokesman* and the *Sikh Review* there has been a steady growth of journals and books about Sikhism written in English. The Punjabi-based renaissance has given way to one in which Sikhism has become conscious of itself as a world faith which is prepared to express itself in English. The process has been hesitant. Ernest Trumpp did not endear himself to the Sikhs by his arrogance and the slighting remarks which prefaced his translation of part of the Adi Granth 100 years ago. M. A. Macauliffe worked on a translation of the Adi Granth with the help of Sikh scholars from 1893 to 1909 and completed it to the satisfaction of many. However, conservatives said that an English translation would.be an act of desecration. It would be carried around like any other book and treated without respect. M. A. Macauliffe had to be satisfied with publishing his monumental *Sikh Religion* (1909) instead. The government which had promised him a grant of 15,000 rupees decided to pay him only one third of that amount, and a session of the Sikh Educational Conference meeting at Rawalpindi not only paid him the uncharacteristic discourtesy of not meeting him at the railway station, it also refused to pass a resolution recommending that his work was worthy of Sikh consideration. Only after his death, four years later, did the Educational Conference pass a resolution of appreciation.

Times have changed. The problem of conservatives is no longer whether the Adi Granth should be translated into English but what the parameters of criticism and analysis should be. Western-style biblical critical methods applied to the janam sakhis by Hew McLeod (McLeod, 1968) were not received with universal enthusiasm. More recently Dr Fauja Singh's article, 'Execution of Guru Tegh Bahadur' (*Sikh Review*, January 1976), in which he raised questions about traditional views in a moderate tone, has raised a storm of protest in the *Spokesman* as well as the *Review*. However, such a price Sikhism must be prepared to pay if it wishes to be regarded as a world faith worthy of serious study in New Zealand, Britain and the USA as well as the Punjab.

Sikhism has become a world faith in a geographical sense. Sikhs are now to be found world-wide. The very different developments in the USA and the UK demand particular consideration though Sikhs are also to be found in many parts of Australia, South-east Asia, Africa and Canada.

Canada and the USA

Early migration from the Punjab was to other parts of India, but by 1904 the census of British Columbia disclosed the presence of 258 'Hindus' in that province of Canada. Most, if not all of them, were probably Sikh. Though easily discernible by their turbans, statistically Sikh migrants have seldom been distinguished from Hindus and in fact the UK census figures put together all people of Indian origin, though perhaps 80 per cent of these are Sikhs. By 1905 there were racists in Vancouver protesting against 'oriental grasp and greed' and voicing the slogan 'white Canada for ever'. At this time also Sikhs, as well as Chinese and Japanese, were settling in California and others were providing a middle class in East Africa.

American Sikhism is currently being influenced by a movement which is too recent for it to be analysed or critically assessed. In January 1969 Harbhajan Singh Puri began to teach yoga at West San Gabriel Valley YMCA, Los Angeles. Since then the popularity of his movement, known as 3HO (Healthy, Happy,

Holy Organisation), has steadily grown and Yogi Bhajan, as he is affectionately called, has become a popular figure. In November 1969 the first converts were initiated into the Sikh faith and there have been other conversions since. America being a byword for novelty, experiment and superficiality, some Sikhs have been cautiously sceptical of the Yogi Bhajan's work. However, the teacher seems to enjoy good relations with Sikh gurdwaras in the USA and one Sikh scholar who recently returned from America concluded his survey thus: 'By the end of 1975, 3HO was a huge organisation with over 110 centres and 250,000 people involved in its various activities and programmes. The growth of 3HO represents the course of the Sikh Renaissance in the Western Hemisphere' (Dr G. S. Mansukhani, Baisakhi Number, *Spokesman*, 1976, p. 22).

Statistical information about the number of Sikhs in Canada and the USA does not exist. It is estimated that there are about 100,000 practising Sikhs of Indian origin in each country. After the initial influx before the First World War few Indians entered Canada until 1953, when a liberal immigration policy attracted them. Anyone who obtained employment could easily obtain permission to stay. In the 1970s a policy change, requiring entry permits, has reduced the number of Sikhs entering Canada. Sikhs are mainly to be found in Vancouver (which has five gurdwaras and perhaps half the total Sikh population), Toronto, Ottawa, Montreal, Edmonton and Calgary. Many of the post-1953 arrivals have come from Britain or East Africa. Business, banking and, in British Columbia, the timber trade, provide the chief means of livelihood.

Stockton, El Centro and Yuba City in California were among the earliest Sikh settlements in the USA. In California many Sikhs are farmers in climatic conditions reminiscent of the Punjab. Other cities such as Washington and New York also have Sikh populations, but the main concentration is along the west coast.

Britain

Rather different but no less influential is the settlement of Sikhs in Britain. Most of them came from the Punjab, but a large minority entered Britain from East Africa. The total Sikh population of the UK is about a quarter of a million and it is distributed among most of the major industrial cities, especially London (Ealing and Southall), Birmingham and the surrounding towns, Leicester and west Yorkshire (Leeds, Bradford and Huddersfield). There are at present over fifty gurdwaras in England, three in Scotland (two in Glasgow, one in Edinburgh) and one in Wales (Cardiff). A survey of Sikh distribution, like that of other Asians as well as West Indians and East Europeans, shows that they settled in areas where there was a shortage of labour, not in districts of considerable unemployment. Though some Sikhs entered Britain between the wars, and the first gurdwara was opened in Putney in 1911, most Sikhs came to Britain in the 1950s or early 1960s. The majority originated from a small area between the rivers Beas and Sutlej called the Jullundur Doab. Their reasons for coming to Britain were economic and many of them quickly fell victim to a rumour that unless they shaved their beards, cut their hair and discarded their turbans they would not find work. This was a mistake, for the Sikhs had won respect in two world wars and once they shed their distinguishing external characteristics they became part of the general classification 'Paki', meaning Pakistani but popularly used even of West Indians!

This largest Sikh population outside India has established itself successfully in Britain. Its numbers include a High Court Judge, JPs and city councillors but as yet no Members of Parliament. In fact the politics of the Punjab often seem to an outsider to occupy Sikhs more than the politics of their new homeland. At present British Sikhs have not finally decided that their residence in Britain is permanent. There is a natural longing for the Punjab, but their children, born in Britain, speaking poor Punjabi and often not being able to read it, are likely to compel most Sikhs to root themselves emotionally to a new homeland. Being adaptable, Sikhs who were often landowners in the Punjab have become labourers, skilled workmen or business men in Britain, often owning their own garages, warehouses or shops.

Sometimes Sikhs have encountered difficulties, and occasionally anomalies occur as when one meets a Sister Singh working in a hospital, or even a Mr Kaur! (Presumably official documents showed the 'surname' of their next of kin to be Singh or Kaur and bureaucracy therefore created an absurdity.) Sometimes the disposal of the dead has also caused anxiety. After cremation the ashes should be thrown into a river but this practice is forbidden in Britain. Provision has been made in London by two boat firms for families to take the ashes out to the open sea (*Community Relations Commission News*, July/August 1971), but often they are flown back to India. The turban issue has attracted more public attention than any other, but the right of Sikhs to wear it instead of regulation caps seems to have been acknowledged and the Sikhs have been exempted from wearing crash helmets when riding motor bikes so long as they wear turbans. In other matters of religious observance – worshipping at the gurdwara or celebrating gurpurbs – there has been a general shift to Sunday as the day for the main service, though many elderly Sikhs gather each evening in the gurdwara to sing kirtan. The gurdwara has often become a social centre to a greater extent than it ever was in the Punjab; on the other hand, for climatic reasons and perhaps as a response to the 'British way of life', open-air processions seldom take place. When the Guru Granth Sahib is moved from the gurdwara to someone's home for an akhand path it travels by car.

The future of Sikhs in Britain cannot be predicted with any ease. The community has a strong sense of identity and the signs indicate that it will keep its distinctiveness. Marriages are still often arranged between the Punjab and Britain, and whilst this may result in east-west tension as boy or girl from the Punjab settles down with someone born and educated in Britain, it can also encourage the conservation of Sikh values. As a general rule it may be said that gurdwaras have not yet addressed themselves to difficulties of Sikh children born in Britain and speaking little Punjabi. Manjit Kaur, a well-known convert and ardent worker, has conducted services in English for a number of years and many gurdwaras hold Punjabi classes, but less than a quarter of the children passing through the British education system attend them and the next generation of Sikhs will, for the most part, find worship literally meaningless. Eventually, Sikhs will have to decide at a practical level whether English or Punjabi is to be the language of worship. So far they have expected children to master Punjabi, quite properly recognising the historic relationship between language and culture, but one day in the fairly near future they must decide whether or not to use English as a medium for preaching and teaching if not singing kirtan. The bilingual gurdwara may be the trend of the future; otherwise Sikhism will prove itself to be the ethnic religion that Ismail Ragi al Faruqi has stated it to be in his *Historical Atlas of the Religions of the World* (Collier-Macmillan, 1974).

India

The Sikh homeland is still the Punjab. In 1947 this term changed its meaning, so far as Sikhs were concerned. Hitherto it had referred to the geographical region of north-west India stretching from Peshawar almost to Delhi. Now it was a state only a third of that size in the newly independent India. Into it poured Sikhs from what is now Pakistan, over two million of them. Not all of them could be settled in the Punjab, where they might have been landless and would have been in competition with the already established, economically successful population. Many went to Delhi which by 1971 had a population of 291,123 Sikhs, the largest community anywhere in the world outside the Punjab. The population of Delhi is 7·16 per cent Sikh compared with the national Indian percentage of 1·89. Other states with large Sikh minorities are Haryana (631,048), Uttar Pradesh (369,673), Maharashtra (101,762), and Jammu and Kashmir (105,873). The Punjab still has by far the highest number of Sikhs (8,159,972), but there are now over two million living elsewhere in India.

If a social survey of Sikhs in India were undertaken it would describe the way in which Sikhs who have moved away from the Punjab and adjacent areas have often abandoned farming for town life and the occupations which go with it, becoming skilled electricians, masons, carpenters, business men, teachers, doctors, social workers and government employees. The army and police force have always attracted Sikh recruits. Many recent migrants from the Punjab are simply examples of the Indian movement from countryside to town. Those over the age of forty probably represent the dispossessed refugees of 1947. Bombay, Cawnpore, Lucknow, Calcutta, Ranchi and Dhanbad are the cities, other than Delhi and Chandigarh, in which many Sikhs are to be found.

Caste

The place of caste in Sikhism is a matter of dispute. In Britain there are gurdwaras which are under the effective control of particular groups – Jat, Ramgarhia or Battra. There are also examples of marriages in which caste plays a minor part or none at all. There are no reliable statistics for the caste distribution of Sikhs, but early census figures (1881 and 1891) showed a preponderance of Jats (farmers) followed by Ramgarhias, a skilled craftsman, artesan group. In 1891 these numbered 134,000 against a Jat total of over one million. Khsatriya and Arora, though higher than Jats or Ramgarhias socially, numbered 52,000 and 60,000 respectively. It would be wrong to regard social considerations as paramount when judging the influence of particular castes. Whatever the power of the Jats militarily during the time of the Gurus and in the eighteenth century, individuals from every stratum of the community have been able to contribute to Sikh life and thought. It is in marriage relationships that caste is seen to be most important, especially in Britain, but doubtless in many Indian villages community politics is dominated by the majority caste group.

Conclusion

As Appendix 3 shows, Sikhism has done more than hold its own in India during the twentieth century. The Sikhs of the dispersion even now would probably add only another 600,000 or 700,000 to the population of India. Sikhism is not a missionary faith; its mission is to proclaim the truth but not to seek converts. Where there are missionary societies their aim is to call Sikhs back to their faith. In Britain and East Africa Sant Puran Singh, for example, has been responsible for thousands of patit Sikhs renewing their vows in the amrit ceremony.

What the future holds for any religion or political philosophy no one can guess. We can only conclude this survey of Sikhism by observing the current strength of Sikh identity. Educational institutions, hospitals and social relief centres named after the Gurus are flourishing in India; the quincentenary of Guru Nanak (1969), with the tercentenaries of Guru Gobind Singh (1966) and Guru Tegh Bahadur (1975), have stimulated conferences and publication. Books on world religions now tend to include some mention of Sikhism and interest seems to be growing. All this means is that Sikhism is flourishing in the eyes of India and the world. The health of the faith deep down cannot be as easily discerned. Time alone can tell what the lasting quality and worth of the current renaissance will be.

Rehat Maryada (a guide to the Sikh way of life)

The Gurdwara Act of 1925 placed the management of Sikh shrines in the hands of the Shiromani Gurdwara Parbandhak Committee (SGPC). As a result it found itself in the position of having to define belief and practice, as there had been no uniformity in these matters for 200 years, during which many Hindu rituals had crept into Sikh worship. In 1931 a meeting was held at the Akal Takht, Amritsar, and it was decided to draw up a code to regulate individual and corporate life. The views of all prominent scholars and associations were canvassed. Teja Singh (convenor), Jodh Singh and Sher Singh, whose writings are mentioned in the section on sources, were three of the scholars; three others who should be named were Bhai Kahan Singh who had assisted M. A. Macauliffe, Bhai Vir Singh the poet and Ganga Singh of the Sikh Shahid Missionary College, Amritsar. Overseas Sikhs in Stockton USA provided responses as well as those nearer home in Burma, Malaya, Karachi and Calcutta. On 3 February 1945 the 'Rehat Maryada' was approved by SGPC. The result strongly reflects the influence of the Singh Sabha and Akali movements of the early twentieth century. The following is a translation of the SGPC document. Words enclosed in square brackets indicate additions by the present authors.

Introduction

DEFINITION OF A SIKH

A Sikh is any person whose faith is in one God, the Ten Gurus and their teaching and the Adi Granth. In addition he or she must believe in the necessity and importance of amrit (initiation) and must not adhere to any other religion.

Sikhism is concerned with individual life and corporate life as a member of the Sikh community.

SECTION ONE

Individual life

The individual Sikh should,
I Be constant in studying the scriptures and meditating upon God.
II Live according to the Gurus' teachings.
III Be active in serving the community (sewa).

I Study of the scriptures and meditation on God

1 A Sikh should rise early, take a bath and then meditate on the one true God.
2 The following hymns should be read or recited daily:
  (a) Japji Sahib.
  (b) Jap Sahib and Ten Swayyas of Guru Gobind Singh. } Early morning.
  (c) Sodar, Rahiras (evening prayer).
  (d) Sohilla (late evening prayer said before retiring).
3 The Ardas [see Appendix 2] should be offered regularly.
4 Every Sikh should participate in congregational worship.

THE GURDWARA

Studying and meditating upon the scriptures as part of the congregation is very important, therefore Sikhs should visit the gurdwara as often as possible.

The Adi Granth should be opened each day for people to read but it should not be left open at night unless it is still being read.

The Adi Granth is usually closed after the Rahiras but may be kept open as long as the granthi or any other true Sikh is present to ensure that it will not be handled irreverently.

The Adi Granth should be opened, read and closed reverently. It should be placed in an elevated position on a form or stool (manji) in a clean place. It should be opened carefully. Small cushions should be used to support it and a romalla [square of cloth] used to cover it between readings whilst it is open. An awning (chanini) should be erected over the Adi Granth and a chauri should be available for waving over the Book.

No articles other than those mentioned above should be used. Rituals derived from other religions, such as the ceremonial use of lamps or fire, the burning of joss sticks, worship with lamps (aarti) and the ceremonial ringing of bells is strictly forbidden. Candles or ghee lamps may be used to give light and joss sticks or flowers allowed in order to purify the air.

No book should be given the same reverence as the Adi Granth in the gurdwara and no secular event should be held there. The gurdwara may be used for any gathering whose purpose is the encouragement of religion.

Such practices as touching the nose or forehead against the manji on which the Adi Granth is placed or placing a jug of water under it [a vessel of water is often used by Hindus to ward off evil], worshipping statues or even bowing to pictures of the Gurus are strictly forbidden.

Ardas should be offered before the Adi Granth is moved from one place to another. A person who carries the Adi Granth should walk barefoot but shoes may be worn if circumstances make it desirable. When it is installed elsewhere Ardas should be said before the Book is opened and consulted.

After Ardas has been offered a passage from the Adi Granth should be selected at random and read out [this is called a hukam].

Whenever another copy of the Adi Granth is brought into the gurdwara everyone present should stand up as an act of respect.

People should take off their shoes before entering a gurdwara and should wash their feet if they are dirty.

If anyone walks around the Adi Granth or the gurdwara it should be in a clockwise direction.

A gurdwara is open to anyone regardless of caste or creed providing they are not carrying tobacco or anything else which is specifically forbidden by the Sikh religion.

After paying homage to the Adi Granth a Sikh should quietly greet the congregation with the words 'Waheguru ji ka Khalsa, sri Waheguru ji ki fatch' ('The Khalsa owes allegiance to God, sovereignty belongs to God alone') and then take his place in the congregation.

In the congregation there should be no distinction of social status or caste or between Sikh and non-Sikh.

Sitting on special cushions, chairs, couches or sofas or in any other way demonstrating social distinction or superiority whilst in the congregation is deemed contrary to Sikhism.

No one should sit bareheaded in the congregation or when the Adi Granth is open. It is contrary to Sikh belief for women to veil their faces.

The four seats of religious authority are:

Sri Akal Takht Sahib, Amritsar,
Takht Sri Patna Sahib, Patna,
Takht Sri Keshgarh Sahib, Anandpur,
Takht Sri Hazur Sahib, Nander.

Only Sikhs who have taken amrit and who possess the Five K's may enter certain parts of the Takhts. With the exception of patit [lapsed] or tankahia [lapsed Sikhs under penance] anyone may ask for prayers to be offered.

The flag (nishan sahib) should be flown prominently from every gurdwara. Its colour should be saffron or blue and it should bear the distinctive symbols of Sikhism incorporating the khanda [double-edged sword].

A large kettledrum should be kept in the gurdwara and beaten at appropriate times [e.g. when langar is ready].

KIRTAN [THE PRAISE OF GOD]

Kirtan consists of singing hymns from the scriptures.

Only a Sikh can perform kirtan in the congregation.

Kirtan consists of musical arrangements of the hymns of the Gurus or the explanations of the Guru's instruction by Bhai Nandlal or Bhai Gurdas.

No additions or subtractions to the original words should be made in the course of producing musical arrangements.

To show respect to the Adi Granth and the congregation is proper, to read the Adi Granth or hear it read is the same as being in the presence of the Sat Guru. However, merely to open the Book and glance at it is meaningless.

Only one expression of worship should take place at a time, be it the singing of hymns, reading the scriptures, listening to sermons or to lectures.

Whoever sits in attendance of the Adi Granth during a service (diwan) must be a Sikh.

Only a Sikh may read the Adi Granth during diwan but anyone may read or sing them elsewhere at other times.

The Adi Granth is frequently used to take advice (vak) from a page chosen at random. When this is done the lesson chosen is at the top of the left-hand page. If this portion begins on the previous page the reading should begin there.

If a Var [ode] has been selected the whole pauri [stanza], including sloks [couplets], should be read as far as the sentence which ends with the word 'Nanak'.

Random readings (vaks) as described above should be used to end a service after the offering of Ardas.

SIDHARAN PATH [NORMAL READING OF THE ADI GRANTH]

Every Sikh should attempt to maintain a place at home where the Adi Granth can be installed and read.

Every Sikh should learn Gurmukhi to be able to read the Adi Granth.

Every Sikh should read a lesson [hukam] from the Adi Granth before taking a morning meal. However, when this is not possible the reading should be done later. If this requirement cannot be met and the Adi Granth cannot be consulted, perhaps during a long journey, there should be no feeling of guilt.

It is desirable that over a period of time a Sikh should read the Adi Granth from beginning to end.

Before embarking upon a new reading of the Adi Granth the first five and the last verse of the Anand Sahib should be read, then Ardas and the taking of a vak, then the new reading should begin with the Japji Sahib.

AKHAND PATH [UNINTERRUPTED COMPLETE READING OF THE ADI GRANTH]

Akhand paths are undertaken on special occasions of joy, sorrow or distress. The complete reading is carried out by a relay of Sikhs and takes approximately forty-eight hours. The reading should be clear, audible, accurate and not too fast so that it can be understood easily.

Anyone who asks for an akhand path or arranges one should try to ensure that the reading is carried out by himself, his family or his friends. If such a person cannot help with the reading he should listen to it for as long as possible. It is wrong for someone to ask for an akhand path and not be prepared either to read or to listen. Those who are invited to assist with the reading may be given food or sustenance according to the means of the person arranging the akhand path. There is no regulation governing either the minimum or maximum number of participants in an akhand path.

No other book may be read during an akhand path or sidharan path [sometimes people read the Japji continuously during a path, this practice is forbidden]. No jug of water, coconut or ghee lamp should be placed near the Adi Granth.

Before commencing any path karah parshad should be prepared then the first five and the final verse of the Anand Sahib should be read followed by Ardas and a hukam. This should be followed by the distribution of karah parshad to the congregation after which the path may begin.

A path should be concluded by reading the mundavani, and, if that is the tradition of the local congregation, Rag Mala. The usual verses of the Anand Sahib are then read followed by Ardas and a hukam. After a path karah parshad is distributed to the congregation.

At the time of an akhand path it is customary to give a romalla, a chauri or a chanini [cloth canopy with fringes for the Adi Granth] and a donation for the upkeep of the gurdwara and the support of Sikhism. The size of the gift should be related to one's means.

KARAH PARSHAD

It is made from plain flour cooked with equal quantities of ghee and sugar. Hymns should be sung during its preparation. When it is ready the karah parshad should be placed on a small stool near the Adi Granth The customary verses of the Anand Sahib should then be spoken clearly followed by the Ardas and a hukam. A kirpan should then be used to touch the karah parshad. The first five portions should be given to Khalsa members in memory of the panj pyares. The person behind the Guru Granth Sahib should be given his portion on a plate so that he can eat it when he has completed his service.

Karah parshad may be prepared at the gurdwara or at home and then offered to the gurdwara which must accept it and distribute it. A small amount of money should be offered at the same time.

No favouritism or greed should be demonstrated in distributing or receiving karah parshad.

KETHA [DISCOURSE BASED UPON THE GURUS' TEACHINGS]

A ketha should only be given to the congregation by a practising Sikh. It should be based upon the gurbani, the teaching of the Tenth Guru or the explanations given by Bhai Gurdas and Bhai Nandlal. Other books may be used to illustrate the talk.

LECTURES

No lecture which contradicts the tenets of Sikhism may be given in a gurdwara.

LITURGY

There is no stipulated liturgy. Diwan should consist of opening the Adi Granth, reading from it, singing kirtan, explaining the gurbani, discourses, customary passages from the Anand Sahib, Ardas, the Fateh [the Fateh is the cry 'Jo bole so nihal' (whosoever knows he is blessed should say') – followed by the reply 'Sat sri akal!' ('the immortal Lord is true')] and a hukam.

II Living according to the Gurus' teachings

A Sikh's life and work should be based upon the principles of Sikhism. They should be guided by the following:

He should be a monotheist and should not take part in any form of idolatry.

To attain liberation he should live a life based on the Gurus' teaching and the Adi Granth.

Sikhs should believe in the unity of the Ten Gurus, that is that a single soul existed in the bodies of the Ten Gurus.

A Sikh should have nothing to do with caste, ideas of pollution, black magic, clairvoyance, seeking boons, superstitious practices involving horoscopes, auspicious times, eclipses, full moon ceremonies, havan, jajana, wearing a sacred thread, or a tuft of unshorn hair, shaving the head at birth, putting a tilak on the forehead, using a tulsi mala, fasting, idolatry, praying at the graves of Hindu or Muslim holy men, going to the pilgrimage centres of other faiths and following Hindu funeral rites. The Vedas, shastras, Gayatri Mantra, Bhagavad Gita, Qur'an and Bible may be read with profit and should be respected but faith should be based on the Sikh scriptures.

It is the duty of parents to instruct their children in the faith.

Sikhs should not cut their children's hair. Boys should be given the name Singh and girls the name Kaur.

Sikhs should not take alcohol, drugs such as opium, or other intoxicants, or use tobacco. They should be content with a normal diet.

Sikhism condemns infanticide outright, particularly female infanticide, and Sikhs should have no dealings with any who condone it.

Sikhs should only live on money that has been earned honestly.

Sikhs should give generously to charity. 'A poor man's mouth is the Guru's treasure chest.'

No Sikh should gamble or steal.

Sikhs must not commit adultery.

A Sikh should respect another man's wife as he would his own mother, and another man's daughter as his own daughter.

A man should enjoy his wife's company and women should be loyal to their husbands.

A Sikh should live his life from birth to death according to the Sikh faith.

A Sikh should greet other Sikhs with the salutation, 'Waheguru ji ka Khalsa, sri Waheguru ji ki fateh' (see p. 126).

It is contrary to Sikhism for women to veil themselves.

Any clothing may be worn by a Sikh provided it includes kachcha and, in the case of males, a turban.

BIRTH (JANAM SANSKAR)

[The naming ceremony has been described in the section on family life, p. 112]

Hindu prohibitions against accepting and eating food from the child's family should not be observed. Any food may be eaten at this or any other time.

A romalla should not be taken from the gurdwara and made into a dress for the baby.

MARRIAGE (ANAND SANSKAR)

Caste or status should not have a place in Sikh marriages.

A Sikh's daughter should marry a Sikh.

The marriage rite should be according to the Anand Karaj ceremony.

Child marriages are not permitted. A girl should marry only when she has attained physical and mental maturity.

A formal betrothal is unnecessary but if both parties desire a token betrothal can be made by the girl's parents visiting the boy's parents on a day which has been mutually agreed. In the presence of the Adi Granth after Ardas has been said they should be presented with a kirpan and a kara for their son and a gift of sweets.

A wedding may be celebrated on any mutually acceptable date; looking for auspicious days or using horoscopes is contrary to Sikh belief.

The tying of head bands, feigning sulking or grief, engaging professional dancers, worshipping ancestors, drinking alcohol, burning sacred fires and engaging in other practices derived from other religious traditions is contrary to Sikh belief.

At the time of the marriage, the boy and his family, accompanied by no more friends and relatives than the girl and her family wish, should go to the girl's home, greet her family with the Fateh when they meet and then sing hymns of praise to God.

Neither a girl nor a boy should be married for money. The Anand form of wedding may only be performed when both partners are Sikhs. [Anand karaj as laid down in Rehat Maryada has been described in the section on family life, pp. 114–19.]

Sikhs should not follow the custom of refusing to eat at the home of their married daughter. [This referred to the danger of imposing upon the son-in-law and his family; sometimes this was averted by not visiting his home.]

There is no prohibition against widows or widowers remarrying if they wish. The ceremony should be the same as that of the first marriage.

Married Sikhs who have undergone initiation should encourage their partners to do likewise.

DEATH (MIRTIK SANSKAR)

No rituals derived from other religions or of any other origin should be performed when a death occurs. A dying person should not be taken from his bed and placed on the ground, as is the Hindu custom. No lamps should be burned and there should be no giving of cows. Comfort should be derived from reading the Adi Granth and meditating upon God.

Deliberate exhibitions of grief or mourning such as the beating of breasts or screaming [to frighten away demons] are contrary to Sikh teaching. The bereaved should seek comfort and guidance in the hymns of the Adi Granth and try to accept God's will.

The dead, even one who dies in early infancy, should be cremated. However, if facilities for cremation do not exist any other method of disposal may be used.

Cremation may be carried out at any convenient time, day or night.

The Five K's should be left on the dead body, which should be washed and clothed in clean garments, if possible, before being put in a coffin or placed on a bier.

A close relative should light the pyre and the mourners should sing appropriate hymns from the Adi Granth. [Other details are contained in the chapter on family life, pp. 119–22.]

OTHER OCCASIONS

Apart from the sanskars there are many happy or sad occasions, for example, house-warming, starting a new business, sending the children to school. A Sikh should invoke God in all he does by saying Ardas.

III Active service to the community

Sewa is an important part of Sikh life and the Gurdwara is a school where community service may be learned, for example cleaning it, and carrying out repairs, fanning the congregation, looking after the shoes, giving water to drink and preparing or serving food in the langar. Langar serves a dual purpose, it trains people in sewa and it overcomes caste distinction. It also supplies the needy with food. There should be no privileged seating or priority in feeding people in the langar and no ideas of pollution should be entertained. The emphasis should be upon brotherhood. Sikhs who have taken amrit should not eat with other Sikhs. [The purpose of this was to encourage Sikhs to be initiated.]

SECTION TWO

Panthic [community] discipline

This section relates to the following aspects of Sikhism:
1 The Guru Panth [Sikh community].
2 Amrit sanskar [initiation].
3 Tankhah [act of reinstatement].
4 Gurmatta [decisions on religious issues].
5 Appeals against local decisions.

The Guru Panth

Sewa does not stop at langar or such acts as fanning the congregation. It is best done by collective effort. This organism to which a Sikh belongs is called the Guru Panth. It was given its final shape by Guru Gobind Singh who conferred the status of Guru upon it. Only Sikhs who have been properly initiated and who keep the Five K's may be considered full members of it.

Amrit sanskar [initiation into the Khalsa]

[The regulations covering this rite have been given in the section on family life and practices, pp. 122–9.]

Tankhah [reinstatement procedure for those who have failed to keep the discipline]

Those who have erred or broken their amrit vows should apologise publicly to the congregation and perform whatever act of contrition is suggested by five designated members of the congregation. The penance should not be harsh and should be some act, preferably of a physical nature, which the penitent should perform himself. The task must be accepted cheerfully without question. Ardas should be offered when the nature of the penance has been declared.

Gurmatta [decisions on religious questions]

All decisions affecting the whole community are made by a meeting of the Panth. The decisions are called gurmattas and are taken to clarify and support the fundamental principles of the faith concerning the position of the Gurus, the Adi Granth, purity of ritual and the public organisation. Gurmattas are binding upon all Sikhs. Other questions, such as political, social or educational matters may be settled locally by a matta [resolution].

Appeals against local decisions

These can be made to the Akal Takht.

APPENDIX TWO

Ardas

The practice of meditation, nam simran, is so important in Sikhism, and so much part of the Indian religious tradition, that it is easy to overlook the fact that prayer is also an essential part of Sikh worship. The purpose of this appendix is therefore to act as a reminder and to provide an English version of the prayer which is used wherever the sangat gathers in worship.

The word for prayer is 'ardas'. Its ultimate origin is the Sanskrit root 'ard', to ask or beg; its more immediate source was the Persian 'arzdasht', a petition or address made by an inferior to a superior. At the time when the prayer is offered the whole congregation stands as a sign of respect and humility with palms pressed together in the eastern manner, facing the throne of the Guru Granth Sahib. A member of the congregation, man or woman and of any social status, comes forward to offer the prayer on behalf of the sangat. Guru Amar Das, said 'The Lord is himself, is the one who knows, who acts, and does what is right, So stand before him and make supplication' (AG 1093).

It is not easy to describe the atmosphere as Ardas is being offered. To an observer it seems to be the most sacred part of the service, a few minutes in which past and present and geographical distance become insignificant. The sangat stands in the presence of God as it did when the Gurus led the prayers, and it feels itself surrounded by a mighty cloud of witnesses.

The prayer is in three parts. First the Sikhs are told to remember God and the Gurus in the words taken from the Dasam Granth. Particular mention is made of the boy Guru, Har Krishan, who compensated for his father's sorrow at the inadequacy of Ram Rai and who, though a child, was seen to possess the spirit of guruship by those who visited him in Delhi. During his brief stay there he became known as a healer. The portion attributed to Guru Gobind Singh ends with words of respect for his father Guru Tegh Bahadur. The nine treasures is a phrase frequently used in Hindu writings to describe spiritual and material prosperity.

The congregation is then told to keep the Guru Granth Sahib, the repository of God's word, in mind as being the manifest form of God. They are then instructed to remember the faithfulness of other devout Sikhs. The 'beloved five' are the first Khalsa members who were prepared to give their lives to the Guru. His four sons died in the struggle against tyranny as did many others, particularly forty Sikhs who deserted him at Anandpur but later changed their minds. As they were returning to the Guru they encountered a Mughal force. They fought with it until the last Sikh was struck down. Later the Guru came to the place and found one Sikh alive. The dying soldier asked for forgiveness which the Guru immediately gave and the place, Khidrana, was renamed Muktsar, the place of deliverance. This part of the prayer also remembers many other martyrs of Sikhism and certainly keeps alive the memory of persecution in commending loyalty. The seats of authority are the seats of doctrinal authority held by the granthis of the Akal Takht, Amritsar, Keshgarh Sahib, Anandpur, Patna Sahib gurdwara and Hazur Sahib at Nander near Hyderabad.

The final section of Ardas is supplicatory and God is asked to keep the Khalsa faithful, to bless the whole of mankind, and heed individual petitions. Particular items may be added to this part of the prayer. The sangat may remember its sick or bereaved, or a newly married couple if Ardas is being offered at a wedding service. At the time of writing Nankana Sahib, Guru Nanak's birthplace in Pakistan, is not accessible to Sikh pilgrims and often a petition for the restoration of access is included in Ardas.

The prayer begins with invocation before proceeding to supplication. It reads as follows:

Victory to the one Lord.
May the almighty God protect us.

First remember almighty God, then call to mind Guru Nanak,
Guru Amar Das and Guru Ram Das, may they help us.
Remember Gurus Arjan, Hargobind, Har Rai and Guru
Har Krishan whose sight removes away all sorrows. May
we remember Guru Tegh Bahadur at whose invocation
the nine treasures come hastening to our home. May they
help and protect us at all times. May we always enjoy the
protection of the Tenth Guru, Guru Gobind Singh be
with us always.
Disciples of the Guru meditate on the Guru Granth Sahib,
the visible form of the Guru. Repeat the name of God.
Waheguru!
Think of the glorious deeds of the five beloved ones, the
Guru's four sons, the forty saved ones and others who
were steadfast and long suffering. Remember them, and
call on God.
Waheguru!
Call to mind those who kept the name in their hearts and
shared their earnings with others.
Waheguru!
Those who allowed themselves to be cut limb from limb,
had their scalps scraped off, were broken on the wheel,
were sawn or flayed alive, remember them.
Waheguru!
Think of those who cleansed the gurdwaras, permitted them-
selves to be beaten, imprisoned, shot, maimed or burned
alive with neither resistance nor complaint, and call on
God.
Waheguru!
As you remember the seats of authority and other places
touched by the Gurus' feet, call on God.
Waheguru!
May the whole Khalsa remember the wonderful Lord, and
as it does so may it be blessed.
May his protection be upon all members of the Khalsa
wherever they may be. May his glory be acclaimed and
his way prevail.

May victory attend our charity and our arms. Let us trust
in his grace.

May the Khalsa always be victorious.

May the Sikh choirs, flags and mansions remain forever.

May the kingdom of justice come.

May the Sikhs be united in love and humility, but exalted
in the wisdom of remembering God. O Khalsa, say the
Lord is wonderful.

Waheguru!

O true King and loving Father, we have sung your sweet
hymns, heard your word which gives life and talked of
your many blessings. May these find a place in our hearts
so that our souls may be drawn towards you.

O Father, save us from lust, anger, greed, worldly attachment and pride: keep us always attached to your feet.

Grant to your Sikhs the gift of discipleship, the gift of your
Name, the gift of faith, the gift of discernment, the gift of
reading your word with understanding.

O kind and loving Father, through your mercy we have
passed our days in peace and happiness: grant that we
may be obedient to your will.

Give us light and understanding so that we may please you.

We offer this prayer in your presence, wonderful Lord.

Forgive us our wrong acts, help us to remain pure.

Bring us into the good company of those who love you
and remember your Name.

Through Nanak may the glory of your Name increase and
may the whole world be blessed by your grace.

Waheguru ji ka Khalsa, Waheguru ji ki fateh!

Sikh population statistics

TABLE 3.1 *Sikhs in their total Indian context*

	Punjab	India	Total population of India
1881	1,706,909[1]	1,853,426	253,896,330
1891	1,849,371	1,907,833	287,314,671
1901	2,130,987	2,195,339	294,361,056
1911	2,883,729	3,014,466	315,156,396
1921	3,110,060	3,238,803	318,942,480
1931	4,071,624	4,333,771	352,837,778
1941	5,116,185	5,691,447	388,997,955
1951	After 1947 the	6,219,134[2]	360,950,365[3]
1961	term Punjab	7,845,843	439,072,582
1971	assumes a	10,378,797	548,159,652
	different meaning		
	and the figures		
	cease to be		
	comparable with		
	those of the		
	1881–1941 period.		

1 Including Delhi.
2 Fire destroyed 268,602 enumeration records of the Punjab census.
3 Pakistan had now come into existence, hence the apparent decline in India's population.

Note to Table 3.1

A certain amount of caution must be exercised in using the figures in this table. First there is the meaning of the term 'Punjab'. In 1868 and 1881 the statistics included Sikhs in Delhi. Since 1951 the 'Punjab' denotes one of the states of what is now the Republic of India. More serious is the definition of a Sikh for census purposes. In 1901 and in the earlier censuses of 1891 and 1881 the term Sikh was defined as a person who, 'besides accepting the religious doctrines of the earlier Gurus', wore the long hair (kesh) and refrained from smoking. All Sahajdaris were listed as Hindus in 1881 and 1901. This led to difficulties. Therefore, 'in 1911 the statement of the persons enumerated regarding religion was accepted with question.' This discussion, which may be found in the *Census of India*, 1921, vol. 15, Punjab and Delhi, part I, Report, page 183, goes a considerable way to explaining the steep rise in the number of Sikhs in a ten-year period when the population of India rose by less than 21 millions and that of the Punjab province actually declined. The explanation given in 1921 may be preferred to that contained in the report of 1911, which commented:

> The rate of increase is much too high for the natural development of the population, under the unhygienic conditions which presided during the decade. The gain seems to have occurred mainly by accretions from the Hindus. It has not been possible to ascertain the number of people who have taken the pahul during the last ten years, but the Singh Sabhas have been very active in enforcing the tenets of Guru Gobind Singh on all the followers of Guru Nanak, whether Sikhs or Hindus, and they have been assisted greatly in their efforts by the fact that only Keshdari Sikhs are enlisted in the army.

This statement is correct in that the total numbers registered as Sahajdaris in 1911 was only 310,740, but as the onus of responsibility for declaring a person to be a Hindu or Sikh, Keshdari or Sahajdari, fell upon the head of a family or upon individual members and not upon the returning officer the increase in numbers could be explained by a relaxation of the definition of 'Sikh'. In 1911 there were 9,209 Namdharis (Kukas) included as

Keshdari Sikhs along with Udasis, Nirankaris and Radhasoamis (the latter as Sahajdari Sikhs). The report itself (p. 120) estimates that half a million people registered as Sikhs in 1911 would have been assessed as Hindus in 1901.

The report of 1911 (India, vol. 7, part I, p. 72) also makes the following point: 'The two earlier censuses of 1855 and 1868 did not include the whole Punjab, nor were they very reliable.' Therefore, we have not included statistics from them in this appendix. It also cites one particular province to highlight the problem which existed in the 1881–1911 period:

The difficulty of drawing the line between Sikh and Hindu is well illustrated by the statistics for Sind. In 1881 127,000 persons were returned as Sikhs, in 1891 the number was less than a thousand, in 1901 it was nil, while in 1911 about 12,000 were then returned. These variations are due mainly to differences of opinion as to the correct classification of the followers of Guru Nanak. (*Census of India*, 1911, vol. 1, part I, p. 119)

Until 1911 the opinion referred to would be that of the returning officer. The 1911 solution did not resolve all difficulties – 476,598 people registered themselves as both Hindu and Sikh and were treated as Sikh-Hindus! (*Census of India*, 1931, vol. 17, Punjab, part I, Report, p. 290.)

TABLE 3.2   *Totals per 10,000 of population 1881–1941 in India*

	1881	1891	1901	1911	1921	1931	1941
Hindus	7,432	7,231	7,034	6,931	6,841	6,824	6,593
Muslims	1,974	1,996	2,122	2,126	2,174	2,216	2,381
Christians	73	79	99	124	150	179	163
Jains	48	40	45	40	37	36	37
Sikhs	73	67	75	96	103	124	147

Note to Table 3.2

Here another factor must be considered. In 1931 it became possible for people to register themselves as Ad-Dharmi, 'religion-less' in census terms. Previously members of the depressed

TABLE 3.3 *Census of India, 1931, vol. 17, Punjab, part I, Report, p. 308*

Caste and religion		1881	1891	1901	1911	1921	1931
Jat	(Hindu)	1,445,374	1,697,177	1,539,574	1,000,085	1,046,396	992,309
	(Sikh)	1,122,673	1,116,417	1,388,877	1,617,532	1,822,881	2,133,152
Tarkhan (Carpenter)[1]	(Hindu)	213,070	215,561	233,934	162,305	161,833	146,727
	(Sikh)	113,067	134,110	146,904	180,447	139,327	158,446
Lohar (Blacksmith)	(Hindu)	101,190	110,338	110,816	82,204	83,385	74,463
	(Sikh)	24,361	23,287	30,455	34,862	20,025	16,460
Chuhra (Scavenger)	(Hindu)	613,434	859,571	934,553	777,821	693,393	368,224
	(Sikh)	40,501	90,321	21,673	49,937	40,345	157,341
Darzi (Tailor)	(Hindu)	9,674	10,218	9,680	7,657	8,178	9,823
	(Sikh)	186	660	716	1,406	1,587	3,630
Chamar (Shoemaker)	(Hindu)	931,915	1,029,335	1,089,003	909,499	968,298	684,963
	(Sikh)	100,014	106,328	75,753	164,110	161,862	155,717

1 Among Sikhs this caste is normally called Ramgarhia.

classes who refused to enter a religion, for example Chuhras (scavengers), were included as Hindus. A few Brahmins called themselves Ad-Dharmis in 1931 but the term was usually adopted by members of the depressed classes.

Bearing all these faults in mind, although it is impossible to produce an accurate picture of the growth of Sikhism in India the general impression is clear. A little more detail is provided by Table 3.3 which shows the major castes which have both Sikh and Hindu members and indicates movements in affiliation between 1891 and 1931 when questions about caste membership ceased to be asked.

Note to Table 3.3

Of other castes only Aroras (114,329), Rajputs (52,829) and Sainis (86,688) included appreciable numbers of Sikhs in the 1931 census. It should be noted that the figures

furnish no more than a mere indication of the caste distribution of Sikhs as except in the case of higher castes such as Jat or Rajput, converts to Sikhism do not as a rule return any caste, being content with the entry of 'Sikh' in the column of caste. (*Census of India*, 1931, Part I, Report, p. 308)

The structure of the Guru Granth Sahib

At first glance the structure of the Guru Granth Sahib is extremely complicated but upon analysis the order is logical and fairly simple. The scripture is arranged in subdivisions according to the musical settings to which Guru Arjan set the hymns. There are thirty-one divisions with variant subsections to nine of them. The names of the sections are those of Indian musical arrangements. The organisation of each section is uniform. First come the hymns of Guru Nanak followed by those of the Third, Fourth, Fifth and Ninth Gurus. After these come the verses of Kabir, Farid, Namdev and Ravidas in that order. Table 4.1 indicates where the rags occur in each. It should be noted that pages 1 to 13 contain major hymns used in daily meditation, the Japji followed by Sodar, Sopurkh and Sohilla, which are commonly given the one name Rahiras (or Rachras). These were not set to musical rags.

The total number of hymns attributed to each of these writers is: Guru Nanak 974; Guru Angad 62; Guru Amar Das 907; Guru Ram Das 679; Guru Arjan 2,218; Guru Tegh Bahadur 116; Kabir 541; Farid 116; Namdev 60; Ravidas 41. Slight variations upon these figures may be found in some books as some passages (e.g. the Epilogue of the Jāpji and pages 8 to 13 occur in more than one place and may be counted twice). The Sloks of Farid which are to be found on pages 1377 to 1384

TABLE 4.1 *The structure of the Guru Granth Sahib*

Rag	Guru				IX	Kabir	Farid	Nambev	Ravidas	Pages of Adi Granth
	I	III	IV	V						
1 Sri Rag	✓	✓	✓	✓	✓				✓	14 93
2 Majh Rag	✓	✓	✓	✓						94 150
3 Gauri	✓	✓	✓	✓	✓			✓	✓	151 346¹
4 Asa	✓	✓	✓	✓	✓	✓		✓	✓	347 488
5 Gujri	✓	✓	✓	✓	✓			✓	✓	489 526
6 Devgandhari		✓	✓	✓	✓					527 536
7 Bihagra		✓	✓	✓						537 556
8 Vadhans	✓	✓	✓	✓						557 594
9 Sorath	✓	✓	✓	✓	✓				✓	595 659
10 Dhanasri	✓	✓	✓	✓	✓			✓	✓	660 695
11 Jaitsri	✓	✓	✓	✓	✓				✓	696 710
12 Todi		✓	✓	✓				✓		711 718
13 Bairari		✓	✓	✓						719 720
14 Tilang	✓			✓	✓		✓			721 727

¹ includes one variant Kafi

190

No.	Raga	Pages	Notes
15	Suhi	728 794	includes one variant Lalit
16	Bilawal	795 858	includes one variant Bilawalgaund
17	Gaund	858 875	
18	Ramkali	876 974	includes variant Dakhni
19	Natnarain	975 983	
20	Mali Gaura	984 988	
21	Maru	989 1106	includes variant Dakhni
22	Tukhari	1107 1117	
23	Kedara	1118 1124	
24	Bhairo	1125 1167	
25	Basant	1168 1196	includes variant Hindol
26	Sarang	1197 1253	
27	Malar	1254 1293	
28	Kanara	1294 1318	
29	Kalyan	1319 1326	includes variant Bhopali
30	Prabhati	1327 1351	includes variant Bibhas
31	Jaijawanti	1352 1353	

Guru Angad has written 62 sloks which are scattered over in ten Vars of the Gurus.

1 Variants to Gauri and Guareri, Dakhni, Cheti, Bhairagan, Purbi, Deepki, Majh, Malwa, Mala, Thitti.

191

provide a specific example of the difficulty of enumeration and attribution. Eighteen of the sloks are not his though some authorities assign them to Farid and therefore give the total as 134 hymns (including four sabads found elsewhere). The sloks which are not his are 32, 113, 120 and 124 (Guru Nanak), 13, 52, 104, 122, and 123 (Guru Amar Das), 121 (Guru Ram Das), 75, 82, 83, 105, 108, 109, 110 and 111 (Guru Arjan). His total is 116 hymns, not 134 as given in many books.

From pages 1353 to 1430 the arrangement is different. The compositions are mostly short items which could not be fitted satisfactorily into the major structure. The sections are primarily assembled on the basis of poetic form and are as follows:

AG 1353–60	Slok Sahskriti of Gurus One and Five.
AG 1360–1	Gatha of Guru Arjan
AG 1361–3	Funhe of Guru Arjan

These titles refer to language and poetic form.

AG 1363–4	Chaubole by Guru Arjan, a poem addressed to four persons
AG 1364–77	Sloks of Kabir
AG 1377–84	Sloks of Farid
AG 1385–9	Swayyas of Guru Arjan
AG 1389–1409	Swayyas of the bhatts (musicians) at Guru Arjan's court
AG 1410–26	Sloks of the Gurus
AG 1426–9	Sloks of Guru Tegh Bahadur
AG 1429	two concluding sabads of Guru Arjan called Mundavani (the Seal), explaining the meaning of the Adi Granth
AG 1429–30	Rag Mala. This is an enunciation of Indian ragas, some of which are found in the Adi Granth. It is not considered part of the bani and seldom read. Akhand paths end with Mundavani.

The day may come when scholars will see page numberings of the Adi Granth to indicate the location of a particular reference, until then students will find themselves confronted with such terms as Guru 3, Sloks, Gauri Rag, Fifth Guru or Sloks of Farid. From the two tables in this section it will be possible to find the approximate position of a quotation but we cannot plead too strongly for writers to provide page numberings!

Of the non-Sikh contributors Kabir (1440–1518) is the one who is best known in the west, who stands nearest to Guru Nanak in his teachings and has most sabads included in the Adi Granth (541). He was a member of the weaver (Jullaha) caste which had probably become Muslim by Kabir's time though Islamic thought has little place in his ideas. 'Ram' is a name which he commonly uses to describe God but like Guru Nanak the sant tradition of northern India is his spiritual context rather than Vaishnavism or Islam.

In the seventeenth century there can be no doubt that Ramanand was the most important of pre-Nanak saints, being regarded as the guru not only of Kabir but of Raidas, Sena (Sain), Pipa and Dhanna. These poets, who are also represented in the Adi Granth, are numbered among his twelve most important missionary disciples. However, both Ramanand's original teaching and his biography are now regarded as uncertain. It is suggested that he may have lived in the thirteenth century (born 1299) and not the fifteenth. His links with these low-caste disciples may be evidence of a sixteenth-century attempt to tie these sects into the main stream of Vaishnavite bhakti by giving them a famous Brahmin as their Adi-Guru. Dhanna was a Rajasthani Jat Vaishnavite who wrote in Hindi. Pipa was a Rajput prince who had once been a devotee of Durga. Sena was a Vaishnavite and by employment barber to the raja of Banddgarh. Raidas (also known as Ravidas or Rohidas) was a leather worker (Chamar) who came to be revered as one of the greatest north Indian saints. Forty-one of his hymns are contained in the Guru Granth Sahib; Dhanna has four and the others, including Ramanand, are represented by one each.

Jaidev, the Bengali Brahmin who was Sanskrit poet at the court of a twelfth-century king of Lakshmana, was author of the famous Gita-Govinda. Two of his Hindi poems are contained in the Adi Granth. Sixty of Namdev's hymns were included. He was a tailor by trade and came from Maharasthra. Namdev is usually listed among members of the sant tradition of northern India. The Sindhi, Sadhna, a butcher, and Beni, a Punjabi about whom no other biographical details are known, and Trilochan, a Bombay Vaishya, are the only other Hindu saints whose poems, one and three and four respectively, are contained in the Sikh scriptures.

Mardana, Guru Nanak's companion, is included among the twelve Sikh bards whose total contributions amount to 126 hymns.

One hundred and thirty-four hymns of one Sufi, Sheikh Farid (1173–1265), are found in the Guru Granth Sahib. They present something of a problem because some may be by the famous Chisti's successors rather than the original head of the order's centre at Pak Pattan in the Punjab. 'Farid' was certainly the name of the pir of Pak Pattan when Guru Nanak visited it. All the Sikh Gurus used the word 'O Nanak' in their hymns and were it not for Guru Arjan assigning the various contributions to Nanak 1, Nanak 2, and so on, it would be impossible to distinguish between them. The Farid bani might similarly represent a school rather than an individual.

TABLE 4.2 *Location of the Bhagat Bani in the Adi Granth*

Jai Dev	Rag Gujri – 1 526	
	Rag Maru – 1 1106	2 hymns
Trilochan	Sri Rag – 1 92	
	Gujri – 2 525	4 hymns
	Dhanasri – 1 695	
Sadna	Rag Bilawal – 1 858	
Beni	Sri Rag – 1 93	
	Ramkali – 1 874	3 hymns
	Parbhati – 1 1351	
Ramanand	Rag Basant 1195	1 hymn
Pipa	Rag Dhanasri 695	1 hymn
Sain	Rag Dhanasri 695	1 hymn

TABLE 4.2 *continued*

Dhanna	Asa – 2 Dhanasri – 1 487–8, 695	3 hymns
Bhikhan	Sorath 659	2 hymns
Parmanand	Sarang 1253	1 hymn
Surdas	Sarang 1253	1 hymn
Satta and Balwand	Ramkali 966–8	8 hymns
Sunder	Ramkali Sad 923–4	6 hymns
Mardana	Bihagra 553	3 hymns

Secondary sources and additional bibliography

Secondary sources are listed under particular section headings which correspond to the major interests of this book. However, as we have not attempted to write an historical survey of Sikhism it is necessary to nominate a number of books which fill this intentional gap. Khushwant Singh is the most famous contemporary writer on the subject and his two-volume *History of the Sikhs* (Oxford University Press, 1966) is an essential guide. The interpretation of the Sikh faith which as a synthesis of Hinduism and Islam is open to dispute but that is another matter. A few years earlier he had written *The Sikhs Today* (Orient Longmans, Calcutta, 1959, revised 1967). This useful little book might be revised yet again in the light of the last ten years, and brought up to date. H. R. Gupta's *History of the Sikh Gurus* (U. C. Kapur & Sons, New Delhi, 1973) provides more biographical information about the Gurus than Khushwant Singh does. Other important recent studies of Sikh history are: *A History of the Sikh People, 1469–1708*, Gopal Singh, New Delhi, 1979, and *The Heritage of the Sikhs*, Harbans Singh, Punjabi University, Patiala, 1983. On particular apects of Sikh history, J. S. Grewal has written two important books, *Guru Nanak in History* (Punjab University, Chandigarh, 1969) and *From Guru Nanak to Maharaja Ranjit Singh* (Guru Nanak University, Amritsar, 1972). These analytical studies are supplements to

Khushwant Singh's survey. W. H. McLeod, *The Evolution of the Sikh Community* (Oxford University Press, 1976) projects J.S. Grewal's analysis into the seventeenth and eighteenth centuries in general, in its examination of the Sikh community and its institutions, the Guru Granth Sahib and the janam sakhis. This is a book for the specialist. *The Sikh Religion* by M. A. Macauliffe (Oxford University Press, 1909, reprinted in three volumes in 1963) still deserves mention. It provides comprehensive if uncritical biographies of the Ten Gurus and is the best compendium of the Sikh tradition covering the period 1469–1708.

Biographical studies of the Gurus are often anecdotal. Lacking any scholarly analysis some of them do not even supplant Macauliffe's work of three generations ago! The following are the most important examinations of the life of Guru Nanak: *Life of Guru Nanak Dev* by Kartar Singh (Lahore Book Shop, Ludhiana, 1937, revised 1958). This has been popular among Sikhs and may be regarded as providing the standard portrait. In *Guru Nanak and the Sikh Religion* (Oxford University Press, 1968) W. H. McLeod subjected the janam sakhi traditions to severe historical scrutiny. This piece of research provides a datum line for all future studies and within a year two biographies had been published which gave some consideration to his findings. These were *Guru Nanak and Origins of the Sikh Faith* by Harbans Singh (Asia Publishing House, Bombay, 1969) and *Guru Nanak Founder of Sikhism* by Trilochan Singh (Gurdwara Parbandhak Committee, Delhi, 1969). Both writers feel the necessity to discuss the value of the janam sakhis but Dr Trilochan Singh eventually presents the reader with a considerable, conservative biography of 488 pages. This is well annotated, but as the first edition lacks an index its value as a quarry for discovering what the janam sakhis have to say about the Guru's visits to Mecca or Bengal is sadly diminished in the tedious process of searching for it. It is understood that the second edition will possess an index.

Guru Nanak, His Personality and Vision by G. S. Talib (Gur Das Kapur & Sons, Delhi, 1969) owes its value more to its examination of the Guru's teaching than the attempt to construct a biography. *Guru Nanak and His Times* by A. C. Bannerjee (Punjabi University, Patiala, 1971) is much more interested in placing the Guru within his social, religious and historical context. This is the distinctive and important quality of this book which, with Talib (1969), might provide a bridge between history and the theological works cited below.

The questions which Hew McLeod has posed will not be answered speedily, even if replies can be made. His analysis might now stimulate scholars to examine the janam sakhis as religious rather than historical sources. But it would be a pity if the force of his work was to result in a pursuit of literary, form-critical studies to the exclusion of seeking an understanding of the religion itself.

Only one serious biographical study of the next eight Gurus exists. That is Trilochan Singh's *Guru Tegh Bahadur* (Gurdwara Parbandhak Committee, Delhi, 1967). Sources are fully listed and the footnotes and index make it a valuable aid to study. *Transformation of Sikhism* by G. C. Narang (New Book Society of India, New Delhi, 1960) spans the gap in his discussion of significant episodes in the history of the Guru period.

Guru Gobind Singh Retold by Narain Singh (1966, privately published) and *Guru Gobind Singh* by Kartar Singh (Lahore Bookshop, Ludhiana, 1951) are traditional biographies of the Guru; much more analytical is *Guru Gobind Singh* by J. S. Grewal and S. S. Bal (Punjab University, Chandigarh, 1967).

Sikh theology really means an analysis of the teachings of the Gurus as contained in the Adi Granth and particularly the ideas of Guru Nanak. There has been little development in what might be regarded as the areas of historical or systematic theology. McLeod (1968) contains an important succinct exposition of the major teachings of Guru Nanak which must be added to the contributions of Bannerjee (1971) and Talib (1969) already mentioned. *Guru Nanak and Indian Religious Thought* ed. Taran Singh (Punjabi University, Patiala, 1966) contains essays by Jodh Singh, B. L. Kapur and B. S. Anand which examine the Guru's teaching in the context of Raj-Yoga, Vedanta and other Indian traditions. These essays attempt to show how Guru Nanak rediscovered, reformulated and developed in a distinctive way ancient Indian concepts. Sher Singh, *Philosophy of Sikhism* (Sterling Publishers, Delhi, India, 1966) gave considerable attention to the traditions which may have influenced the Guru. The two books fit usefully together. S. S. Kohli, *Philosophy of*

Guru Nanak (Punjab University, Chandigarh, 1969) considered the main aspects of the Guru's thought and placed it within a world-wide philosophical and religious context, thus supplementing the narrower task he had set himself in *Outlines of Sikh Thought* (Punjabi Prakashak, New Delhi, 1966) which briefly describes such concepts as Brahman (God), jiva (soul) and hukam (divine will). *Guru Nanak and the Logos of Divine Manifestation* by S. C. Varma (Gurdwara Parbandhak Committee, Delhi, 1969) is a rather pretentious volume in both title and appearance but does contain a considerable exposition of the Japji. This important hymn has also been commented upon by Dewan Singh, *Guru Nanak's Message in Japji* (Faqir Singh & Sons, Amritsar, 1970), Harman Singh, *The Japji* (S. Surinder Singh, New Delhi, 1957) and Teja Singh, *The Japji* (Khalsa Brothers, Amritsar, 1964), who has also published a translation, with introduction, of Guru Arjan's important hymn, the Sukhmani, *The Psalm of Peace* (Khalsa Brothers, Amritsar, 1937).

The Guru's quincentenary in 1969 saw the publication of a number of volumes of essays devoted to the teachings of Guru Nanak. These provide useful introductions written by leading scholars to most aspects of the Guru's thought and the background to Sikhism. The most important collections are *Guru Nanak* (Publication Division, Government of India, 1969), Gurmukh Nihal Singh (ed.), *Guru Nanak, His Life, Times and Teachings* (National Publishing House, New Delhi, 1969), *Sikhism* (Punjabi University, Patiala, 1969), K. R. Srinivasar Iyengar (ed.), *Guru Nanak, a Homage* (Sahitya Akadami, New Delhi, 1973) and *Perspectives on Guru Nanak*, ed. Harbans Singh (Punjabi University, Patiala, 1975). This volume contains fifty-four essays and is really the proceedings of an international seminar held in Patiala in 1969.

Three books which are useful for understanding particular aspects of the background to Guru Nanak's teaching are, first, *A Cultural History of India* by A. L. Basham (Oxford University Press, 1975), containing an excellent essay on Sikhism by Hew McLeod and useful chapters on the Hindu and Muslim scene of Guru Nanak's time; *Kabir* by C. Vaudeville (Oxford University Press, 1974) not only analyses the sant tradition of which Guru Nanak seems to have been a product, it also includes a collection of his sakhis (devotional poems) – the comments on these are valuable in understanding the terms used by Guru Nanak; *Gorakhnath and the Kanpatha Yogis* by G. W. Briggs (Motilal Banarsidass, Bombay, 1938, reprinted 1973) is a study of another group which seems to have had considerable influence upon the Guru either directly or through the sant tradition. Essential for the understanding of Sikh society in Punjab and in Britain is M. Juergensmeyer's *Religion as Social Vision*, University of California, 1982. It is especially relevant to studies of the Valmiki and Ravidasi communities.

Vaudeville's *Kabir* is extremely useful because no explanatory commentary of the Adi Granth is available in English. *A Critical Study of the Adi Granth* by S. S. Kohli (Punjabi Writers' Co-operative, New Delhi, 1961) discusses metre, musical form, language and some of its religious and ethical concepts but it gives no assistance to anyone wishing to understand the text. A brief introduction to the musical settings of the Adi Granth may be found in *Sikh Sacred Music* (Sikh Sacred Music Society, 1967) and a more complete one in *Indian Music* by P. Holroyde (Allen & Unwin, 1972).

The practices and ceremonies of Sikhism together with their underlying concepts may be found in a variety of books such as *Sikhism, Its Ideals and Institutions* by Teja Singh (Orient Longmans, Calcutta, 1964) and *Sikh Ceremonies* by Sir Joginder Singh (Religious Book Society, Chandigarh, 1968). Both of these are frequently consulted by gurdwara committees. *The Sikh Gurus and the Temple of Bread* by Parkash Singh (Dharam Parchar Committee SGPC, Amritsar, 2nd edn, 1971) is a specialised study of the langar (Guru's kitchen). *Parasharprasna* by Kapur Singh (Hind Publishers, Jullundur, 1959) is a very interesting analysis of the profound meaning of Guru Gobind Singh's institution of the Khalsa. As action should never be divorced from belief in Sikhism this is perhaps as good a place as any to mention *Sikh Ethics* by S. S. Kohli (Munshiram Manoharlal, New Delhi, 1975) and *Ethics of the Sikhs* by Avtar Singh (Punjabi University, Patiala, 1970). Detailed studies of other aspects of the religion are *The Guru in Sikhism* and *Sikhism in its Indian Context, 1469–1708*, both by W. O. Cole and published by Darton, Longman & Todd in 1982 and 1984. Also Madanjit Kaur, *The Golden Temple*, Amritsar, 1983.

Such topics as the Sikh attitude to other religions is covered in some of the collections of essays listed above, for example *Sikhism* (1969) contains a contribution by Sohan Singh. The journals listed below also include articles on the same theme, for it is one which has always been of interest to Sikh writers, placed as they have always been between Hinduism and Islam, holding the view that Guru Nanak is to be regarded as a world teacher.

The student of the Adi Granth will soon encounter references to Hindu beliefs and mythology. *Hindu Polytheism* by A. Danielou (Routledge & Kegan Paul, 1964), *Hindu Myths* by W. D. O'Flaherty (Penguin, 1975), *Hinduism* ed. J. R. Hinnells and E. J. Sharpe (Oriel Press, 1972) and *Hindu World* by B. Walker (Allen & Unwin, 1968) will be found to provide most of the necessary information. *Epics*, Myths and Legends of India (13th edn., 1973) and *Hindu Religion Customs and Manners* (1960), both by P. Thomas (Taraporevala, Bombay) provide insights into some of the references to religious and social customs as well as festivals and mythology.

Occasionally the journals listed below contain information about the Sikh dispersion in America, Europe, South-east Asia or Africa. *Sikh Children in Britain* by A. G. James (Oxford University Press, 1974) is warmly recommended to students interested in the UK community. R. and C. Ballard's essay in *Between Two Cultures: Migrants and Minorities in Britain*, ed. J. Watson (Blackwell, 1977) brings the picture up to date and refers to important articles. Communities in other parts of the world have still to be documented in detail. *Sikhs in England*, A. W. Helweg, O.U.P., 1979, is really an account of the Gravesend community. While possessing depth it does not convey the impression of an author conversant with the British Sikh community as a whole. A number of books and articles have been written about the Sikh crisis in India. The most balanced account to date is *The Sikhs*, by Christopher Shackle, Minority Rights Group, 29 Craven Street, London WC2N 5NT.

Journals

There are a number of periodicals and journals but the quality of articles varies considerably because editorial boards seem to draw no distinguishing line between devotional eulogies and scholarly academic contributions. *Punjab Past and Present* (Punjabi University, Patiala) is a clear exception to this rule. As the name implies, the articles are historical or sociological as well as religious, and range beyond Sikhism to include such topics as the education of girls at the time of annexation by the British or the history of Christianity in the Punjab. Often important essays from books which are now out of print are reproduced. This periodical appears twice yearly and was first published in 1967. It is worth purchasing past copies which currently cost forty rupees. The *Journal of Sikh Studies* (Guru Nanak University, Amritsar) also appears twice a year at an annual subscription cost of ten rupees. It was first published in 1974 and is a serious academic journal covering all aspects of Sikh life and thought. The *Spokesman*, founded in 1951, is a weekly newspaper (Northend Complex, R. K. Ashram Marg, New Delhi), which also publishes interesting anniversary issues at such times as Baisakhi or the birthday of Guru Nanak. Its interests are domestic and political as well as religious. Sikhs in Canada, the UK and other countries also have their own journals. The *Sikh Courier* (88 Mollison Way, Edgware, London) was founded as a quarterly in 1960. The *Sikh Sansar* (Sikh Foundation, PO Box 727, Redwood City, California 94064) is the corresponding quarterly journal for Sikhs in Canada and the USA. It was established in 1972. Both these periodicals include articles about Sikhism in general as well as covering British and American aspects of the religion.

The *Journal of Religious Studies* (Punjabi University, Patiala) which is published twice a year must be appended to this list because of its importance. However, only a minority of its articles are concerned with Sikhism. The annual rate of subscription is currently fifteen rupees. The Guru Nanak Foundation, Near Qutab Hotel, New Delhi, 110067, which was established in 1981, issues *Studies in Sikhism and Comparative Religion* twice yearly. The current subscription rate is thirty rupees.

Finally, a Sikh studies section of the British Association for the History of Religions was established in 1984. Its annual bulletin is available from West Sussex Institute of Higher Education, College Lane, Chichester, and costs £1.

Audio-visual aids to the study of Sikhism

It may seem odd to include such a section in a book of this nature. However, Sikhism has to do with people as well as ideas and whilst Christian theologians have usually written for people who have a cultural affinity with the religion which they are studying this is not likely to be true of most people who read this book. Even if something of the spirit of Sikhism has been conveyed through its pages, the difficulty of understanding an alien culture remains. The theological and psychological problems which may arise cannot be discussed here. Turning to the practical one, short of visiting the Punjab we would urge students to make contact with the local Sikh community if there is one. A few minutes sitting quietly and watching carefully in the gurdwara can be a great source of learning. Failing this there are the following slides or filmstrips which have been published in the UK.

Sikhism, Educational Products (Bradford Road, East Ardsley, Wakefield). This filmstrip was photographed in India and covers most aspects of the faith.

The Sikh Religion, Concordia (117–123 Golden Lane, London EC1) was filmed in Leeds. This filmstrip concentrates on worship and the gurdwara and a wedding. A taped commentary to accompany it is available.

The Sikh Amrit Ceremony (Educational Productions) is a filmstrip which was also made in Leeds. It shows the initiation of a man and four women into the Khalsa. A separate tape study of the ceremony is also available.

Excellent slide sets covering the Ten Gurus, the Golden Temple, a Sikh wedding and the Martyrdom of Guru Tegh Bahadur (twelve slides in each set) are available from Bury Peerless, 22 King's Avenue, Birchington, Kent.

Video films are now a valuable resource in religious studies. Covering Sikhism are: *Sikhs in Britain* (Open University), *Believe it or Not – Sikhism* (ITV), *Sikhism through the Eyes of Sikh Children* (Christian Education Movement), and *Aspects of Sikhism* (Exmouth School).

For those wishing to listen to some of the hymns of the Gurus there are many recordings available. Here we will list the following few on the basis of importance or variety.

Japji/Raehraas, EMI ECLP 2355. A recording of some of the most important sabads recited as a part of daily prayer. The sleeve notes are in English.

Asa di Var, HVM EMI ECLP 2307/08 (another version is on Polydor 2675 053). This is another very important collection of hymns.

Shabads of Guru Nanak, ELR 235–40. This is a six-record set of forty-seven sabads and was made to celebrate the quincentenary. Records can be bought separately. Sleeve notes are in Punjabi.

Kaisi Aarti Hoye, Polydor 2392 832, contains seven sabads by various Gurus including the Tenth and provides variety on one disc.

Khushwant Singh has recorded a two-disc set entitled *Sikhism Through the Songs of the Gurus*, Polydor Set No. 2675 068. The commentary and sleeve notes are in English. This is a very interesting and useful introduction to Sikhism, though again Khushwant Singh presents his thesis that Guru Nanak evolved an eclectic faith combining what he thought was best in Hinduism and Islam.

Anyone wishing to pass beyond Sikhism into Punjabi culture might enjoy listening to *Baisakhi Mela* EMI ECLP 2439 which includes bhangra and gidha dances and captures the atmosphere of the great Amritsar fair. Some novels will enable this exploration to go further, for example *Punjabi Century* by Prakash Tandon (Hind Pocket Books, Delhi, 1972) which is the autobiography of a family and covers the period 1849 to 1955. There are also *I Shall Not Hear the Nightingale* by Khushwant Singh (India Bookhouse, Delhi, 1959) which is the story of an untypical Sikh family, *Train to Pakistan* by Khushwant Singh (India Bookhouse, Delhi, 1975) and *Nails and Flesh* by K. S. Duggal (Hind Pocket Books, Delhi, 1969). The last two stories are set in the troubles of 1947. *An Indian Attachment*, Sarah Lloyd, Harvill Press, London 1984, is an intimate study of Sikh life through the eyes of a British woman who lived among them in Punjab.

Additional bibliography

Ahluwalia, M. M., *Kukas, The Freedom Fighters of the Punjab*, Bombay, 1965.
Archer, J. C., *The Sikhs*, Princeton University Press, 1946.
Basham, A. L., *The Wonder That Was India*, Collins Fontana, 1970.
Bhattacharya, H. (ed.), *Cultural Heritage of India*, volumes 3 and 4, 2nd edn., Calcutta, 1956.
Brent, P., *Godmen of India*, Penguin edn., 1972.
Carpenter, J. E., *Theism in Medieval India*, Williams and Norgate, 1921
Cunningham, J.D., *A History of the Sikhs*, Indian edn., S. Chand, New Delhi, 1960.
Darshan Singh, *Indian Bhakti Tradition and the Sikh Gurus*, Lyall Book Depot, Chandigarh, 1968.
De Bary, W. T. (ed.), *Sources of Indian Tradition*, Columbia University Press, 1958.
Hinnells, J. R., and Sharpe, E. J., *Hinduism*, Oriel Press, 1972.
Lannoy, R., *The Speaking Tree*, Oxford University Press, 1971.
Noss, J. D., *Man's Religions*, Collier-Macmillan, 1963, 4th edn., 1974.
Parrinder, E. G., *Worship in the World's Religions*, Faber & Faber, 1961.
Parrinder, E. G., *Avatar and Incarnation*, Faber & Faber, 1970.
Renou, L., *Religions of Ancient India*, Schocken, London, 1953; reprinted 1968.
Sen, K. M., *Hinduism*, Penguin, 1970.
Smart, N., *Religious Experience of Mankind*, Collins Fontana, 1972.

Index

Index

207

Index

Golden Temple, 22, 51, 58, 61, 130, 153, 159; see also Darbar Sahib
Gorakhnath (Gorakhnāth), 4, 99
grace, 74, 79, 80, 81, 82, 83
granthi, 64, 108, 112, 113, 144
Grewal, J. S., 125, 196, 198
grihastha, 14, 118, 121, 124, 136
Gupta, H. R., 105, 196
gurbani (gurbāṇī), 44
Gurdas, Bhai (Gurdās, Bhāī), xvi, xvii, 14, 15, 16, 26, 30, 31, 44, 45, 54, 80, 92, 100, 103, 107, 122, 123, 129, 171, 174
gurdwara (gurdwārā), 14, 43, 50, 51, 52, 58–66, 106–19, 120, 159, 164, 170, 178
gurmatta, 111, 179
gurmukh, 68, 84, 86
Gurmukh Nihal Singh, 199
gurmukhi (gurmukhī), 50, 52, 55, 57, 62, 172
gurpurb, 123, 124, 132–5, 164
Guru (Gurū) (Sikh Gurus are listed under their individual names): as God, 37, 45, 53, 56, 62, 63, 65, 67, 73, 80, 82, 149; as man, 7, 10, 28, 43, 44, 79, 81, 95, 101, 103, 110, 120, 122–32, 132–5, 152, 155, 180–3; as scripture, 100–5; see also Adi Granth; Guru Granth Sahib; installation of, 16, 37, 104, 105, 123
Guru Granth Sahib (Gurū Granth Sāhib), 10, 15, 18, 32, 38, 44, 45, 50, 51, 53, 58, 60, 64, 100–5 (Guru concept), 108, 112–19, 134–5, 142, 164, 180–3, 189–95, 197
Guru Panth, 37
gutka (guṭkā), 113

hair, 106, 111
Har Gobind (Guru), 23, 25, 27, 29–31, 33, 59, 60, 131, 138
Har Krishan (Guru), 33
Har Rai (Guru) (Har Rāi), 32–3
Harbans Singh, 197, 199
Harbhajan Singh Puri, 161
Hardwar, 2, 12
Harmandir, 22, 25, 26, 34; see also Darbar Sahib

Harnam Singh, 199
haumai, 68, 77, 78
heaven, 87
hell, 87
Hinduism/Hindu, 2, 3, 8, 9, 10, 12, 13, 14, 24, 26, 27, 31, 34, 35, 49, 52, 53, 57, 70, 100, 102, 105, 124, 129, 137, 145–51
Hinnells, J. R., 200
Hola Mohalla, 131–2
hukam, 68, 73, 81, 89, 172, 173, 199
Humayan (emperor) (Humāyān), 19

ignorance, 76
initiation (amrit sanskar), 36, 57, 122–9, 151, 169, 177, 179
Islam/Muslim, 2, 3, 9, 10, 12, 13, 24, 26, 27, 31, 32, 34, 35, 40, 41, 49, 52, 59, 70, 99, 102, 124, 145–51
Ismail Bokharai (sheikh), 2
Iyengar, K. R. S., 199

Jai Ram, 9
Jaidev, 46, 193
James, A. G., 201
Janam sakhi (Janam sākhi), xvi, xvii, 12, 13, 21, 41, 42, 134, 150, 161, 197; Bala (Bālā), 8, 19, 20, 89, 134, 142; Hafizabad, 54; Handaliya, 23, 41; India Office Library (B 40), 59, 61; Meharban (Meharbān), 8, 41; Puratan (Purātan), 9, 12, 45, 103
Jap Sahib (Jāp Sāhib), 56, 57, 107, 126, 127, 169
Japji (Japjī), 13, 14, 50, 56, 65, 74, 80, 93, 107, 112, 126–9, 169, 172, 173, 199
jat (jāṭ), 23, 25, 36, 127, 166, 187, 188
Jehangir (emperor) (Jehāngīr), 25, 31
Jesus, 95, 97
jiva (jīva), 90, 199
jivan mukti (jīvan mukti), 85, 95, 96
jizya, 3, 34
Jodh Singh, xvii, 168, 198
Joginder Singh, 200
Journal of Religious Studies, 202
Journal of Sikh Studies, 201
judgment, 87

208

Index

Index

Namdhari Satgurus: Baba Ram Singh (Bābā Rām Siṅgh), 156; Baba Balak Singh (Bābā Balak Siṅgh), 157; Partap Singh (Partāp Siṅgh), 158; Jagjit Singh (Jagjīt Siṅgh), 158
names (naming of children), 44, 112–14
names, Sikh, 36, 113, 114, 138, 163, 175
Nanak, Guru (Nānak, Guru), xvi, 2, 6, 8–18, 22, 30, 32, 38–42, 43, 45, 46, 47, 51, 59, 61, 63, 69, 70, 73, 76, 78, 82, 89, 97, 101, 102, 123, 133–4, 153, 154, 166, 185, 189–95
Nanak panthi (Nānak panthi), 156
Nanaki (Nānaki), 9
Nand Lal, Bhai (Nand Lāl, Bhāī), 111, 171, 174
Nander, 152, 157, 171, 181
Narain Singh, 198
Narang, G. C., 198
nath yogi (nāth yogī), 3, 4, 88, 101
nirankari (niraṅkārī), 155–6, 158, 160, 186
nirguna (nirguṇa), 67, 70, 95
nishan sahib, 48, 63, 132, 171
Noss, J. B., 38

Om, 69, 92

pacifism, 127, 128, 138–41
Paira, Bhai (Paira, Bhāī), 47
Paira Mokha, Bhai (Paira Mokha, Bhāī), 19
palki, 62
panj pyares (pañj pyares), 124–9, 181
panth, 20, 23, 24, 26, 37, 98
Parkash Singh, 200
Parmanand, 195
Parrinder, E. G., 38
patit, 171
Patna, 171, 181
Peerless, Bury, 203
pilgrimage, 20, 23, 34, 175
Pipa, 193, 194
piri and miri concept, 29, 30, 31
pollution, 11, 18, 175
population, 155, 162, 165, 184–8
Prithi Chand (Prithī Chand), 23, 24, 25, 26

priesthood/ministry, 64
prohibitions, 127–9
Punjab (Puñjāb), 1, 2, 4, 25, 42, 63, 125, 129, 152–8, 163, 165, 184
Punjab Past and Present, 155, 201
purdah, 109

qazi, 11, 12
Qur'an, 40

Radhasoami, 158, 187
rag (rāg), 49
Rag Maru, 49
Rag Wadhans, 49
ragi (rāgī), 51
Rahiras, 169, 170
Rai Bular, 8
Rajput (Rājpūt), 138
Ram Das (Guru) (Rām Dās), 22, 23, 24, 189–95
Ram Rai (Rām Rāi), 32, 33, 34, 49, 50
Rama (Rāma), 41, 43, 62, 70
Ramanand, 5, 98, 99, 151, 189–95
Ramgarhia (Rāmgarhīā), 166
Ranjit Singh (maharaja) (Rañjīt Siṅgh), 30, 42, 110, 153
Ravi Das (Ravi Dās), 46, 189–95
rebirth, 68, 72, 73, 75, 79, 85, 87, 89, 148
Rehat Maryada, 31, 168–79
reinstatement of lapsed Sikhs, 178, 179
Renou, L., 38
revelation, concept of, 52
ritual, attitude to, 40, 54, 80, 107, 111, 124, 147, 148, 170, 175, 177
romalla, 112, 173

sabad/sabd (śabad/śabd), 20, 24, 52, 67, 73, 82, 146, 149
Sadhu (Sādhu), 9, 98, 106
Sadna, 193
saguna (saguṇa), 67, 70
sahaj, 86, 94, 119
sahajdari (sahajdārī), 185
Sahansar Ram (Sahansar Rām), 48
Sain, 46, 193
Sajjan, 12, 59
Salim (prince), 3
sangat (saṅgat), 15, 26, 37, 53, 76, 84, 88, 93, 144, 171

210